W9-ADS-092

THE CONSCIOUS VOICE

AN ANTHOLOGY OF AMERICAN POETRY
FROM THE SEVENTEENTH CENTURY
TO THE PRESENT

THE CONSCIOUS VOICE
AN ANTHOLOGY OF AMERICAN POETRY

THE CONSCIOUS VOICE

AN ANTHOLOGY OF AMERICAN POETRY FROM THE SEVENTEENTH CENTURY TO THE PRESENT

Edited, with an Introduction, by

ALBERT D. VAN NOSTRAND

AND

CHARLES H. WATTS II

Granger Index Reprint Series

BOOKS FOR LIBRARIES PRESS
PLAINVIEW, NEW YORK

INTERNATIONAL STANDARD BOOK NUMBER:
0-8369-6045-9

LIBRARY OF CONGRESS CATALOG CARD NUMBER:
70-76940

PRINTED IN THE UNITED STATES OF AMERICA

ACKNOWLEDGMENTS

For permission to reprint the poems in the present volume, acknowledgment is made to the following authors, publishers, and agents:

PRINCETON UNIVERSITY PRESS—for the poems of Edward Taylor from *The Poetical Works of Edward Taylor*, 1939.

CHARLES SCRIBNER'S SONS—for the poems of Sidney Lanier from *Poems and Poem Outlines*, 1945.
For "Octaves 2, 3, 11, 18" by Edwin Arlington Robinson from *Collected Poems*, 1937.

THE MACMILLAN COMPANY—for "Hillcrest," "The Man Against the Sky," "Demos," "Not Always (I)," "New England," "A Christmas Sonnet," by Edwin Arlington Robinson from *Collected Poems*, copyright 1896 to 1934 by E. A. Robinson; copyright 1935, 1937 by the Macmillan Company.

HENRY HOLT AND COMPANY, INC.—for the poems of Robert Frost from *Complete Poems of Robert Frost*. Copyright 1930, 1939, 1943, 1947, 1949, by Henry Holt and Company, Inc. Copyright 1936, 1942, 1945, 1948 by Robert Frost.
For the following poems by Carl Sandburg from *Chicago Poems:* "Chicago," "Bunkshooter," "I Am the People," "Languages," copyright 1916 by Henry Holt and Company, Inc. Copyright 1944 by Carl Sandburg. For the following Carl Sandburg poems from *Cornhuskers:* "Joliet," "Oldtimers," copyright 1918 by Henry Holt and Company, Inc. Copyright 1946 by Carl Sandburg.

HARCOURT, BRACE AND COMPANY, INC.—for the following poems by Carl Sandburg from *Smoke and Steel:* "They All Want to Play Hamlet," "The Sins of Kalamazoo," "Slabs of the Sunburnt West," copyright 1920 by Harcourt, Brace and Company, Inc.; renewed by Carl Sandburg. For the following poems by Carl Sandburg from *The People, Yes:* Number 1, 2, 24, 32, 76, 107, copyright 1936 by Harcourt, Brace and Company, Inc.

ALFRED A. KNOPF, INC.—for the poems of Wallace Stevens from *The Collected Poems of Wallace Stevens*, copyright 1923, 1931, 1937, 1942, 1950, 1954 by Wallace Stevens.

NEW DIRECTIONS—for "Canto I" from *The Cantos of Ezra Pound*, copyright 1934, 1937, 1940, 1948 by Ezra Pound; for the other poems of Ezra Pound, reprinted from *Personae*, copyright 1926 by Ezra Pound.

RANDOM HOUSE, INC.—for the poems of Robinson Jeffers: "The Excesses of God" and "Prescription of Painful Ends" from *Be Angry at the Sun*, copyright 1941 by Robinson Jeffers; "New Year's Eve" and "Self-Criticism in February" from *Such Counsels You Gave to Me and Other Poems*, copyright 1937 by Random House, Inc.; "The Beauty of Things" from *Hungerfield and Other Poems*, copyright 1951 by Robinson Jeffers; "Ocean" from *Hungerfield and Other Poems*, copyright 1954 by Robinson Jeffers; "Rearmament" and "The Cruel Falcon" and "Flight of Swans" from *The Selected Poetry of Robinson Jeffers*, copyright 1935 by Modern Library, Inc.; "Fire on the Hills," "The Place for No Story," "Second Best" from *The Selected Poetry of Robinson Jeffers*, copyright 1932 by Robinson Jeffers; "Antrim" from *The Selected Poetry of Robinson Jeffers*, copyright 1933 by Random House; "The Old Man's Dream After He Died" from *The Selected Poetry of Robinson Jeffers*, copyright 1928 and renewed 1956 by Robinson Jeffers; "Ante Mortem" and "Roan Stallion" from *The Selected Poetry of Robinson Jeffers*, copyright 1925 and renewed 1953 by Robinson Jeffers.
For the poems of Archibald MacLeish: "Voyage West" from *Act Five and Other Poems*, copyright 1941 by Archibald MacLeish; "Geography of This Time" from *Act Five and Other Poems*, copyright 1942 by Archibald MacLeish.

HOUGHTON MIFFLIN COMPANY—for the poems of Archibald MacLeish: "The End of the World," "Ars Poetica," "Not Marble Nor the Gilded Monuments," "You, Andrew Marvell," "Men," "American Letter," "Seafarer," "Invocation to the Social Muse," "The Old Man to the Lizard," "The Sheep in the Ruins," "Hypocrite Auteur," from *Collected Poems* (1917-1952), copyright by Houghton Mifflin Company 1917, 1924, 1925, 1926, 1928, 1929, 1930, 1932, 1933, 1936, 1939, 1943, 1948, 1951, 1952.

LIVERIGHT PUBLISHING CORPORATION—for the poems of Hart Crane from *The Collected Poems of Hart Crane*, copyright 1933 by Liveright, Inc.

TABLE OF CONTENTS

THE CONSCIOUS VOICE

THE CONSCIOUS VOICE

The concept that a poem is both the reordering of experience and, consequently, an experience in itself suggests the intricacy of the poet's involvement with the world. The poem, in fact, fixes the degree of his involvement, as the tone of voice within that poem reveals the emotional remove of the poet from his world. Some poetry, for instance, has been written in an entirely public fashion, its origin lying in national or communal event, its undertaking either royally or financially decreed, and its intention being to return the public event to the public in a form and manner that renders that event both recognizable and palatable. Testimony to the high art possible under such circumstances is available in British poetry of the eighteenth century. Public poetry in the extreme, or occasional verse, offers a fixed mark by which to measure any poet's commitment to actual circumstances, to actual events and their public consequences. On the other hand, however, when the communal event becomes part of the poet's personal experience, then the poetry itself becomes an experience rather than merely a report of it.

In America, poets have characteristically responded to the environment in terms of the land and its significance. William Cullen Bryant was moved to build a poetry out of native materials; and he domesticated a rational god to preside over the American landscape and its history. Newspaper editors, like Bryant, theologians, naturalists, and political commentators have also been poets; the Miltonic image of the citizen-poet has been popular in America. And sometimes it is difficult to know whether the poet or the public man came first, or to know which occupied the dominant position in the artist's mind, the particulars of his experience, or the abstractions of his beliefs or convictions. Among the earlier generations of poets in this country the facts of experience and the ideals of conviction seemed to reinforce one another, allowing a harmonious involvement of the poet with the world he saw. Edward Taylor's gift for seeing the abstractions of religious conviction moving within daily circumstance reflects the coherence of his world; it also provides the basis for his poetry. Sometimes the involvement was too easy, with a consequent loss of perspective and of the emotional distance necessary for art—that resistance in the writer which Wallace Stevens calls the imagination's pressure thrusting outward to withstand exterior realities. Stevens means a way of perceiving, one which acknowledges the significance of the immediate happening in relation to some larger vision. On many occasions in American verse, the poet's imagination—in Stevens' metaphor —has not withstood the pressure of exterior realities, to the detriment of his poetry. One thinks of Philip Freneau and wonders what this romantic's soul would have perceived of the world had not the immediate horizon of the Revolution obscured his vision and moved him to compose those endless propagandistic verses. Freneau is not alone. Most public poems in America, born of easy involvement with affairs, have not survived the occasions they celebrated: John Greenleaf Whittier's antislavery poems, for instance, and James Russell Lowell's satires. Sidney Lanier's desperate and intermittently successful efforts to graft economic theory to lyric expression mark a more complex involvement with national problems. And there are poems with much less stamina than these: the versified propaganda in behalf of labor, temperance, and dozens of other humanitarian causes in the eighteen forties and fifties; and the countless verse narratives commemorating military events in the struggle between North and South—virtually prescriptions, to be refilled with new names.

But beyond such particular failures of grasp stands the impressive accomplishment of other poets precisely because of a delicate involvement with the exterior and public realities. Walt Whitman's personal commitment to the circumstance of Lincoln's funeral train motivated the most persuasive elegy in the literature. "When Lilacs Last in the Dooryard Bloom'd" arose from his deeply personal identification with a nation's grief.

What we have called the conscious voice in American poetry has something to do with a poet's commitment to the community: his willingness to be involved, in the immediacy of daily affairs, and to use the poem, as a shared experience, to make life more practicable. American poetry has taken much of its tone from the regularity with which the poets find themselves part of the communal experience. The joy or the horror, the warning or the celebration is personal; but the genesis of that emotion or insight most often lies within an atmosphere or condition which affects the community. This is a private voice which testifies to a shared experience; furthermore—and this is significant—whether it speaks of celebration or dismay, it seems always to grow out of a *sense of expectation*, a sense of the imminent possibilities of the community. As Carl Sandburg promises, "When I, the People, learn to remember . . . the mob, the crowd, the mass will arrive then."

This constant sense of possible fulfillment helps explain American poetry. It begins to account for Edgar Allan Poe's theory that the poem must record the striving for supernal beauty; or for Emily Dickinson's central and thematic conviction, itself reminiscent of Edward Taylor, "I dwell in possibility"; for Robert Frost's meliorism; for Henry Wadsworth Longfellow's didactic insistence on human perfectibility; and for the embracing metaphor of Hart Crane's Bridge, which leaps in time and space, connecting a nation to its past and to its possibilities. This anticipation of fulfillment begins also to explain some of the apparent differences between the earlier and the contemporary poets. Thus Bryant could encourage his expectation of an ordered nation with a reassuring look at the prairies and their evidence of a cyclic history of man on the land. Thus Robinson Jeffers, whose expectation for the community has been contradicted by its incestuous weakness, searches a patch of landscape at Sovranes Creek and finds it too noble for humanity, "The Place for No Story."

Somewhere between Bryant and Jeffers, Ralph Waldo Emerson looks at the land of Bulkeley, Hunt, and Willard, in "Hamatreya," and listens to the earth-song ironically contradicting the expectation of these men but fulfilling the poet's.

The juxtaposition of Bryant, Emerson, and Jeffers suggests how the conscious voice—the expression of this expectation—has responded to the affairs of a national community in the course of a hundred and fifty years or more. The native poetry has described a continuous, wave-like motion as it has approached and retreated from the fact of America, as that fact impinges on the poet's consciousness. The significant change in convictions toward a common subject occurs between Emerson and Jeffers. Bryant, after all, expresses the desires of a great many people; and Emerson can still share them. But Jeffers can not. He has not disowned the community—"I would burn my right hand in a slow fire to change the future"—but he has resisted its pressures in favor of a more personal vision. The three poets stand in various degrees of involvement with the community. And their respective positions mark a historical development in America of this sense of expectation.

Consider for a moment the community to which the writer has belonged and some of the tidemarks of its rising anticipation of self-fulfillment. Ponder the climate of Europe and England as the Plymouth founders set sail. Whether their motives were more economic or theological, these men responded to a general sense of expansion and exploration which greeted any adventure, geographic or cerebral. Men had come upon the thought that within their grasp lay a vestige of control over themselves and, in fact, over the world. The God of John Calvin may have insisted upon absolute dominion, but He asked so much that men could but strain themselves to reach Him, and in the straining they found within themselves capacities they had not anticipated. The Covenant Theology—the limiting of Calvin's God—testifies to man's willingness to believe at least partly in his own efficacy; and it was the Covenanters who controlled New England Congregationalism.

Thus the sense of anticipation. Thus the capacity to hope that the Massachusetts shore was the boundary of the New Jerusalem. Thus, despite theological strictures, the increasing awareness of this world's and specifically the North American continent's possibility. As the land proved limitless, and the toehold on life first established in the Northeast grew to a thriving set of colonies, there seemed little that men might not do with this new world.

The land was harsh to those unaccustomed to its ways, and man's finiteness readily apparent; but standing above such confirmation was the hope of the New Jerusalem, a hope which seemed less and less remote as the colonists took hold, even as the outlines of that hope changed from the theological to the political and the social. The evolution from Covenant theology, based on a contract between man and God, to the amenities of nineteenth-century Unitarianism, with the rational mind in control of its destiny, testifies, in the American's view of himself, to the power of the land over the warnings about the finiteness of man's spirit. Congregations needed only to look out of the church window for evidence of their capacity to shape human affairs. After the successes of the Revolution, the growing urbanization of the East and the continuous westward motion of the population left little room for doubt. The ideals of the Declaration of Independence remain significant precisely because men believed they could bring them off. As Robert Penn Warren has demonstrated in *Brother to Dragons* (1953), Thomas Jefferson envisioned the New Jerusalem as clearly as did any Puritan saint. And the statesmanship of that odd triumvirate, Franklin, Jefferson, and Hamilton—no matter what their philosophical differences—proceeded on the premise that this nation was the setting for endless financial growth and cultural development. The stamina of this self-confidence is suggested by that most indicative of American families, the Adamses. Young Henry knew what it meant to sit in church behind a President grandfather and gaze at the portrait of a President great-grandfather; and he agreed that he, in his turn, would be President. This pre-

sumption is less a statement of aristocratic bias than the
normal result of a climate in which one labored for the na-
tion.

The nineteenth century everywhere exhibited workers and
prophets acting in expectation that tomorrow, before their
eyes, would blossom a land democratic in both action and
sentiment, and peaceful in an industrious reaping of natural
wealth which seemed to increase each time someone tried to
measure it. For forty years or more Ralph Waldo Emerson
proclaimed just such a material fulfillment of the spirit. This
lecturer was no thinker, and his place in America's culture
ought rightly to be measured less in terms of the quality of
his Germanic thought than in the conviction of his tone and
the innocence of his belief. He is a distinctly American phe-
nomenon, seizing on ideas compatible with the prosperity he felt
about him, proclaiming the potency of the American Scholar.
Art was democratic; and Emerson was an evangelist, inspiring
Lyceum audiences with the same messages of self-fulfillment
which he preached to the artist. Brahmin or no, radical or
not, Emerson caught that quality of anticipation and belief
in self that moved New Englanders to Ohio and finally to the
coast: the belief that almost anything is possible if you look
long enough and work hard enough.

Many nineteenth-century writers contributed to the sense
of expectation: some of them domesticated other men's ideas,
as Emerson used Swedenborg's. Others looked to a native
past, as did Hawthorne when he considered the destination of
Hester Prynne. This woman finally emerged a self-sufficient
personality, dominating *The Scarlet Letter,* notwithstanding
Hawthorne's acknowledgment of her guilt. Other literary ex-
pressions of confident expectation—like Natty Bumppo's de-
cision to turn westward at the end of *The Pioneers*—combine
political history with Rousseau's ideal. But the most strident
Answerer to the land was Walt Whitman, an epitome of the
nation's willingness to believe in the individual's capacity to
shape a destiny of his own choice. Whitman spoke in the im-
perative: you *shall* be inspired by the land, by the people on

the landscape, by yourself, and by Walt Whitman. When Whitman went to the opera, he soared to beliefs evidently incompatible with the struggle for wealth going on outside. He was no Brahmin, and his air was not the cloistered excitement of Concord or Cambridge, but instead of writing another Susan Lenox he wrote "Song of Myself." And his yawp celebrated the possibilities of self throughout his life, until suddenly and terribly an adversary bore down on him. Suddenly and terribly the human wrecks of the Civil War gainsaid his whole ideology. The men whom he volunteered to nurse were both fact and symbol of a nation falling apart. Their agonies, the dereliction of their bodies and minds, and the smell of mortal infection shattered the bold possibilities of self and the mystical oneness of a nation on which Whitman had built everything. The record of this shock is in the two volumes of *Drum Taps* (1865-66), which hold short, precise accounts of the noises and sensations of fighting and waiting and dying, reported from low down and nearby. They are grotesque fragments: "So fierce you whirr and pound you drums—so shrill you bugles blow." They record paralysis: "would the singer attempt to sing? . . . Then rattle quicker, heavier drums—you bugles wilder blow." The triumph of Lincoln's funeral train, which followed this paralysis, could grow only out of Whitman's lonely reassessment of everything he had believed. One consequence of Whitman's shock and reassessment was his long poem, "Passage to India" (1871). It exhibits both less and more than his earlier poetry: less, in that Whitman tempered his bold mysticism with an orthodox notion of a life after death; and more, in a purely geographical sense. The poem acknowledges the first continental railroad and the opening of the Suez Canal, both in 1869. Whitman celebrated the joining of the New World with the Old, and his catalogues specify new horizons beyond the nation. Consciously or not, here was one way of asserting a new unity on the wreckage of the old, a new world brotherhood where the nation had failed. Whitman proclaimed the "Passage to India" in a conscious voice, raised in renewed commitment to the community, and in this voice he spoke as a native poet. The shocked expectation, the reassessment, and the search for even greater human possibilities, which was Whitman's particular experience, fairly describes the course of American poetry.

Although Whitman's shock and reappraisal were representative, the extent of his renewed affirmation was unique. That some few writers had reasoned differently is clear; their native expectation had long since yielded to apprehension. As far back as the Revolution Freneau had wondered, and wondered again when Tom Paine, his usefulness over, was branded radical. The complaints of Freneau and Hugh Henry Brackenridge were based on the common conviction of a fulfillment that had been missed somewhere along the line. Such was the case with Cooper, returned from Europe, and with Henry Thoreau. Things were not what they seemed, and the violent motion of national expansion and development obscured a deeper trouble. This might be a New Jerusalem, and the land might be more bountiful than man could imagine, and the creeds of the Declaration of Independence might last forever as classic statements of man's hope for himself; but men seemed to remain incorrigibly weak and corruptible. Brackenridge, in *Modern Chivalry* (1792-1815), saw it all in classically simple political terms: backwoods Pennsylvania was a prime place to test the ideal of a mature citizenry; and Teague O'Regen, part fool and part knave, very nearly got elected by this citizenry. Brackenridge's dismayed anticipation for the electorate clearly shows through his satire. And take Cooper, thin-skinned and showing his disgust when he saw at first hand the changes Andrew Jackson had wrought in the political legacy of Thomas Jefferson. Cooper's novel, *Home as Found* (1838), cried foul and begat such unfavorable response that Cooper turned back in time to the youth of his hero, Natty Bumppo, and conjured him into an ideal that could exist only as long as it retreated westward, away from Jackson's democracy.

Different in tone but similar in origin were the convictions of Henry Thoreau. Bumppo went West, and Thoreau went to

Walden Pond; both sought clearer air. Thoreau saw his fellow farmers staggering beneath their possessions and told them to stand up and be men instead of landholders. Cooper, the landholder, never solved the problem of how one might remain a landholder while fulfilling the expectations of manhood exemplified in Natty Bumppo. Thoreau and Cooper both reacted to the changes wrought by a country settling into its harness, and each in his own way felt that the process was stifling a hope. It was as difficult for Thoreau to count the Irish lives sacrificed to the nearby railroad as it was for Cooper to explain to Lafayette that the national dream had apparently failed.

No one of these artists could precisely delineate that dream; no one of them even consciously considered America's promise as a dream near fulfillment. The only continuing and immediately visible contours of any "dream" might be said to be political, those of the Declaration; but these men were artists as well as politicians, and even that part of them labeled politician reacted differently to the changing political creeds: Jackson meant one thing to Cooper, and quite another to Whitman. What we suggest, rather, is not devotion to a cause or a particular belief, but a prevailing attitude.

Another conscious voice in this native chorus was Melville's. What moves us in *Moby Dick* is the intensity of Melville's reaction to the scenes he portrays, and the violence of his hatred and joy. Why such intensity and violence? The story is not new, and Ahab's failure is as inevitable as Ishmael's decision to settle for less than Ahab demanded. Such intensity and violence could come from a shocked innocence, from something within Melville which induced him to fashion a Taji who refuses to accept the rational limits of possibility; and this, after Melville's life had already been cast by family failure and poverty and an education in forecastles and jails. Melville's sense (in *Moby Dick* and in *Pierre*) that something had failed suggests that he was an innocent, that he had somewhere absorbed a sense of possibility, of man's control of his own destiny, and, indeed (remembering certain passages in

Moby Dick), of a nation's firm and democratic control of its growth and future.

Now regard Melville's poetry, which he began by commemorating occasions of the Civil War. How different it is from the prose that preceded it. The intensity and the violence of that prose, which also inheres in the subject of his poetry, is nevertheless missing from the verse itself. That Melville didn't understand the scope and pressures of a poetic line, though curious, is evident. But this does not wholly account for the change. Melville's shock and horror at the sensations of the War are even more obvious in his verse than in Whitman's. His lines compound reportage, dismayed conscience, and sentimentality; and those honest tributes are curiously unmoving. His imagination, as Wallace Stevens would put it, did not withstand the pressures of external realities. And we infer that the subject of the War has once more overwhelmed the artist.

All this evidence supports two observations: that the idea of a national community has impinged on the conscience of the native writer in such a way that he has considered himself a participant in its growth and development; and that the fact of the community, as it has grown and developed, has continuously contradicted his idea of what it might be. The ideologies of the nation—political, religious, educational, economic, social, or whatever—have become explicit, a process necessarily limiting possibilities. The fact of the Civil War hastened the diminishing of possibility into fact. Every one of the propositions in the opening sentences of the Declaration had become irretrievably explicit. The self-evident truth that all men are created equal had somehow worked to dispossess the race it freed. The divine endowment of certain inalienable rights had been resolved by military force. Abruptly, two ideals had become mutually exclusive: that governments derive their just power from the consent of the governed; and that it is the right of the people to abolish a government destructive of these ends. The right to the pursuit of happiness, intermittently incorporated into the majority of state constitutions, became a matter of judicial interpretation.

The ideal of free enterprise had spawned two warring economic philosophies. And the aim of material well-being had somehow diminished into materialism. Perhaps a sign of change and of a consciousness of change is visible in the comment of a magazine correspondent writing not long after the Civil War: "We have found 'realizing the ideal,' to be impracticable in proportion as the ideal is raised high. But 'idealizing the real,' as I shall maintain, is not only practicable but the main secret of the art of living . . . ."

The process of stating the Idea of America and then of gradually realizing that it must remain an ideal, finally just out of reach, surely explains much of the native writing. The eighteenth-century men of letters were directly concerned with making the country a political reality. Melville, Whitman, Emerson, and their contemporaries were born at a time when they could imbibe a sense of hope with their first breath; and their writing tends to extremes: either a determined insistence that the ideal has been achieved, or an anguished admission that things are not as they should be. All of them witnessed the apparently inevitable lessening of the sense of freedom, of fulfillment of self. It is an oversimplification but not an untruth to say that the Civil War grew from the very thing they witnessed, namely, the gradual settling of several economic and political entities into regions and finally into a nation—not a nation as conceived in idea but a nation as it existed in fact. And they did not know precisely how to deal with it.

This frustration has been part of the national legacy to writers who have grown up after the Civil War. We have been speaking all along of the stamina of this native sense of expectation. Among contemporary poets it still persists, and it has taken a singular but not surprising turn. Searching for evidence of the fulfillment of human possibilities, the contemporary has characteristically dislocated himself from the native landscape. Reconsider the kind and quality of Whitman's affirmation after his war poems. His "Passage to India" transcends locality. That is its subject, a prophetic one for American poetry. The homogeneous society of the nineteenth century is no longer. With the increase of immigration, the ease of travel, and a succession of world wars, the native audience has, in fact, changed more than the poet has. His "dislocation" —a familiar comment on the contemporary artist's state of mind—seems scarcely a negative carping or "an escape from reality." On the contrary, still testing the possibilities of the community, he appears to have broadened the horizons of evidence.

To see this we need only inspect the metaphors the poets themselves have used. E. A. Robinson began with the local metaphor of "Tilbury Town." His subject was contemporary morality; but Tilbury Town was the end of the line, and he switched to Arthurian romance to dramatize his subject. And he conducted his most intensive analysis (note the dimensions) of "The Man Against the Sky." Robinson's landscape was about as definite as the garden in which Emily Dickinson pondered the struggle between love and death; her placelessness has been congenial to the succeeding generations of American poets. Robert Frost's landscapes are precisely local, and so are the people on them; but over and over again they dramatize the struggle for what Frost calls "Our Hold on the Planet." Wallace Stevens' "Order at Key West" similarly graduates the local metaphor. E. E. Cummings' city scenes subserve his speculations about "this busy monster, Manunkind." So, too, Robinson Jeffers' Sovranes Creek, "The Place for No Story," is everywhere. The metaphorical evidence is symptomatic; all these poets appear to have embarked on the passage to India. This sense of placelessness has been so pronounced as to bother certain of our poets; witness Archibald MacLeish's "American Letter":

> This, this is our land, this is our people,
> This that is neither a land nor a race. We must reap
> The wind here in the grass for our soul's harvest;
> Here we must eat our salt or our bones starve.
> Here we must live or live only as shadows.

Sometimes this metaphorical passage has become insistently thematic, as in Carl Sandburg's *The People Yes*:

> In the night, and overhead a shovel of stars for
> Keeps, the people march:
>   "Where to? What next?"

Nevertheless it is a minority report which MacLeish renders. Sometimes the passage has been actual, like the endless journey of Ezra Pound. Pound exiled himself successively from America, from England, and from France, and sought a kind of supranational culture in the languages and literatures of a dozen races, covering a period of two thousand years or more. This emigrant is the most formative and influential writer contemporary poetry has had; and his poetic program communicates a familiar sense of commitment, of responsibility, and of expectation—spoken in that conscious voice. Pound has written: "The governor and legislator cannot act effectively or frame his laws, without words and the solidarity of these words is in the care of that damned and despised *literati*. When their work goes rotten . . . when their very medium or the very essence of their work, the application of word to thing goes rotten, i.e., becomes slushy and inexact or excessive or bloated, the whole machinery of social and individual thought and order goes to pot." Pound's self-indulgence in attitudes has sabotaged his own program. Nevertheless, from his peculiar placelessness in the world he has continued to gather evidence to test the human possibility. It seems relevant to remind ourselves that Pound's most obtuse poems, the middle Cantos, which obscurely traffic in many languages, are nevertheless an evaluation of the political philosophy of Jefferson and Adams. The experiment of America appears to have spread beyond the borders of the New Jerusalem.

ALBERT D. VAN NOSTRAND
CHARLES H. WATTS II

NOTE ON THE TEXT

Our purpose in representing major American poets has been to compile a selection balancing two possibilities: poems of true power, whatever their relation to the poet's total work; and poems which reveal what it has meant to him to be a poet. Beyond this, we have aimed at compiling an accurate text, faithful to each writer's intentions, in a precisely meaningful chronology. This purpose accounts for all of our editorial decisions—both the principles of procedure and their exceptions. Our procedure can be briefly stated.

The poems in this volume are based on our study of the complete poetical writings of each author. Consulting a writer's whole canon acknowledges—as well as the immediate problem of selection—certain less obvious editorial responsibilities. Of contemporary poets, for instance, the so-called "collected" or "complete" edition is not always complete, and its assignment of dates to poems, and of poems to previous editions which it reprints, is sometimes more approximate than precise.

The text, cited in the introductory note to each author, is the one we consider the most nearly definitive. Generally, it is the last published text which the poet himself either acknowledged or helped to prepare, or, if posthumously published, the text which acknowledges his latest revision. In the case of Emily Dickinson, where several manuscript versions exist, we have chosen from among the variants the poet has offered; and certain significant changes by her editors we have indicated in brackets.

The sequence of the volume follows the birth dates of the writers; and, within each writer's canon, it follows the date of first publication of each poem. The sequence of poems is occasionally modified to correspond to an author's choice of a particular poem as a preface, regardless of its date, in his own editions or selected volumes.

A word about dates. Excepting the poems of Taylor, Whitman, and Dickinson, most of the poems in the volume first appeared in periodicals and were later published by their authors in selections or collections. Unless otherwise stated in an introductory note, the date following a poem is the date of its first publication. Occasionally two dates follow a poem, for either of two reasons: (1) when a poem is known to have been written considerably earlier than its first publication, we have included both dates, the first marked "w" for its date of writing; (2) when we have used a text of a poem other than the edition cited in the headnote, the date of that edition appears in parentheses following the date of publication. In the case of contemporaries, where a bibliography or check list is only as current as its own date of publication, if the *Readers' Guide* to periodical literature does not cite a poem which has appeared after the latest check list, we have assigned to that poem the date of its author's earliest selection containing it.

The line numbers alongside the text are offered as a convenience. They represent certain editorial, but not literary or critical, decisions on our part. Except for the few instances of obviously prose paragraphs, the numbers indicate verse lines rather than typographical lines. Our rule has been to follow, in our chosen text, the conventions of capitalization and indentation for identifying verse lines. These conventions vary from one text to another.

Poems of T. S. Eliot and E. E. Cummings might have appeared in this volume but for the prohibitions imposed by Eliot's American publisher and the limitations imposed by Cummings' literary agent.

THE CONSCIOUS VOICE

AN ANTHOLOGY OF AMERICAN POETRY
FROM THE SEVENTEENTH CENTURY
TO THE PRESENT

EDWARD TAYLOR

Edward Taylor (*c*. 1644-1729) was born in Leicestershire, England, and trained by a nonconformist schoolteacher. Taylor himself tried teaching, then abandoned it when he could not honor the oath, required for a teaching license, obligating him to uphold the Church of England. He emigrated to America, to complete his education and join the Congregational ministry. He was graduated from Harvard in 1671, a classmate of Samuel Sewall, and answered a call to organize the first parish at Westfield, Massachusetts. As minister and physician he remained in that parish for the rest of his life. Twice married, he was the father of thirteen children, of whom only the six by his second marriage outlived him. Except for the remarks of his college roommate and close friend, Sewall, the scant recollections of Taylor's grandson, his obituary (presumably written by his pastoral assistant), and the record of some of his business travels, little is known about Taylor's life. The poems record the man.

Taylor wrote nearly three hundred poems between the year of his graduation from college and the end of his life. These are contained in a four-hundred-page octavo manuscript volume entitled "Poetical Works." The volume begins with some conventional elegies, a few striking personal lyrics, and the fragment of an epic, and then presents two sustained poetical works: "God's Determinations" and "Sacramental Meditations."

"God's Determinations" is a series of thirty-six individual poems, the majority of which assign speeches to six abstract characters: Christ, The Soul, Satan, a Saint, Justice, and Mercy. The whole work resembles a morality play about the fall of man and the problem of his salvation, and it justifies the Covenant theology. Its complete title defines its plot: "God's Determinations Touching His Elect: and the Elects' Combat in Their Conversion, and Coming Up to God in Christ: Together with the Comfortable Effects Thereof." There is a Prologue and a series of choral epilogues; and the entire work follows a Preface which draws its substance from the book of Job. "God's Determinations" anticipates the

3

dramatic quality of the "Sacramental Meditations," which comprise the largest part of the volume: two hundred and seventeen lyrics of various length, written after 1682. The circumstances of these poems are explained in their title: "Sacramental Meditations . . . Preparatory Meditations upon my Approach to the Lord's Supper, Chiefly upon the Doctrine Preached upon the Day of Administration." The texts of most of these poems are drawn from the New Testament.

Except for two stanzas of one of his lyrics—presumably without Taylor's knowledge—none of the poetry was published during his lifetime. Taylor willed most of his library, including the "Poetical Works," to his son-in-law, the Reverend Mr. Isaac Stiles of New Haven. Subsequently the manuscript passed to another branch of the family, and was presented to the Yale University Library in 1883. More than two hundred years after Taylor's death, a few of his poems first appeared in print, edited by Thomas H. Johnson, in the *New England Quarterly* (June, 1937). Johnson then edited the first collection, *The Poetical Works of Edward Taylor* (New York, 1939), a selection of Taylor's best poems, with notes, a glossary, and a description of the manuscript. Johnson's editing of the text involved regularizing the spelling and abbreviations and modifying some of the punctuation. He followed this with a second edition of selected poems with the same title (1943). The only complete edition of the "Poetical Works" is on microfilm: Donald Elwin Stanford (ed.), *Poetical Works of Edward Taylor* (Ann Arbor, 1954), University Microfilm publication number 6911.

Except for "Meditation Ten" in the original manuscript of *Poetical Works* the poems here printed follow the text of Johnson's first edition. The composition dates of the "Sacramental Meditations" and the sequence of the undated poems, in Johnson's edition, derive from the manuscript.

PREFACE TO "GOD'S DETERMINATIONS"

Infinity, when all things it beheld,
In Nothing, and of Nothing all did build,
Upon what Base was fixt the Lath, wherein
He turn'd this Globe, and riggalld it so trim?
Who blew the Bellows of his Furnace Vast?

5

Or held the Mould wherein the world was Cast?
Who laid its Corner Stone? Or whose Command?
Where stand the Pillars upon which it stands?
Who Lac'de and Fillitted the earth so fine,
With Rivers like green Ribbons Smaragdine?   10
Who made the Sea's its Selvedge, and it locks
Like a Quilt Ball within a Silver Box?
Who spread its Canopy? Or Curtains Spun?
Who in this Bowling Alley bowld the Sun?
Who made it always when it rises set: 15
To go at once both down, and up to get?
Who th' Curtain rods made for this Tapistry?
Who hung the twinckling Lanthorns in the Sky?
Who? who did this? or who is he? Why, know
It's Onely Might Almighty this did doe.   20
His hand hath made this noble worke which Stands
His Glorious Handywork not made by hands.
Who spake all things from nothing: and with ease
Can speake all things to nothing, if he please.
Whose Little finger at his pleasure Can   25
Out mete ten thousand worlds with halfe a Span?
Whose Might Almighty can by half a looks
Root up the rocks and rock the hills by th' roots.
Can take this mighty World up in his hande,
And shake it like a Squitchen or a Wand.   30
Whose single Frown will make the Heavens shake
Like as an aspen leafe the Winde makes quake.
Oh! what a might is this! Whose single frown
Doth shake the world as it would shake it down?
Which All from Nothing fet, from Nothing, All: 35
Hath All on Nothing set, lets Nothing fall.
Gave all to nothing Man indeed, whereby
Through nothing man all might him Glorify.
In Nothing is imbosst the brightest Gem
More pretious than all pretiousness in them.   40
But Nothing man did throw down all by sin:
And darkened that lightsom Gem in him,
    That now his Brightest Diamond is grown
    Darker by far than any Coalpit Stone.

THE JOY OF CHURCH FELLOWSHIP RIGHTLY ATTENDED

[An epilogue to "God's Determinations"]

In Heaven soaring up, I dropt an Eare
On Earth: and oh! sweet Melody!
And 'listening, found it was the Saints who were
Encroacht for Heaven that sang for Joy.
For in Christs Coach they sweetly sing,   5
As they to Glory ride therein.

Oh! joyous hearts! Enfir'de with holy Flame!
Is speech thus tasseled with praise?
Will not your inward fire of Joy contain,
That it in open flames doth blaze?   10
For in Christs Coach Saints sweetly sing,
As they to Glory ride therein.

And if a string do slip by Chance, they soon
Do screw it up again: whereby
They set it in a more melodious Tune   15
And a Diviner Harmony.
For in Christs Coach they sweetly sing,
As they to Glory ride therein.

In all their Acts, publick and private, nay,
And secret too, they praise impart.   20
But in their Acts Divine, and Worship, they
With Hymns do offer up their Heart.
Thus in Christs Coach they sweetly sing,
As they to Glory ride therein.

Some few not in; and some whose Time and Place   25
Block up this Coaches way, do goe
As Travellers afoot: and so do trace
The Road that gives them right thereto;
While in this Goach these sweetly sing
As they to Glory ride therein.   30

AN ADDRESS TO THE SOUL OCCASIONED
BY A RAIN

Ye Flippering Soule,
  Why dost between the Nippers dwell?
Not stay, nor goe. Not yea, nor yet Controle.
  Doth this doe well?
    Rise journy'ng when the skies fall weeping Showers,   5
    Not o're nor under th' Clouds and Cloudy Powers.

Not yea, nor noe:
  On tiptoes thus? Why sit on thorns?
Resolve the matter: Stay thyselfe or goe:
  Ben't both wayes born.   10
    Wager thyselfe against thy surplic'de see,
    And win thy Coate, or let thy Coate win thee.

Is this th' Effect
  To leaven thus my Spirits all?
To make my heart a Crabtree Cask direct?   15
  A Verjuc'te Hall?
    As Bottle Ale, whose Spirits prison'd must
    When jogg'd, the bung with Violence doth burst?

Shall I be made
  A sparkling Wildfire Shop,   20
Where my dull Spirits at the Fireball trade
  Do frisk and hop?
    And while the Hammer doth the Anvill pay,
    The fire ball matter sparkles e'ry way.

One sorry fret,   25
  An anvill Sparke, rose higher,
And in thy Temple falling, almost set
  The house on fire.
    Such fireballs dropping in the Temple Flame
    Burns up the building: Lord, forbid the same.   30

UPON A SPIDER CATCHING A FLY

Thou sorrow, venom Elfe:
  Is this thy play,
To spin a web out of thyselfe
  To Catch a Fly?
    For why?   5

I saw a pettish wasp
  Fall foule therein:
Whom yet thy whorle pins did not hasp
  Lest he should fling
    His sting.   10

But as afraid, remote
  Didst stand hereat,
And with thy little fingers stroke
  And gently tap
    His back.   15

Thus gently him didst treate
  Lest he should pet,
And in a froppish, aspish heate
  Should greatly fret
    Thy net.   20

Whereas the silly Fly,
  Caught by its leg,
Thou by the throate took'st hastily,
  And 'hinde the head
    Bite Dead.   25

This goes to pot, that not
  Nature doth call.
Strive not above what strength hath got,
  Lest in the brawle
    Thou fall.   30

This Frey seems thus to us:
    Hells Spider gets
His entrails spun to whip Cords thus,
    And wove to nets,
        And sets.   35

To tangle Adams race
    In's stratagems
To their Destructions, Spoil'd made base
    By venoms things,
        Damn'd Sins.   40

But mighty, Gracious Lord,
    Communicate
Thy Grace to breake the Cord; afford
    Us Glorys Gate
        And State.   45

We'l Nightingaile sing like,
    When pearcht on high
In Glories Cage, thy glory, bright:
    Yea, thankfully,
        For joy.   50

THE EBB AND FLOW

When first thou on me, Lord, wrough'st thy Sweet Print,
    My heart was made thy tinder box.
    My 'ffections were thy tinder in't:
        Where fell thy Sparkes by drops.
Those holy Sparks of Heavenly fire that came   5
Did ever catch and often out would flame.

But now my Heart is made thy Censar trim,
    Full of thy golden Altars fire,
    To offer up Sweet Incense in
        Unto thyselfe intire: 10
I finde my tinder scarce thy sparks can feel
.That drop out from thy Holy flint and Steel.

Hence doubts out bud for feare thy fire in mee
  'S a mocking Ignis Fatuus,
Or lest thine Altars fire out bee,   15
  It's hid in ashes thus.
Yet when the bellows of thy Spirit blow
Away mine ashes, then thy fire doth glow.

THE EXPERIENCE [MEDITATION THREE]

Canticles I: 3: . . . thy name is as ointment poured forth.

Oh! that I alwayes breath'd in such an aire
  As I suck't in, feeding on sweet Content!
Disht up unto My Soul ev'n in that pray're
  Pour'de out to God over last Sacrament.
    What Beam of Light wrapt up my sight to finde   5
    Me neerer God than ere Came in my minde?

Most strange it was! But yet more strange that shine
  Which fill'd my Soul then to the brim to spy
My nature with thy Nature all Divine
  Together joyn'd in Him that's Thou, and I.   10
    Flesh of my Flesh, Bone of my Bone: there's run
    Thy Godhead and my Manhood in thy Son.

Oh! that that Flame which thou didst on me Cast
  Might me enflame, and Lighten ery where.
Then Heaven to me would be less at last,   15
  So much of heaven I should have while here.
    Oh! Sweet though Short! I'le not forget the same.
    My neerness, Lord, to thee did me Enflame.

I'le Claim my Right: Give place ye Angells Bright.
  Ye further from the Godhead stande than I.
My Nature is your Lord; and doth Unite   20
  Better than Yours unto the Deity.
    Gods Throne is first and mine is next: to you
    Onely the place of Waiting-men is due.

Oh! that my Heart, thy Golden Harp might bee   **25**
  Well tun'd by Glorious Grace, that e'ry string
Screw'd to the highest pitch, might unto thee
  All Praises wrapt in sweetest Musick bring.
I praise thee, Lord, and better praise thee would,
If what I had, my heart might ever hold.   **30**

MEDITATION TEN

John VI: 55: For my flesh is meat indeed, and my blood is
drink indeed.

Stupendious Love! All Saints Astonishment!
  Bright Angells are black Motes in this Suns Light,
Heav'ns canopy, the Pantile to Gods tent,
  Can't cover't neither with its breadth nor height,
Its Glory doth all Glory else outrun,   **5**
  Beams of bright Glory to't are motes i'th'sun.

My Soule had caught an Ague, and like Hell
  Her thirst did burn: she to each spring did fly,
But this bright blazing Love did spring a Well
  Of Aqua-Vitae in the Deity,   **10**
  Which on the top of Heav'ns high Hill out burst
And down came running thence t'allay my thirst.

But how it came, amazeth all communion.
  Gods onely Son doth hug Humanity
Into his very person. By which Union   **15**
  His Humane Veans its golden gutters ly.
And rather than my Soule should dy by thirst,
  These Golden Pipes, to give me drink, did burst.

This Liquour brew'd, thy sparkling Art Divine,
  Lord, in thy Chrystall Vessells did up tun,   **20**
(Thine Ordinances) which all Earth o're shine,
  Set in thy rich Wine Cellars out to run.
Lord, make thy Butlar draw, and fill with speed
  My Beaker full: for this is drink indeed.

Whole Buts of this blesst Nectar shining stand   25
  Lockt up with Saph'rine Taps, whose splendid Flame
Too bright do shine for brightest Angells hands
  To touch, my Lord. Do thou untap the same.
Oh! make thy Chrystall Buts of Red Wine bleed
  Into my Chrystall Glass this Drink-Indeed.   30

How shall I praise thee then? My blottings jar
  And wrack my Rhymes to pieces in thy praise.
Thou breath'st thy Vean still in my Porringer,
  To lay my thirst, and fainting spirits raise.
Thou makest Glory's chiefest Grape to bleed   35
  Into my cup: And this is Drink-Indeed.

Nay, though I make no pay for this Red Wine,
  And scarce do say I thank ye for't; strange thing!
Yet were thy silver skies my Beer bowle fine,
  I finde my Lord would fill it to the brim.   40
Then make my life, Lord, to thy praise proceed
For thy rich blood, which is my Drink-Indeed.

                                                          1684

MEDITATION THIRTY-EIGHT

   I John II: 1: And if any man sin, we have an advocate with
the Father.

Oh! What a thing is Man? Lord, Who am I?
  That thou shouldst give him Law (Oh! golden Line)
To regulate his Thoughts, Words, Life thereby:
  And judge him wilt thereby too in thy time.
A Court of Justice thou in heaven holdst,   5
  To try his Case while he's here housd on mould.

How do thy Angells lay before thine eye
  My Deeds both White and Black I dayly doe?
How doth thy Court thou Pannellst there them try?
  But flesh complains. What right for this? let's know!   10

For right or wrong, I can't appeare unto't.
And shall a sentence Pass on such a suite?

Soft; blemish not this golden Bench, or place.
  Here is no Bribe, nor Colourings to hide,
Nor Pettifogger to befog the Case;   15
    But Justice hath her Glory here well tri'de:
    Her spotless Law all spotted Cases tends;
    Without Respect or Disrespect them ends.

God's Judge himselte, and Christ Atturny is;
  The Holy Ghost Regesterer is founde.   20
Angells the sergeants are, all Creatures kiss
  The booke, and doe as Evidence abounde.
    All Cases pass according to pure Law,
    And in the sentence is no Fret nor flaw.

What saith, my soule? Here all thy Deeds are tri'de.   25
  Is Christ thy Advocate to pleade thy Cause?
Art thou his Client? Such shall never slide.
    He never lost his Case: he pleads such Laws
    As Carry do the same, nor doth refuse
    The Vilest sinners Case that doth him Choose.   30

This is his Honour, not Dishonour: nay,
  No Habeas-Corpus 'gainst his Clients came;
For all their Fines his Purse doth make down pay.
    He Non-Suites Satan's suite or Casts the same.
    He'll plead thy Case, and not accept a Fee.   35
    He'll plead Sub Forma Pauperis for thee.

My Case is bad. Lord, be my Advocate.
  My sin is red: I'me under Gods Arrest.
Thou hast the Hit of Pleading; plead my state.
    Although it's bad, thy Plea will make it best.   40
    If thou wilt plead my Case before the King,
    I'le Waggon Loads of Love and Glory bring.

                        1690

MEDITATION THIRTY

Second Series

Matthew XII: 40: For as Jonas was three days and three
nights in the whale's belly; so shall the Son of man be three
days and three nights in the heart of the earth.

Prest down with sorrow, Lord, not for my Sin,
    But with Saint 'Tonys Cross I crossed groane.
Thus my leane Muses garden thwarts the spring:
    Instead of Anthems, breatheth her a hone.
    But duty raps upon her doore for verse,   5
    That makes her bleed a poem through her searce.

When, Lord, man was a mirror of thy Works
    In happy state, adorn'd with Glory's Wealth,
What heedless thing was hee? The serpent lurks
    Under an apple paring, and by stealth   10
    Destroy'd her Glory. O poor keeper hee
    Was of himselfe: lost God, and lost his Glee.

Christ, as a Turtle Dove, puts out his Wing.
    Lay all on mee; I will, saith hee, Convay
Away thy fault, and answer for thy sin.   15
    Thou'st be the Stewhouse of my Grace, and lay
    It and thyself out in my service pure,
    And I will for thy sake the storm Endure.

Jonas did type this thing, who ran away
    From God and, shipt for Tarsus, fell asleep.   20
A storm lies on the Ship: the Seamen they
    Bestir their stumps, and at wits end do weep:
    'Wake, Jonas:' who saith, 'Heave me over deck;
    The Storm will Cease then; all lies on my neck.'

They cast him overboard out of the ship.   25
    The tempest terrible lies thereby still.

A Mighty Whale nam'd Neptunes Dog doth skip
  At such a Boon, whose greedy gorge can't kill,
Neither Concoct this gudgeon, but its Chest
  Became the Prophets Coffin for the best.   30

He three dayes here lies trancifi'de and prayes,
  Prooves working Physick in the fishes Crop:
Maybe in th' Euxine, or the Issick Bay
  She puking falls, and he alive out drops.
She vomits him alive out on the Land,   35
Whence he to Ninive receives command.

A sermon he unto the Gentiles preach't,
  'Yet fortie dayes, and Nin've is destroy'd!'
Space granted, this Repentance doth them teach:
  God pardons them, and thus they ruine 'void.   40
Oh! Sweet, Sweet Providence, rich Grace hath splic'te
This Overture to be a type of Christ.

Jonas our Turtle Dove, I Christ intend,
  Is in the ship for Tarsus under saile.
A fiery storm tempestiously doth spend   45
  The Vessill and its hands: all Spirits faile;
The ship will sink, or wrack upon the rocks,
Unless the tempest cease the same to box.

None can it Charm but Jonas. Christ up posts,
  Is heaved overboard into the sea: 50
The Dove must die, the storm gives up its Ghost,
  And Neptune's Dogg leapes at him as a Prey,
Whose stomach is his Grave where he doth sleep
Three Dayes sepulchred, Jonas in the Deep.

The Grave him swallow'd down as a rich Pill   55
  Of Working Physick full of Virtue, which
Doth purge Death's Constitution of its ill,
  And womble-Crops her stomach where it sticks.
It heaves her stomach till her hasps off fly:
And out hee comes cast up, rai's up thereby.   60

In glorious Grace he to the Heathen goes,
    Envites them to Repentance. They accept.
Oh! Happy Message squandering Curst foes:
    Grace in her glorious Charriot here rides decks.
    Wrath's Fire is quencht: and Graces sun out shines;   65
    Death on her deathbed lies, Consumes and pines.

Here is my rich Atonement in thy Death;
    My Lord, nought is so sweet, though sweat it cost.
This turns from me Gods wrath: thy sweet sweet breath
    Revives my heart: thy Rising up o're bosst   70
    My Soule with Hope. seeing acquittance in't:
    That all my sins are kill'd, that did mee sinke.

I thanke thee, Lord, thy death hath dead'ned quite
    The Dreadfull Tempest. Let thy Dovy wings
Oreshadow me, and all my Faults benight,   75
    And with Celestiall Dews my soule besprindge.
    In angells Quires I'le then my Michtams sing,
    Upon my Jonah Elem Rechokim.

                                                            1699

MEDITATION FIFTY-SIX

Second Series

John XV: 24: If I had not done among them the works
which none other man did, they had not had sin: but now
have they both seen and hated both me and my Father.

Should I with silver tooles delve through the Hill
    Of Cordilera for rich thoughts, that I
My Lord, might weave with an angelick skill
    A Damask Web of Velvet Verse, thereby
    To deck thy Works up, all my Web would run   5
    To rags and jags: so snick-snarld to the thrum.

Thine are so rich: within, without refin'd:
    No worke like thine. No Fruits so sweete that grow

On th' trees of righteousness of Angell kinde,
   And Saints, whose limbs reev'd with them bow down low.   10
Should I search ore the Nutmeg Gardens shine,
   Its fruits in flourish are but skegs to thine.

The Clove, when in its White-green'd blossoms shoots,
   Some Call the pleasantst scent the World doth show,
None Eye e're saw, nor nose e're smelt such Fruits,   15
   My Lord, as thine, Thou Tree of Life in 'ts blow.
Thou Rose of Sharon, Vallies Lilly true,
Thy Fruits most sweet and glorious ever grew.

Thou are a Tree of Perfect nature trim,
   Whose golden lining is of perfect Grace,   20
Perfum'de with Deity unto the brim,
   Whose fruits, of the perfection, grow, of Grace.
Thy Buds, thy Blossoms, and thy fruits adorne
Thyselfe and Works, more shining than the morn.

Art, natures Ape, hath many brave things done: 25
   As th' Pyramids, the Lake of Meris vast,
The Pensile Orchards built in Babylon,
   Psammitich's Labyrinth, (arts Cramping task)
Archimedes his Engins made for war,
Romes Golden House, Titus his Theater.   30

The Clock of Strasburgh, Dresdens Table-sight,
   Regsamonts Fly of Steele about that flew,
Turrian's Wooden Sparrows in a flight,
   And th' Artificiall man Aquinas slew,
Mark Scaliota's Lock and Key and Chain   35
Drawn by a Flea, in our Queen Betties reign.

Might but my pen in natures Inventory
   Its progress make, 't might make such things to jump,
All which are but Inventions Vents or glory:
   Wits Wantonings, and Fancies frollicks plump: 40
Within whose maws lies buried Times, and Treasures,
Embalmed up in thick dawbd sinfull pleasures.

Nature doth better work than Art, yet thine
   Out vie both works of nature and of Art.
Natures Perfection and the perfect shine   45
   Of Grace attend thy deed in ev'ry part.
   A Thought, a Word, and Worke of thine, will kill
   Sin, Satan, and the Curse: and Law fulfill.

Thou are the Tree of Life in Paradise,
   Whose lively branches are with Clusters hung   50
Of Lovely fruits, and Flowers more sweet than spice.
   Bende down to us, and doe outshine the sun.
   Delightfull unto God, doe man rejoyce
   The pleasant'st fruits in all Gods Paradise.

Lord, feed mine eyes then with thy Doings rare,   55
   And fat my heart with these ripe fruites thou bear'st
Adorn my Life well with thy works; make faire
   My person with apparrell thou prepar'st.
   My Boughs shall loaded bee with fruits that spring
   Up from thy Works, while to thy praise I sing.   60

                                                    1703

PHILIP FRENEAU

Philip Morin Freneau (1752-1832) was born in New York City and made his home in New Jersey and Pennsylvania, except for the fifteen years which he spent variously at sea and in the West Indies. He was a teacher, soldier, printer, postal clerk, translator, merchant seaman, newspaper editor, book publisher, and farmer—as well as a prodigious poet.

Freneau was graduated from the College of New Jersey (Princeton) in 1771, a classmate of James Madison, Hugh Henry Brackenridge, and Aaron Burr, at a time when that college was a "hotbed of Whiggism" and anti-British feeling. After several attempts at schoolteaching and some desultory study in theology, Freneau became secretary to a planter in Santa Cruz (1775-78). On his return to America he joined the Continental Army as a private but saw little action. Sailing back to the West Indies (1780), he was captured, tried, and imprisoned by the British. He was exchanged as a prisoner of war and spent the next three years employed in the Philadelphia post office and writing verse satires on the British. He went to sea again until 1790, the year of his marriage, after which he spent the next ten years editing newspapers. The most important of these papers was the *National Gazette* (1791-93), which Freneau edited while employed as a part-time translator in the Department of State during most of Jefferson's tenure as Secretary. The paper was vigorously and pointedly anti-Federalist, and drew Alexander Hamilton's charges that Freneau was merely Jefferson's mouthpiece. When Washington apparently wanted Freneau removed from the Department of State, Jefferson defended his journalism: "His paper has saved our constitution, which was galloping fast into monarchy. . . ." The animosities in this affair anticipated the beginning of the two-party system.

After four more years at sea (1803-7), on cargo ships between Atlantic and Caribbean ports, Freneau returned to his home in New Jersey and continued to write. In 1832 he was granted a federal pension but did not live to collect it.

Freneau wrote about most of the experiences of this many-sided career; the writer and the public man nourished one another. He wrote descriptive, political, and literary essays; and some of his ideas he developed in fiction. But he wrote more poetry than prose, much of it mediocre. Five collections of his poems were published during his lifetime. The first two (1786, 1788) were edited by Freneau's friend, Francis Bailey, while Freneau was out of the country; the third collection (1795) includes Freneau's earlier poems: the fourth (1809) is the most comprehensive collection and represents the last stage of revision in which he left most of his poems; and the fifth (1815) contains his later poems. There is no complete collection of Freneau's poetry. The most reliable and comprehensive edition is: Fred L. Pattee (ed.), *The Poems of Philip Freneau*, 3 vols. (Princeton, 1902-7). This edition reprints all but about a hundred of Freneau's poems and establishes the dates of first publication.

These selections are presented in the order of their first publication, but since Freneau revised most of his verse, the text in most cases is the text of the latest edition published during his lifetime.

THE VANITY OF EXISTENCE

To Thyrsis

In youth, gay scenes attract our eyes,
    And not suspecting their decay
Life's flowery fields before us rise,
    Regardless of its winter day.

But vain pursuits and joys as vain,   5
    Convince us life is but a dream.
Death is to wake, to rise again
    To that true life you best esteem.

So nightly on some shallow tide,
    Oft have I seen a splendid show;   10
Reflected stars on either side,
    And glittering moons were seen below.

But when the tide had ebbed away,
    The scene fantastic with it fled,

A bank of mud around me lay,   15
And sea-weed on the river's bed.

First titled "A Moral Thought" 1781 (1786)

ON THE EMIGRATION TO AMERICA
AND PEOPLING THE WESTERN COUNTRY

To western woods, and lonely plains,
Palemon from the crowd departs,
Where Nature's wildest genius reigns,
To tame the soil, and plant the arts—
What wonders there shall freedom show,   5
What mighty states successive grow!

From Europe's proud, despotic shores
Hither the stranger takes his way,
And in our new found world explores
A happier soil, a milder sway,   10
Where no proud despot holds him down,
No slaves insult him with a crown.

What charming scenes attract the eye,
On wild Ohio's savage stream!
There Nature reigns, whose works outvie   15
The boldest pattern art can frame;
There ages past have rolled away,
And forests bloomed but to decay.

From these fair plains, these rural seats,
So long concealed, so lately known,   20
The unsocial Indian far retreats,
To make some other clime his own,
When other streams, less pleasing, flow,
And darker forests round him grow.

Great Sire of floods! whose varied wave   25
Through climes and countries takes its way,

To whom creating Nature gave
Ten thousand streams to swell thy sway!
No longer shall they useless prove,
Nor idly through the forests rove;   30

Nor longer shall your princely flood
From distant lakes be swelled in vain,
Nor longer through a darksome wood
Advance,˙unnoticed, to the main,
Far other ends, the heavens decree—   35
And commerce plans new freights for thee.

While virtue warms the generous breast,
There heaven-born freedom shall reside,
Nor shall the voice of war molest,
Nor Europe's all-aspiring pride—   40
There Reason shall new laws devise,
And order from confusion rise.

Forsaking kings and regal state,
With all their pomp and fancied bliss,
The traveller owns, convinced though late,   45
No realm so free, so blest as this—
The east is half to slaves consigned,
Where kings and priests enchain the mind.

O come the time, and haste the day,
When man shall man no longer crush,   50
When Reason shall enforce her sway,
Nor these fair regions raise our blush,
Where still the African complains,
And mourns his yet unbroken chains.

Far brighter scenes a future age,   55
The muse predicts, these States will hail,
Whose genius may the world engage,
Whose deeds may over death prevail,
And happier systems bring to view,
Than all the eastern sages knew.   60

1785 (1809)

ON RETIREMENT

(By Hezekiah Salem)

A hermit's house beside a stream,
  With forests planted round,
Whatever it to you may seem
More real happiness I deem
  Than if I were a monarch crown'd.   5

A cottage I could call my own,
  Remote from domes of care;
A little garden walled with stone,
The wall with ivy overgrown,
  A limpid fountain near,   10

Would more substantial joys afford,
  More real bliss impart
Than all the wealth that misers hoard,
Than vanquish'd worlds, or worlds restored—
  Mere cankers of the heart!   15

Vain, foolish man! how vast thy pride,
  How little can your wants supply!—
'Tis surely wrong to grasp so wide—
You act as if you only had
  To vanquish—not to die!   20

        [Later titled "The Wish of Diogenes"] 1786

THE WILD HONEY SUCKLE

Fair flower, that dost so comely grow,
Hid in this silent, dull retreat,
Untouch'd thy honey'd blossoms blow,
Unseen thy little branches greet:
  No roving foot shall crush thee here,   5
  No busy hand provoke a tear.

By Nature's self in white array'd,
She bade thee shun the vulgar eye,
And planted here the guardian shade,
And sent soft waters murmuring by;   10
   Thus quietly thy summer goes,
   Thy days declining to repose.

Smit with those charms, that must decay,
I grieve to see your future doom;
They died—nor were those flowers more gay,   15
The flowers that did in Eden bloom;
   Unpitying frosts, and Autumn's power
   Shall leave no vestige of this flower.

From morning suns and evening dews
At first thy little being came: 20
If nothing once, you nothing lose,
For when you die you are the same;
   The space between, is but an hour,
   The frail duration of a flower.

                                        1786 (1809)

ON A BOOK CALLED UNITARIAN THEOLOGY

   In this choice work, with wisdom penned, we find
The noblest system to reform mankind,
Bold truths confirmed, that bigots have denied,
By most perverted, and which some deride.
   Here, truths divine in easy language flow,   5
Truths long concealed, that now all climes shall know
Here, like the blaze of our material sun,
Enlightened Reason proves, that God is One—
As that, concentered in itself, a sphere,
Illumes all Nature with its radiance here,   10
Bids towards itself all trees and plants aspire,
Awakes the winds, impels the seeds of fire,
And still subservient to the Almighty plan,
Warms into life the changeful race of man;

So—like that sun—in heaven's bright realms we trace   15
One Power of Love, that fills unbounded space,
Existing always by no borrowed aid,
Before all worlds—eternal, and not made—
To That indebted, stars and comets burn,
Owe their swift movements, and to That return!   20
Prime source of wisdom, all-contriving mind,
First spring of Reason, that this globe designed;
Parent of order, whose unwearied hand
Upholds the fabric that his wisdom planned,
And, its due course assigned to every sphere,   25
Revolves the seasons, and sustains the year!—
    Pure light of Truth! where'er thy splendours shine,
Thou art the image of the power divine;
Nought else, in life, that full resemblance bears,
No sun, that lights us through our circling years,   30
No stars, that through yon' charming azure stray,
No moon, that glads us with her evening ray,
No seas, that o'er their gloomy caverns flow,
No forms beyond us, and no shapes below!
    Then slight—ah slight not, this instructive page,   35
For the mean follies of a dreaming age:
Here to the truth, by Reason's aid aspire,
Nor some dull preacher of romance admire;
See One, Sole God, in these convincing lines,
Beneath whose view perpetual day-light shines;   40
At whose command all worlds their circuits run,
And night, retiring, dies before the sun!
    Here, Man no more disgraced by Time appears,
Lost in dull slumbers through ten thousand years;
Plunged in that gulph, whose dark unfathomed wave   45
Men of all ages to perdition gave;
An empty dream, or still more empty shade,
The substance vanished, and the form decayed:—
    Here Reason proves, that when this life decays,
Instant, new life in the warm bosom plays,   50
As that expiring, still its course repairs
Through endless ages, and unceasing years.
    Where parted souls with kindred spirits meet,
Wrapt to the bloom of beauty all complete;

In that celestial, vast, unclouded sphere,   55
Nought there exists but has its image here!
All there is Mind!—That Intellectual Flame,
From whose vast stores all human genius came,
In which all Nature forms on Reason's plan—
Flows to this abject world, and beams on Man!   60

[First titled "On the Honourable Emanuel Swedenborg's Uni-
versal Theology"]   1786 (1809)

TO AN AUTHOR

Your leaves bound up compact and fair,
In neat array at length prepare,
To pass their hour on learning's stage,
To meet the surly critic's rage;
The statesman's slight, the smatterer's sneer—   5
Were these, indeed, your only fear,
You might be tranquil and resigned:
What most should touch your fluttering mind;
Is that, few critics will be found
To sift your works, and deal the wound.   10

Thus, when one fleeting year is past
On some bye-shelf your book is cast—
Another comes, with something new,
And drives you fairly out of view:
With some to praise, but more to blame,   15
The mind returns to—whence it came;
And some alive, who scarce could read
Will publish satires on the dead.

Thrice happy Dryden, who could meet
Some rival bard in every street!   20
When all were bent on writing well
It was some credit to excel:—

Thrice happy Dryden, who could find
A Milbourne for his sport designed—

And Pope, who saw the harmless rage   25
Of Dennis bursting o'er his page
Might justly spurn the critic's aim,
Who only helped to swell his fame.

On these bleak climes by Fortune thrown,
Where rigid Reason reigns alone,   30
Where lovely Fancy has no sway,
Nor magic forms about us play—
Nor nature takes her summer hue
Tell me, what has the muse to do?—

An age employed in edging steel   35
Can no poetic raptures feel;
No solitude's attracting power,
No leisure of the noon day hour,
No shaded stream, no quiet grove
Can this fantastic century move;   40

The muse of love in no request—
Go—try your fortune with the rest,
One of the nine you should engage,
To meet the follies of the age:—

On one, we fear, your choice must fall—   45
The least engaging of them all—
Her visage stern—an angry style—
A clouded brow—malicious smile—
A mind on murdered victims placed—
She, only she, can please the taste!   50

1788 (1809)

HATTERAS

In fathoms five the anchor gone;
While here we furl the sail,
No longer vainly labouring on
Against the western gale:

While here thy bare and barren cliffs,   5
O Hatteras, I survey,
And shallow grounds and broken reefs—
What shall console my stay!

The dangerous shoal, that breaks the wave
In columns to the sky;   10
The tempests black, that hourly rave,
Portend all danger nigh:
Sad are my dreams on ocean's verge!
The Atlantic round me flows,
Upon whose ancient angry surge   15
No traveller finds repose!

The Pilot comes!—from yonder sands
He shoves his barque, so frail,
And hurrying on, with busy hands,
Employs both oar and sail.   20
Beneath this rude unsettled sky
Condemn'd to pass his years,
No other shores delight his eye,
No foe alarms his fears.

In depths of woods his hut he builds,   25
Devoted to repose,
And, blooming, in the barren wilds
His little garden grows:
His wedded nymph, of sallow hue,
No mingled colours grace—   30
For her he toils—to her is true,
The captive of her face.

Kind Nature here, to make him blest,
No quiet harbour plann'd;
And poverty—his constant guest,   35
Restrains the pirate band:
His hopes are all in yonder flock,
Or some few hives of bees,
Except, when bound for Ocracock,
Some gliding barque he sees: 40

His Catharine then he quits with grief,
And spreads his tottering sails,
While, waving high her handkerchief,
Her commodore she hails:
She grieves, and fears to see no more   45
The sail that now forsakes,
From Hatteras' sands to banks of Core
Such tedious journies takes!

Fond nymph! your sighs are heav'd in vain,
Restrain those idle fears: 50
Can you—that should relieve his pain—
Thus kill him with your tears!
Can absence, thus, beget regard,
Or does it only seem?
He comes to meet a wandering bard   55
That steers for Ashley's stream.

Though disappointed in his views,
Not joyless will we part;
Nor shall the god of mirth refuse
The Balsam of the Heart: 60
No niggard key shall lock up Joy—
I'll give him half my store
Will he but half his skill employ
To guard us from your shore.

Should eastern gales once more awake,   65
No safety will be here:—
Alack! I see the billows break,
Wild tempests hovering near:
Before the bellowing seas begin
Their conflict with the land,   70
Go, pilot, go—your Catharine join,
That waits on yonder sand.

                                1789 (1795)

STANZAS TO AN ALIEN

Remote, beneath a sultry star
Where Mississippi flows afar
I see you rambling, God knows where.

Sometimes, beneath a cypress bough,
When met in dreams, with spirits low,   5
I long to tell you what I know.

How matters go, in this our day,
When monarchy renews her sway,
And royalty begins her play.

I thought you wrong to come so far   10
Till you had seen our western star
Above the mists ascended clear.

I thought you right, to speed your sails
If you were fond of loathsome jails,
And justice with uneven scales.   15

And so you came and spoke too free
And soon they made you bend the knee,
And lodged you under lock and key.

Discharged at last, you made your peace
With all you had, and left the place   20
With empty purse and meagre face.—

You sped your way to other climes
And left me here to teaze with rhymes
The worst of men in worst of times.

Where you are gone the soil is free   25
And freedom sings from every tree,
"Come quit the crowd and live with me!"

Where I must stay, no joys are found;
Excisemen haunt the hateful ground,
And chains are forged for all around.   30

The scheming men, with brazen throat,
Would set a murdering tribe afloat
To hang you for the lines you wrote.

If you are safe beyond their rage
Thank heaven, and not our ruling sage,   35
Who shops us up in jail and cage.

Perdition seize that odious race
Who, aiming at distinguish'd place,
Would life and liberty efface;

With iron rod would rule the ball   40
And, at their shrine, debase us all,
Bid devils rise and angels fall.

Oh wish them ill, and wish them long
To be as usual in the wrong
In scheming for a chain too strong.   45

So will the happy time arrive
When coming home, if then alive,
You'll see them to the devil drive.

                                        1799 (1815)

ON THE UNIFORMITY AND PERFECTION OF NATURE

On one fix'd point all nature moves,
Nor deviates from the track she loves;
Her system, drawn from reason's source,
She scorns to change her wonted course.

Could she descend from that great plan   5
To work unusual things for man,
To suit the insect of an hour—
This would betray a want of power,

Unsettled in its first design
And erring, when it did combine   10
The parts that form the vast machine,
The figures sketch'd on nature's scene.

Perfections of the great first cause
Submit to no contracted laws,
But all-sufficient, all-supreme,   15
Include no trivial views in them.

Who looks through nature with an eye
That would the scheme of heaven descry,
Observes her constant, still the same,
In all her laws, through all her frame.   20

No imperfection can be found
In all that is, above, around,—
All, nature made, in reason's sight
Is order all, and *all is right*.

                                              1815

WILLIAM CULLEN BRYANT

William Cullen Bryant (1794-1878), editor, poet, lawyer, and abolitionist, was born in Cummington, Massachusetts, son of a country physician, and was buried from a Unitarian church in Roslyn, Long Island. Educated partly in the rural district schools of western Massachusetts and partly by tutors, he trained for the bar and practiced in Massachusetts from 1815 to 1825. His reputation as a poet began with the publication of "Thanatopsis" in the *North American Review* in 1817, six years after he had written the poem, and his literary stature grew rapidly. He published an edition of poems (1821), and, while still practicing law, he agreed to furnish the *United States Literary Gazette* a hundred lines of poetry a month. In 1825 he became coeditor of the *New York Review and Athenaeum Magazine* and, later, editor and part owner of the New York *Evening Post*. The *Post* was a vigorous force in the Democratic party until Bryant's abolitionism allied the paper with the new Republican party in 1856. His editorial career effectively limited his literary energies, and the 1832 edition of his poems represents substantially his canon of poetry, although he later translated the *Iliad* and the *Odyssey* and published a half-dozen or more titles of his own.

Bryant's poetic program is simply stated. He intended to help build a native American literature; his lecture, "On Poetry in its Relation to Our Age and Country" (1825), concludes with his estimate of the probability of achieving it: "I infer, then, that all the materials of poetry exist in our own country, with all the ordinary encouragements and opportunities for making a successful use of them. The elements of beauty and grandeur, intellectual greatness and moral truth, the stormy and the gentle passions, the casualties and the changes of life, and the light shed upon man's nature by the story of past times and the knowledge of foreign manners, have not made their sole abode in the old world beyond the waters. If under these circumstances our poetry should finally fail of rivalling that of Europe, it will be because Genius sits idle in the midst of its treasures." Part of Bryant's task was to domesticate the forms and conventions of eighteenth-century

English poetry, which he did with the substance of many of
his poems: the physical properties of the new country.
The text of these poems is: Parke Godwin (ed.), *The
Poetical Works of William Cullen Bryant*, 2 vols. (New York,
1883).

THANATOPSIS

To him who in the love of Nature holds
Communion with her visible forms, she speaks
A various language; for his gayer hours
She has a voice of gladness, and a smile
And eloquence of beauty, and she glides   5
Into his darker musings, with a mild
And healing sympathy, that steals away
Their sharpness, ere he is aware. When thoughts
Of the last bitter hour come like a blight
Over thy spirit, and sad images   10
Of the stern agony, and shroud, and pall,
And breathless darkness, and the narrow house,
Make thee to shudder, and grow sick at heart;—
Go forth, under the open sky, and list
To Nature's teachings, while from all around—   15
Earth and her waters, and the depths of air—
Comes a still voice.—

                Yet a few days, and thee
The all-beholding sun shall see no more
In all his course; nor yet in the cold ground,   20
Where thy pale form was laid, with many tears,
Nor in the embrace of ocean, shall exist
Thy image. Earth, that nourished thee, shall claim
Thy growth, to be resolved to earth again,
And, lost each human trace, surrendering up   25
Thine individual being, shalt thou go
To mix for ever with the elements,
To be a brother to the insensible rock
And to the sluggish clod, which the rude swain
Turns with his share, and treads upon. The oak   30
Shall send his roots abroad, and pierce thy mould.

Yet not to thine eternal resting-place
Shalt thou retire alone, nor couldst thou wish
Couch more magnificent. Thou shalt lie down
With patriarchs of the infant world—with kings,   35
The powerful of the earth—the wise, the good,
Fair forms, and hoary seers of ages past,
All in one mighty sepulchre. The hills
Rock-ribbed and ancient as the sun,—the vales
Stretching in pensive quietness between;   40
The venerable woods—rivers that move
In majesty, and the complaining brooks
That make the meadows green; and, poured round all,
Old Ocean's gray and melancholy waste,—
Are but the solemn decorations all   45
Of the great tomb of man. The golden sun,
The planets, all the infinite host of heaven,
Are shining on the sad abodes of death,
Through the still lapse of ages. All that tread
The globe are but a handful to the tribes   50
That slumber in its bosom.—Take the wings
Of morning, pierce the Barcan wilderness,
Or lose thyself in the continuous woods
Where rolls the Oregon, and hears no sound,
Save his own dashings—yet the dead are there: 55
And millions in those solitudes, since first
The flight of years began, have laid them down
In their last sleep—the dead reign there alone.
So shalt thou rest, and what if thou withdraw
In silence from the living and no friend   60
Take note of thy departure? All that breathe
Will share thy destiny. The gay will laugh
When thou art gone, the solemn brood of care
Plod on, and each one as before will chase
His favorite phantom; yet all these shall leave   65
Their mirth and their employments, and shall come
And make their bed with thee. As the long train
Of ages glides away, the sons of men,
The youth in life's fresh spring, and he who goes
In the full strength of years, matron and maid,   70
The speechless babe, and the gray-headed man—

Shall one by one be gathered to thy side,
By those, who in their turn shall follow them.

So live, that when thy summons comes to join
The innumerable caravan, which moves   75
To that mysterious realm, where each shall take
His chamber in the silent halls of death,
Thou go not, like the quarry-slave at night,
Scourged to his dungeon, but, sustained and soothed
By an unfaltering trust, approach thy grave.   80
Like one who wraps the drapery of his couch
About him, and lies down to pleasant dreams.

                                                        1817

INSCRIPTION FOR THE ENTRANCE TO A WOOD

Stranger, if thou hast learned a truth which needs
No school of long experience, that the world
Is full of guilt and misery, and hast seen
Enough of all its sorrows, crimes, and cares,
To tire thee of it, enter this wild wood   5
And view the haunts of Nature. The calm shade
Shall bring a kindred calm, and the sweet breeze
That makes the green leaves dance, shall waft a balm
To thy sick heart. Thou wilt find nothing here
Of all that pained thee in the haunts of men,   10
And made thee loathe thy life. The primal curse
Fell, it is true, upon the unsinning earth,
But not in vengeance. God hath yoked to guilt
Her pale tormentor, misery. Hence, these shades
Are still the abodes of gladness; the thick roof   15
Of green and stirring branches is alive
And musical with birds, that sing and sport
In wantonness of spirit; while below
The squirrel, with raised paws and form erect,
Chirps merrily. Throngs of insects in the shade   20
Try their thin wings and dance in the warm beam
That waked them into life. Even the green trees
Partake the deep contentment; as they bend

To the soft winds, the sun from the blue sky
Looks in and sheds a blessing on the scene.   25
Scarce less the cleft-born wild-flower seems to enjoy
Existence, than the wingèd plunderer
That sucks its sweets. The mossy rocks themselves,
And the old and ponderous trunks of prostrate trees
That lead from knoll to knoll a causey rude   30
Or bridge the sunken brook, and their dark roots,
With all their earth upon them, twisting high,
Breathe fixed tranquillity. The rivulet
Sends forth glad sounds, and tripping o'er its bed
Of pebbly sands, or leaping down the rocks,   35
Seems, with continuous laughter, to rejoice
In its own being. Softly tread the marge,
Lest from her midway perch thou scare the wren
That dips her bill in water. The cool wind,
That stirs the stream in play, shall come to thee,   40
Like one that loves thee nor will let thee pass
Ungreeted, and shall give its light embrace.

                                                       1817

A FOREST HYMN

The groves were God's first temples. Ere man learned
To hew the shaft, and lay the architrave,
And spread the roof above them—ere he framed
The lofty vault, to gather and roll back
The sound of anthems; in the darkling wood,   5
Amid the cool and silence, he knelt down,
And offered to the Mightiest solemn thanks
And supplication. For his simple heart
Might not resist the sacred influences
Which, from the stilly twilight of the place,   10
And from the gray old trunks that high in heaven
Mingled their mossy boughs, and from the sound
Of the invisible breath that swayed at once
All their green tops, stole over him, and bowed
His spirit with the thought of boundless power   15
And inaccessible majesty. Ah, why

Should we, in the world's riper years, neglect
God's ancient sanctuaries, and adore
Only among the crowd, and under roofs
That our frail hands have raised? Let me at least,   20
Here, in the shadow of this aged wood,
Offer one hymn—thrice happy, if it find
Acceptance in His ear.

             Father thy hand
Hath reared these venerable columns, thou
Didst weave this verdant roof. Thou didst look down   25
Upon the naked earth, and, forthwith, rose
All these fair ranks of trees. They, in thy sun,
Budded, and shook their green leaves in thy breeze,
And shot toward heaven. The century-living crow,
Whose birth was in their tops, grew old and died   30
Among their branches, till, at last, they stood,
As now they stand, massy, and tall, and dark,
Fit shrine for humble worshipper to hold
Communion with his Maker. These dim vaults,
These winding aisles, of human pomp or pride   35
Report not. No fantastic carvings show
The boast of our vain race to change the form
Of thy fair works. But thou art here—thou fill'st
The solitude. Thou art in the soft winds
That run along the summit of these trees   40
In music; thou art in the cooler breath
That from the inmost darkness of the place
Comes, scarcely felt; the barky trunks, the ground,
The fresh moist ground, are all instinct with thee.
Here is continual worship;—Nature, here,   45
In the tranquillity that thou dost love,
Enjoys thy presence. Noiselessly, around,
From perch to perch, the solitary bird
Passes; and yon clear spring, that, midst its herbs,
Wells softly forth and wandering steeps the roots   50
Of half the mighty forest, tells no tale
Of all the good it does. Thou hast not left
Thyself without a witness, in the shades,
Of thy perfections. Grandeur, strength, and grace

Are here to speak of thee. This mighty oak—   55
By whose immovable stem I stand and seem
Almost annihilated—not a prince,
In all that proud old world beyond the deep,
E'er wore his crown as loftily as he
Wears the green coronal of leaves with which   60
Thy hand has graced him. Nestled at his root
Is beauty, such as blooms not in the glare
Of the broad sun. That delicate forest flower,
With scented breath and look so like a smile,
Seems, as it issues from the shapeless mould,   65
An emanation of the indwelling Life,
A visible token of the upholding Love,
That are the soul of this great universe.

My heart is awed within me when I think
Of the great miracle that still goes on,   70
In silence, round me—the perpetual work
Of thy creation, finished, yet renewed
Forever. Written on thy works I read
The lesson of thy own eternity.
Lo! all grow old and die—but see again,   75
How on the faltering footsteps of decay
Youth presses—ever gay and beautiful youth
In all its beautiful forms. These lofty trees
Wave not less proudly that their ancestors
Moulder beneath them. Oh, there is not lost   80
One of the earth's charms: upon her bosom yet,
After the flight of untold centuries,
The freshness of her far beginning lies
And yet shall lie. Life mocks the idle hate
Of his arch-enemy Death—yea, seats himself   85
Upon the tyrant's throne—the sepulchre,
And of the triumphs of his ghastly foe
Makes his own nourishment. For he came forth
From thine own bosom, and shall have no end.

There have been holy men who hid themselves   90
Deep in the woody wilderness, and gave
Their lives to thought and prayer, till they outlived

The generation born with them, nor seemed
Less aged than the hoary trees and rocks
Around them;—and there have been holy men   95
Who deemed it were not well to pass life thus.
But let me often to these solitudes
Retire, and in thy presence reassure
My feeble virtue. Here its enemies,
The passions, at thy plainer footsteps shrink   100
And tremble and are still. O God! when thou
Dost scare the world with tempests, set on fire
The heavens with falling thunderbolts, or fill,
With all the waters of the firmament,
The swift dark whirlwind that uproots the woods   105
And drowns the villages; when, at thy call,
Uprises the great deep and throws himself
Upon the continent, and overwhelms
Its cities—who forgets not, at the sight
Of these tremendous tokens of thy power,   110
His pride, and lays his strifes and follies by?
Oh, from these sterner aspects of thy face
Spare me and mine, nor let us need the wrath
Of the mad unchained elements to teach
Who rules them. Be it ours to meditate,   115
In these calm shades, thy milder majesty,
And to the beautiful order of thy works
Learn to conform the order of our lives.

                                                    1825

TO COLE, THE PAINTER, DEPARTING
FOR EUROPE

Thine eyes shall see the light of distant skies;
    Yet, COLE! thy heart shall bear to Europe's strand
    A living image of our own bright land,
Such as upon thy glorious canvas lies;
Lone lakes—savannas where the bison roves—   5
    Rocks rich with summer garlands—solemn streams—
    Skies, where the desert eagle wheels and screams—
Spring bloom and autumn blaze of boundless groves.

Fair scenes shall greet thee where thou goest—fair,
But different—everywhere the trace of men,   10
To where life shrinks from the fierce Alpine air.
Gaze on them, till the tears shall dim thy sight,
But keep that earlier, wilder image bright.

1830

THE PRAIRIES

These are the gardens of the Desert, these
The unshorn fields, boundless and beautiful,
For which the speech of England has no name—
The Prairies. I behold them for the first,
And my heart swells, while the dilated sight   5
Takes in the encircling vastness. Lo! they stretch,
In airy undulations, far away,
As if the ocean, in his gentlest swell,
Stood still, with all his rounded billows fixed,
And motionless forever. Motionless?—   10
No—they are all unchained again. The clouds
Sweep over with their shadows, and, beneath,
The surface rolls and fluctuates to the eye;
Dark hollows seem to glide along and chase
The sunny ridges. Breezes of the South!   15
Who toss the golden and the flame-like flowers,
And pass the prairie-hawk that, poised on high,
Flaps his broad wings, yet moves not—ye have played
Among the palms of Mexico and vines
Of Texas, and have crisped the limpid brooks   20
That from the fountains of Sonora glide
Into the calm Pacific—have ye fanned
A nobler or a lovelier scene than this?
Man hath no power in all this glorious work:
The hand that built the firmament hath heaved   25
And smoothed these verdant swells, and sown their slopes
With herbage, planted them with island groves,
And hedged them round with forests. Fitting floor
For this magnificent temple of the sky—
With flowers whose glory and whose multitude   30

Rival the constellations! The great heavens
Seem to stoop down upon the scene in love,—
A nearer vault, and of a tenderer blue,
Than that which bends above our eastern hills.

As o'er the verdant waste I guide my steed,   35
Among the high rank grass that sweeps his sides
The hollow beating of his footstep seems
A sacrilegious sound. I think of those
Upon whose rest he tramples. Are they here—
The dead of other days?—and did the dust   40
Of these fair solitudes once stir with life
And burn with passion? Let the mighty mounds
That overlook the rivers, or that rise
In the dim forest crowded with old oaks,
Answer. A race, that long has passed away,   45
Built them;—a disciplined and populous race
Heaped, with long toil, the earth, while yet the Greek
Was hewing the Pentelicus to forms
Of symmetry, and rearing on its rock
The glittering Parthenon. These ample fields   50
Nourished their harvests, here their herds were fed,
When haply by their stalls the bison lowed,
And bowed his manèd shoulder to the yoke.
All day this desert murmured with their toils,
Till twilight blushed, and lovers walked, and wooed   55
In a forgotten language, and old tunes,
From instruments of unremembered form,
Gave the soft winds a voice. The red man came—
The roaming hunter-tribes, warlike and fierce,
And the mound-builders vanished from the earth.   60
The solitude of centuries untold
Has settled where they dwelt. The prairie-wolf
Hunts in their meadows, and his fresh-dug den
Yawns by my path. The gopher mines the ground
Where stood their swarming cities. All is gone;   65
All—save the piles of earth that hold their bones,
The platforms where they worshipped unknown gods,
The barriers which they builded from the soil
To keep the foe at bay—till o'er the walls

The wild beleaguerers broke, and, one by one,   70
The strongholds of the plain were forced, and heaped
With corpses. The brown vultures of the wood
Flocked to those vast uncovered sepulchres,
And sat unscared and silent at their feast.
Haply some solitary fugitive,   75
Lurking in marsh and forest, till the sense
Of desolation and of fear became
Bitterer than death, yielded himself to die.
Man's better nature triumphed then. Kind words
Welcomed and soothed him; the rude conquerors   80
Seated the captive with their chiefs; he chose
A bride among their maidens, and at length
Seemed to forget—yet ne'er forgot—the wife
Of his first love, and her sweet little ones,
Butchered, amid their shrieks, with all his race.   85

Thus change the forms of being. Thus arise
Races of living things, glorious in strength,
And perish, as the quickening breath of God
Fills them, or is withdrawn. The red-man, too
Has left the blooming wilds he ranged so long,   90
And, nearer to the Rocky Mountains, sought
A wilder hunting-ground. The beaver builds
No longer by these streams, but far away,
On waters whose blue surface ne'er gave back
The white man's face—among Missouri's springs,   95
And pools whose issues swell the Oregon—
He rears his little Venice. In these plains
The bison feeds no more. Twice twenty leagues
Beyond remotest smoke of hunter's camp,
Roams the majestic brute, in herds that shake   100
The earth with thundering steps—yet here I meet
His ancient footprints stamped beside the pool.

Still this great solitude is quick with life.
Myriads of insects, gaudy as the flowers
They flutter over, gentle quadrupeds,   105
And birds, that scarce have learned the fear of man,
Are here, and sliding reptiles of the ground,

Startlingly beautiful. The graceful deer
Bounds to the wood at my approach. The bee,
A more adventurous colonist than man,   110
With whom he came across the eastern deep,
Fills the savannas with his murmurings,
And hides his sweets, as in the golden age,
Within the hollow oak. I listen long
To his domestic hum, and think I hear   115
The sound of that advancing multitude
Which soon shall fill these deserts. From the ground
Comes up the laugh of children, the soft voice
Of maidens, and the sweet and solemn hymn
Of Sabbath worshippers. The low of herds   120
Blends with the rustling of the heavy grain
Over the dark brown furrows. All at once
A fresher wind sweeps by, and breaks my dream,
And I am in the wilderness alone.

                                                        1833

EARTH

A midnight black with clouds is in the sky;
I seem to feel, upon my limbs, the weight
Of its vast brooding shadow. All in vain
Turns the tired eye in search of form; no star
Pierces the pitchy veil; no ruddy blaze,   5
From dwellings lighted by the cheerful hearth,
Tinges the flowering summits of the grass.
No sound of life is heard, no village hum,
Nor measured tramp of footstep in the path,
Nor rush of wind, while, on the breast of Earth,   10
I lie and listen to her mighty voice:
A voice of many tones—sent up from streams
That wander through the gloom, from woods unseen
Swayed by the sweeping of the tides of air,
From rocky chasms where darkness dwells all day,   15
And hollows of the great invisible hills,
And sands that edge the ocean, stretching far
Into the night—a melancholy sound.

O Earth! dost thou too sorrow for the past
Like man thy offspring? Do I hear thee mourn 20
Thy childhood's unreturning hours, thy springs
Gone with their genial airs and melodies,
The gentle generations of thy flowers,
And thy majestic groves of olden time,
Perished with all their dwellers? Dost thou wail 25
For that fair age of which the poets tell,
Ere yet the winds grew keen with frost, or fire
Fell with the rains or spouted from the hills,
To blast thy greenness, while the virgin night
Was guiltless and salubrious as the day? 30
Or haply dost thou grieve for those that die—
For living things that trod thy paths awhile,
The love of thee and heaven—and now they sleep
Mixed with the shapeless dust on which thy herds
Trample and graze? I too must grieve with thee, 35
O'er loved ones lost. Their graves are far away
Upon thy mountains; yet, while I recline
Alone, in darkness, on thy naked soil,
The mighty nourisher and burial-place
Of man, I feel that I embrace their dust. 40

Ha! how the murmur deepens! I perceive
And tremble at its dreadful import. Earth
Uplifts a general cry for guilt and wrong,
And heaven is listening. The forgotten graves
Of the heart-broken utter forth their plaint. 45
The dust of her who loved and was betrayed,
And him who died neglected in his age;
The sepulchres of those who for mankind
Labored, and earned the recompense of scorn;
Ashes of martyrs for the truth, and bones 50
Of those who, in the strife for liberty,
Were beaten down, their corses given to dogs,
Their names to infamy, all find a voice.
The nook in which the captive, overtoiled,
Lay down to rest at last, and that which holds 55
Childhood's sweet blossoms, crushed by cruel hands,
Send up a plaintive sound. From battle-fields,

Where heroes madly drave and dashed their hosts
Against each other, rises up a noise,
As if the armèd multitudes of dead   60
Stirred in their heavy slumber. Mournful tones
Come from the green abysses of the sea—
A story of the crimes the guilty sought
To hide beneath its waves. The glens, the groves,
Paths in the thicket, pools of running brook,   65
And banks and depths of lake, and streets and lanes
Of cities, now that living sounds are hushed,
Murmur of guilty force and treachery.

Here, where I rest, the vales of Italy
Are round me, populous from early time,   70
And field of the tremendous warfare waged
'Twixt good and evil. Who, alas! shall dare
Interpret to man's ear the mingled voice
That comes from her old dungeons yawning now
To the black air, her amphitheatres,   75
Where the dew gathers on the mouldering stones,
And fanes of banished gods, and open tombs,
And roofless palaces, and streets and hearths
Of cities dug from their volcanic graves?
I hear a sound of many languages,   80
The utterance of nations now no more,
Driven out by mightier, as the days of heaven
Chase one another from the sky. The blood
Of freemen shed by freemen, till strange lords
Came in their hour of weakness, and made fast   85
The yoke that yet is worn, cries out to heaven.

What then shall cleanse thy bosom, gentle Earth,
From all its painful memories of guilt?
The whelming flood, or the renewing fire,
Or the slow change of time?—that so, at last,   90
The horrid tale of perjury and strife,
Murder and spoil, which men call history,
May seem a fable, like the inventions told
By poets of the gods of Greece. O thou,
Who sittest far beyond the Atlantic deep,   95

Among the sources of thy glorious streams,
My native Land of Groves! a newer page
In the great record of the world is thine;
Shall it be fairer? Fear, and friendly Hope,
And Envy, watch the issue, while the lines,   100
By which thou shalt be judged, are written down.

    1835

THE ANTIQUITY OF FREEDOM

Here are old trees, tall oaks, and gnarlèd pines,
That stream with gray-green mosses; here the ground
Was never trenched by spade, and flowers spring up
Unsown, and die ungathered. It is sweet
To linger here, among the flitting birds   5
And leaping squirrels, wandering brooks, and winds
That shake the leaves, and scatter, as they pass,
A fragrance from the cedars, thickly set
With pale-blue berries. In these peaceful shades—
Peaceful, unpruned, immeasurably old—   10
My thoughts go up the long dim path of years,
Back to the earliest days of liberty.

O FREEDOM! thou art not, as poets dream,
A fair young girl, with light and delicate limbs,
And wavy tresses gushing from the cap   15
With which the Roman master crowned his slave
When he took off the gyves. A bearded man,
Armed to the teeth, art thou, one mailèd hand
Grasps the broad shield, and one the sword; thy brow,
Glorious in beauty though it be, is scarred   20
With tokens of old wars; thy massive limbs
Are strong with struggling. Power at thee has launched
His bolts, and with his lightnings smitten thee;
They could not quench the life thou hast from heaven;
Merciless Power has dug thy dungeon deep,   25
And his swart armorers, by a thousand fires,
Have forged thy chain; yet, while he deems thee bound,
The links are shivered, and the prison-walls

Fall outward; terribly thou springest forth,
As springs the flame above a burning pile,   30
And shoutest to the nations, who return
Thy shoutings, while the pale oppressor flies.

Thy birthright was not given by human hands:
Thou wert twin-born with man. In pleasant fields,
While yet our race was few, thou sat'st with him,   35
To tend the quiet flock and watch the stars,
And teach the reed to utter simple airs.
Thou by his side, amid the tangled wood,
Didst war upon the panther and the wolf,
His only foes; and thou with him didst draw   40
The earliest furrow on the mountain-side,
Soft with the deluge. Tyranny himself,
Thy enemy, although of reverend look,
Hoary with many years, and far obeyed,
Is later born than thou; and as he meets   45
The grave defiance of thine elder eye,
The usurper trembles in his fastnesses.

Thou shalt wax stronger with the lapse of years,
But he shall fade into a feebler age—
Feebler, yet subtler. He shall weave his snares,   50
And spring them on thy careless steps, and clap
His withered hands, and from their ambush call
His hordes to fall upon thee. He shall send
Quaint maskers, wearing fair and gallant forms
To catch thy gaze, and uttering graceful words   55
To charm thy ear; while his sly imps, by stealth,
Twine round thee threads of steel, light thread on thread,
That grow to fetters; or bind down thy arms
With chains concealed in chaplets. Oh! not yet
Mayst thou unbrace thy corslet, nor lay by   60
Thy sword; nor yet, O Freedom! close thy lids
In slumber; for thine enemy never sleeps,
And thou must watch and combat till the day
Of the new earth and heaven. But wouldst thou rest
Awhile from tumult and the frauds of men,   65
These old and friendly solitudes invite

Thy visit. They, while yet the forest-trees
Were young upon the unviolated earth,
And yet the moss-stains on the rock were new,
Beheld thy glorious childhood, and rejoiced.   70

                                    1842

THE POET

Thou, who wouldst wear the name
  Of poet mid thy brethren of mankind,
And clothe in words of flame
  Thoughts that shall live within the general mind!
Deem not the framing of a deathless lay   5
The pastime of a drowsy summer day.

But gather all thy powers,
  And wreak them on the verse that thou does weave,
And in thy lonely hours,
  At silent morning or at wakeful eve,   10
While the warm current tingles through thy veins,
Set forth the burning words in fluent strains.

No smooth array of phrase,
  Artfully sought and ordered though it be,
Which the cold rhymer lays   15
  Upon his page with languid industry,
Can wake the listless pulse to livelier speed,
Or fill with sudden tears the eyes that read.

The secret wouldst thou know
  To touch the heart or fire the blood at will?   20
Let thine own eyes o'erflow;
  Let thy lips quiver with the passionate thrill;
Seize the great thought, ere yet its power be past,
And bind, in words, the fleet emotion fast.

Then, should thy verse appear   25
  Halting and harsh, and all unaptly wrought,
Touch the crude line with fear,

Save in the moment of impassioned thought;
Then summon back the original glow, and mend
The strain with rapture that with fire was penned.   30

Yet let no empty gust
    Of passion find an utterance in thy lay,
A blast that whirls the dust
    Along the howling street and dies away;
But feelings of calm power and mighty sweep,   35
Like currents journeying through the windless deep.

Seek'st thou, in living lays,
    To limn the beauty of the earth and sky?
Before thine inner gaze
    Let all that beauty in clear vision lie;   40
Look on it with exceeding love, and write
The words inspired by wonder and delight.

Of tempests wouldst thou sing,
    Or tell of battles—make thyself a part
Of the great tumult; cling   45
    To the tossed wreck with terror in thy heart;
Scale, with the assaulting host, the rampart's height,
And strike and struggle in the thickest fight.

So shalt thou frame a lay
    That haply may endure from age to age,   50
And they who read shall say:
    "What witchery hangs upon this poet's page!
What art is his the written spells to find
That sway from mood to mood the willing mind!"

                                                      1864

RALPH WALDO EMERSON

Ralph Waldo Emerson (1803-1882) was born in Boston and raised in a Unitarian household. He was graduated from Harvard and, after several years of schoolteaching, from the Harvard Divinity School. In 1832 he resigned his pulpit at the Second [Unitarian] Church of Boston, because he could no longer serve the sacrament of Communion. He traveled in Europe for two years and began to absorb certain philosophical ideas of Coleridge, Carlyle, and the German idealists. Because of these associations, his study compassed Platonism, Neoplatonism, Eastern religious thought, and the teaching of Emanuel Swedenborg. Upon his return to Boston, armed with new convictions and with the entries in his journal, which he had continued since his undergraduate days, Emerson began a lecturing career.

His long essay, *Nature* (1836), and his orations, *The American Scholar* (1837) and *An Address Delivered Before the Senior Class in Divinity College, Cambridge* (1838), established his premises for the doctrine of Transcendentalism and the principles of his whole canon of writing. Two series of essays (1841, 1844), and *Representative Men: Seven Lectures* (1850) variously dramatized these principles and acknowledged their implications. Three volumes of poems (1847, 1867, 1876) and a dozen other titles of lectures and essays comprise most of Emerson's published writing. Ten volumes of his journals and six volumes of his letters were posthumously published.

Emerson wrote and published poetry all his life, and he also translated many poems from foreign languages. He once wrote in a letter: "I am a born poet; of a low class without doubt, yet a poet. . . . My singing, to be sure, is very husky, and is for the most part prose. Still I am a poet." According to Emerson's essay, "The Poet" (1844), language is symbolic and is therefore an extension of the entire natural world. Each poem—each new structure of language—must therefore find its own characteristic shape and development. What makes each poem, he declared, is "a thought so passionate

51

and alive that, like the spirit of a plant or an animal, it has an architecture of its own. . . ." His theory was prophetic, and his verse inclines toward the symbolic and suggestive. But his practice often departed from his theory, and he used traditional verse forms without particular innovation. Notwithstanding his remarks, moreover, inspiration did not carry the whole poem, for his manuscripts reveal the process of repeated and lengthy revisions.

The first collection of Emerson's works after his death is the text of these poems: James Elliot Cabot (ed.), *The Works of Ralph Waldo Emerson*, 14 vols. (Cambridge, 1883-95), of which the last two volumes contain Cabot's memoir of Emerson.

EACH AND ALL

Little thinks, in the field, yon red-cloaked clown
Of thee from the hill-top looking down;
The heifer that lows in the upland farm,
Far-heard, lows not thine ear to charm;
The sexton, tolling his bell at noon,   5
Deems not that great Napoleon
Stops his horse, and lists with delight,
Whilst his files sweep round yon Alpine height;
Nor knowest thou what argument
Thy life to thy neighbor's creed has lent.   10
All are needed by each one;
Nothing is fair or good alone.
I thought the sparrow's note from heaven,
Singing at dawn on the alder bough;
I brought him home, in his nest, at even;   15
He sings the song, but it cheers not now,
For I did not bring home the river and sky;—
He sang to my ear,—they sang to my eye.
The delicate shells lay on the shore;
The bubbles of the latest wave   20
Fresh pearls to their enamel gave,
And the bellowing of the savage sea
Greeted their safe escape to me.

I wiped away the weeds and foam,
I fetched my sea-born treasures home;   25
But the poor, unsightly, noisome things
Had left their beauty on the shore
With the sun, and the sand, and the wild uproar.
The lover watched his graceful maid,
As mid the virgin train she strayed,   30
Nor knew her beauty's best attire
Was woven still by the snow-white choir.
At last she came to his hermitage,
Like the bird from the woodlands to the cage;—
The gay enchantment was undone,   35
A gentle wife, but fairy none.
Then I said, "I covet truth;
Beauty is unripe childhood's cheat;
I leave it behind with the games of youth."—
As I spoke, beneath my feet   40
The ground-pine curled its pretty wreath,
Running over the club-moss burrs;
I inhaled the violet's breath;
Around me stood the oaks and firs;
Pine-cones and acorns lay on the ground;   45
Over me soared the eternal sky,
Full of light and of deity;
Again I saw, again I heard,
The rolling river, the morning bird;—
Beauty through my senses stole;   50
I yielded myself to the perfect whole.

                                                    1839

THE PROBLEM

I like a church; I like a cowl;
I love a prophet of the soul;
And on my heart monastic aisles
Fall like sweet strains, or pensive smiles;
Yet not for all his faith can see
Would I that cowlèd churchman be.

Why should the vest on him allure,
Which I could not on me endure?

Not from a vain or shallow thought
His awful Jove young Phidias brought,   10
Never from lips of cunning fell
The thrilling Delphic oracle;
Out from the heart of nature rolled
The burdens of the Bible old;
The litanies of nations came,   15
Like the volcano's tongue of flame,
Up from the burning core below,—
The canticles of love and woe:
The hand that rounded Peter's dome,
And groined the aisles of Christian Rome,   20
Wrought in a sad sincerity;
Himself from God he could not free;
He builded better than he knew;—
The conscious stone to beauty grew.

Know'st thou what wove yon woodbird's nest   25
Of leaves, and feathers from her breast?
Or how the fish outbuilt her shell,
Painting with morn each annual cell?
Or how the sacred pine-tree adds
To her old leaves new myriads?   30
Such and so grew these holy piles,
Whilst love and terror laid the tiles.
Earth proudly wears the Parthenon,
As the best gem upon her zone,
And Morning opes with haste her lids,   35
To gaze upon the Pyramids;
O'er England's abbeys bends the sky,
As on its friends, with kindred eye;
For, out of Thought's interior sphere,
These wonders rose to upper air;   40
And Nature gladly gave them place,
Adopted them into her race,
And granted them an equal date
With Andes and with Ararat.

These temples grew as grows the grass;   45
Art might obey, but not surpass.
The passive Master lent his hand
To the vast soul that o'er him planned;
And the same power that reared the shrine
Bestrode the tribes that knelt within.   50
Ever the fiery Pentecost
Girds with one flame the countless host,
Trances the heart through chanting choirs,
And through the priest the mind inspires.
The word unto the prophet spoken   55
Was writ on tables yet unbroken;
The word by seers or sibyls told,
In groves of oak, or fanes of gold,
Still floats upon the morning wind,
Still whispers to the willing mind.   60
One accent of the Holy Ghost
The heedless world hath never lost.
I know what say the fathers wise,—
The Book itself before me lies,
Old *Chrysostom*, best Augustine,   65
And he who blent both in his line,
The younger *Golden Lips* or mines,
Taylor, the Shakspeare of divines.
The words are music in my ear,
I see his cowled portrait dear;   70
And yet, for all his faith could see,
I would not the good bishop be.

                                    1840

HAMATREYA

Bulkeley, Hunt, Willard, Hosmer, Meriam, Flint,
Possessed the land which rendered to their toil
Hay, corn, roots, hemp, flax, apples, wool and wood.
Each of these landlords walked amidst his farm,
Saying, ' 'Tis mine, my children's and my name's: 5
How sweet the west-wind sounds in my own trees!
How graceful climb those shadows on my hill!

I fancy these pure waters and the flags
Know me, as does my dog: we sympathize;
And, I affirm, my actions smack of the soil.'   10
Where are these men? Asleep beneath their grounds;
And strangers, fond as they, their furrows plough.
Earth laughs in flowers, to see her boastful boys
Earth-proud, proud of the earth which is not theirs;
Who steer the plough, but cannot steer their feet   15
Clear of the grave.
They added ridge to valley, brook to pond,
And sighed for all that bounded their domain;
'This suits me for a pasture; that's my park;
We must have clay, lime, gravel, granite-ledge,   20
And misty lowland, where to go for peat.
The land is well,—lies fairly to the south.
'Tis good, when you have crossed the sea and back,
To find the sitfast acres where you left them.'
Ah! the hot owner sees not Death, who adds   25
Him to his land, a lump of mould the more.
Hear what the Earth says:—

                        Earth-song

    Mine and yours;
    Mine, not yours.
    Earth endures;   30
    Stars abide—
    Shine down in the old sea;
    Old are the shores;
    But where are old men?
    I who have seen much   35
    Such have I never seen.

    The lawyer's deed
    Ran sure,
    In tail,
    To them and to their heirs   40
    Who shall succeed,
    Without fail,
    Forevermore.

Here is the land,
Shaggy with wood,   45
With its old valley,
Mound and flood.
But the heritors?
Fled like the flood's foam,—
The lawyer, and the laws,   50
And the kingdom,
Clean swept herefrom.

They called me theirs,
Who so controlled me;
Yet every one   55
Wished to stay, and is gone,
How am I theirs,
If they cannot hold me,
But I hold them?

When I heard the Earth-song,   60
I was no longer brave;
My avarice cooled
Like lust in the chill of the grave.

1847

ODE

Inscribed to W. H. Channing

Though loath to grieve
The evil time's sole patriot,
I cannot leave
My honied thought
For the priest's cant,   5
Or statesman's rant.

If I refuse
My study for their politique,

Which at the best is trick,
The angry Muse   10
Puts confusion in my brain.

But who is he that prates
Of the culture of mankind,
Of better arts and life?
Go, blindworm, go,   15
Behold the famous States
Harrying Mexico
With rifle and with knife!

Or who, with accent bolder,
Dare praise the freedom-loving mountaineer?   20
I found by thee, O rushing Contoocook!
And in thy valleys, Agiochook!
The jackals of the negro-holder.

The God who made New Hampshire
Taunted the lofty land   25
With little men;—
Small bat and wren
House in the oak;—
If earth-fire cleave
The upheaved land, and bury the folk,   30
The Southern crocodile would grieve.
Virtue palters; Right is hence;
Freedom praised, but hid;
Funereal eloquence
Rattles the coffin-lid.   35

What boots thy zeal,
O glowing friend,
That would indignant rend
The Northland from the South?
Wherefore? to what good end?   40
Boston Bay and Bunker Hill
Would serve things still;—
Things are of the snake.

The horseman serves the horse,
The neatherd serves the neat, 45
The merchant serves the purse,
The eater serves his meat;
'Tis the day of the chattel,
Web to weave, and corn to grind;
Things are in the saddle, 50
And ride mankind.

There are two laws discrete,
Not reconciled,—
Law for man, and law for thing;
The last builds town and fleet, 55
But it runs wild,
And doth the man unking.

'Tis fit the forest fall,
The steep be graded,
The mountain tunnelled, 60
The sand shaded,
The orchard planted,
The glebe tilled,
The prairie granted,
The steamer built. 65

Let man serve law for man;
Live for friendship, live for love,
For truth's and harmony's behoof;
The state may follow how it can,
As Olympus follows Jove. 70

   Yet do not I implore
The wrinkled shopman to my sounding woods,
Nor bid the unwilling senator
Ask votes of thrushes in the solitudes.
Every one to his chosen work;— 75
Foolish hands may mix and mar;
Wise and sure the issues are.
Round they roll till dark is light,

Sex to sex, and even to odd;
The over-god   80
Who marries Right to Might,
Who peoples, unpeoples,—
He who exterminates
Races by stronger races,
Black by white faces,—   85
Knows to bring honey
Out of the lion;
Grafts gentlest scion
On pirate and Turk.

The Cossack eats Poland,   90
Like stolen fruit;
Her last noble is ruined,
Her last poet mute;
Straight, into double band
The victors divide;   95
Half for freedom strike and stand;—
The astonished Muse finds thousands at her side.

                                             1847

GIVE ALL TO LOVE

Give all to love;
Obey thy heart;
Friends, kindred, days,
Estate, good-fame,
Plans, credit and the Muse,—   5
Nothing refuse.

'Tis a brave master;
Let it have scope:
Follow it utterly,
Hope beyond hope: 10
High and more high
It dives into noon,
With wing unspent,
Untold intent;

But it is a god,   15
Knows its own path
And the outlets of the sky.

It was never for the mean;
It requireth courage stout.
Souls above doubt,   20
Valor unbending,
It will reward,—
They shall return
More than they were,
And ever ascending.   25

Leave all for love;
Yet, hear me, yet,
One word more thy heart behoved,
One pulse more of firm endeavor,—
Keep thee to-day,   30
To-morrow, forever,
Free as an Arab
Of thy beloved.

Cling with life to the maid;
But when the surprise,   35
First vague shadow of surmise
Flits across her bosom young,
Of a joy apart from thee,
Free be she, fancy-free;
Nor thou detain her vesture's hem,   40
Nor the palest rose she flung
From her summer diadem.

Though thou loved her as thyself,
As a self of purer clay,
Though her parting dims the day,   45
Stealing grace from all alive;
Heartily know,
When half-gods go,
The gods arrive.

                                            1847

MERLIN

I

Thy trivial harp will never please
Or fill my craving ear;
Its chords should ring as blows the breeze,
Free, peremptory, clear.
No jingling serenader's art,   5
Nor tinkle of piano strings,
Can make the wild blood start
In its mystic springs.
The kingly bard
Must smite the chords rudely and hard,   10
As with hammer or with mace;
That they may render back
Artful thunder, which conveys
Secrets of the solar track,
Sparks of the supersolar blaze.   15
Merlin's blows are strokes of fate,
Chiming with the forest tone,
When boughs buffet boughs in the wood;
Chiming with the gasp and moan
Of the ice-imprisoned flood;   20
With the pulse of manly hearts;
With the voice of orators;
With the din of city arts;
With the cannonade of wars;
With the marches of the brave;   25
And prayers of might from martyrs' cave.

Great is the art,
Great be the manners, of the bard.
He shall not his brain encumber
With the coil of rhythm and number;   30
But, leaving rule and pale forethought,
He shall aye climb
For his rhyme.

'Pass in, pass in,' the angels say,
'In to the upper doors,   35
Nor count compartments of the floors,
But mount to paradise
By the stairway of surprise.'

Blameless master of the games,
King of sport that never shames,   40
He shall daily joy dispense
Hid in song's sweet influence.
Forms more cheerly live and go,
What time the subtle mind
Sings aloud the tune whereto   45
Their pulses beat,
And march their feet,
And their members are combined.

By Sybarites beguiled,
He shall no task decline;   50
Merlin's mighty line
Extremes of nature reconciled,—
Bereaved a tyrant of his will,
And made the lion mild.
Songs can the tempest still,   55
Scattered on the stormy air,
Mould the year to fair increase,
And bring in poetic peace.

He shall not seek to weave,
In weak, unhappy times,   60
Efficacious rhymes;
Wait his returning strength.
Bird that from the nadir's floor
To the zenith's top can soar,—
The soaring orbit of the muse exceeds that journey's length.   65
Nor profane affect to hit
Or compass that, by meddling wit,
Which only the propitious mind
Publishes when 't is inclined.
There are open hours   70

When the God's will sallies free,
And tne dull idiot might see
The flowing fortunes of a thousand years;—
Sudden, at unawares,
Self-moved, fly-to the doors,   75
Nor sword of angels could reveal
What they conceal.

                                                    1847

BACCHUS

Bring me wine, but wine which never grew
In the belly of the grape,
Or grew on vine whose tap-roots, reaching through
Under the Andes to the Cape,
Suffer no savor of the earth to scape.   5

Let its grapes the morn salute
From a nocturnal root,
Which feels the acrid juice
Of Styx and Erebus;
And turns the woe of Night,   10
By its own craft, to a more rich delight.

We buy ashes for bread;
We buy diluted wine;
Give me of the true,—
Whose ample leaves and tendrils curled   15
Among the silver hills of heaven
Draw everlasting dew;
Wine of wine,
Blood of the world,
Form of forms, and mould of statures,   20
That I intoxicated,
And by the draught assimilated,
May float at pleasure through all natures;
The bird-language rightly spell,
And that which roses say so well.   25

Wine that is shed
Like the torrents of the sun
Up the horizon walls,
Or like the Atlantic streams, which run
When the South Sea calls.   30

Water and bread,
Food which needs no transmuting,
Rainbow-flowering, wisdom-fruiting,
Wine which is already man,
Food which teach and reason can.   35

Wine which Music is,—
Music and wine are one,—
That I, drinking this,
Shall hear far Chaos talk with me;
Kings unborn shall walk with me;   40
And the poor grass shall plot and plan
What it will do when it is man.
Quickened so, will I unlock
Every crypt of every rock.

I thank the joyful juice   45
For all I know;—
Winds of remembering
Of the ancient being blow,
And seeming-solid walls of use
Open and flow.   50

Pour, Bacchus! the remembering wine;
Retrieve the loss of me and mine!
Vine for vine be antidote,
And the grape requite the lote!
Haste to cure the old despair,—   55
Reason in Nature's lotus drenched,
The memory of ages quenched;
Give them again to shine;
Let wine repair what this undid;
And where the infection slid,   60

A dazzling memory revive;
Refresh the faded tints,
Recut the aged prints,
And write my old adventures with the pen
Which on the first day drew,   65
Upon the tablets blue,
The dancing Pleiads and eternal men.

                                                                    1847

DAYS

Daughters of Time, the hypocritic Days,
Muffled and dumb like barefoot dervishes,
And marching single in an endless file,
Bring diadems and fagots in their hands.
To each they offer gifts after his will,   5
Bread, kingdoms, stars, and sky that holds them all.
I, in my pleached garden, watched the pomp,
Forgot my morning wishes, hastily
Took a few herbs and apples, and the Day
Turned and departed silent. I, too late,   10
Under her solemn fillet saw the scorn.

                                                                    1857

BRAHMA

If the red slayer think he slays,
  Or if the slain think he is slain,
They know not well the subtle ways,
  I keep, and pass, and turn again.

Far or forgot to me is near;   5
  Shadow and sunlight are the same;
The vanished gods to me appear;
  And one to me are shame and fame.

They reckon ill who leave me out;
  When me they fly, I am the wings;   10

I am the doubter and the doubt,
  And I the hymn the Brahmin sings.

The strong gods pine for my abode,
  And pine in vain the sacred Seven;
But thou, meek lover of the good!   15
  Find me, and turn thy back on heaven.

                                        1857

TERMINUS

It is time to be old,
To take in sail:—
The god of bounds,
Who sets to seas a shore,
Came to me in his fatal rounds,   5
And said: 'No more!
No farther shoot
Thy broad ambitious branches, and thy root.
Fancy departs: no more invent;
Contract thy firmament   10
To compass of a tent.
There's not enough for this and that,
Make thy option which of two;
Economize the failing river,
Not the less revere the Giver,   15
Leave the many and hold the few.
Timely wise accept the terms,
Soften the fall with wary foot;
A little while
Still plan and smile,   20
And,—fault of novel germs,—
Mature the unfallen fruit.
Curse, if thou wilt, thy sires,
Bad husbands of their fires,
Who, when they gave thee breath,   25
Failed to bequeath
The needful sinew stark as once,
The Baresark marrow to thy bones,

But left a legacy of ebbing veins,
Inconstant heat and nerveless reins,—   30
Amid the Muses, left thee deaf and dumb,
Amid the gladiators, halt and numb.'

    As the bird trims her to the gale,
I trim myself to the storm of time,
I man the rudder, reef the sail,   35
Obey the voice at eve obeyed at prime;
'Lowly faithful, banish fear,
Right onward drive unharmed;
The port, well worth the cruise, is near,
And every wave is charmed.'   40

                                                1867

HENRY WADSWORTH LONGFELLOW

Henry Wadsworth Longfellow (1807-1882) was born in Portland, Maine, and attended Bowdoin College, a classmate of Nathaniel Hawthorne. Upon graduation in 1825, Longfellow accepted an appointment at Bowdoin as professor of modern languages, beginning with a year's leave of absence for study in Europe. A similar appointment from Harvard College ten years later enabled him again to travel to Europe for a year. Upon his return, in 1836, Longfellow began his tenure—succeeding George Ticknor—as Smith Professor of Modern Languages at Harvard, which he held until his resignation in 1854. These extensive journeys to Europe prepared him for more than teaching. The idioms and conventions of other national literatures were the subject of his constant study as a poet, as evidenced by his translations of poems from Spanish, Swedish, Danish, German, Italian, and Portuguese, as well as from Anglo-Saxon and Latin. His first published translation—of the Spanish *Copla de Manrique*—appeared in 1832, and he continued his translations for his remaining fifty years. With the aid of James Russell Lowell and Charles Eliot Norton, Longfellow accomplished his major translation, Dante's *Divine Comedy*, which was published in 1867.

Longfellow's desire to be a professional man of letters was both early and constant. Still a senior in college, he wrote to his father: "I most eagerly aspire after future eminence in literature. . . . Surely there never was a better opportunity offered for exertion of literary talent in our own country than is now offered. To be sure, most of our literary men thus far have not been profoundly so, until they have studied and entered the practice of theology, law, or medicine. I do believe that we ought to pay more attention to the opinion of philosophers, that 'nothing but nature can qualify a man for knowledge'. . . ." Thirty years later the intrusion of academic demands on his writing prompted Longfellow to resign from teaching.

Longfellow's major poetic work, *Christus* (1872-73), was more than thirty years in preparation. It is a long account in dramatic form, as Longfellow tells us, of "the various aspects of Christendom in the Apostolic, Middle, and Modern Ages." The last of these three parts dramatizes the faith and intolerance of the Puritan religion in the New England colonies. Longfellow's canon includes also long narrative poems, among them *Evangeline* (1847), *Hiawatha* (1855), and *The Courtship of Miles Standish* (1858), as well as the collection of narratives in *Tales of a Wayside Inn* (1863-86). The scope and bulk of Longfellow's poetry defy an editor's selection. But the quality of his verse and the typical structure, which speculatively develops a given visual situation, are readily represented in the best of his shorter poems.

The text of these poems is: Horace E. Scudder (ed.), *The Complete Poetical Works of Henry W. Longfellow* (Boston, 1893), which reproduces the entire poetical text of Longfellow's *Complete Works*, also edited by Scudder, in the Riverside Edition, 11 vols. (Boston, 1886).

THE ARSENAL AT SPRINGFIELD

This is the Arsenal. From floor to ceiling,
  Like a huge organ, rise the burnished arms;
But from their silent pipes no anthem pealing
  Startles the villages with strange alarms.

Ah! what a sound will rise, how wild and dreary,   5
  When the death-angel touches those swift keys!
What loud lament and dismal Miserere
  Will mingle with their awful symphonies!

I hear even now the infinite fierce chorus,
  The cries of agony, the endless groan,   10
Which, through the ages that have gone before us,
  In long reverberations reach our own.

Our helm and harness rings the Saxon hammer,
  Through Cimbric forest roars the Norseman's song,
And loud, amid the universal clamor,   15
  O'er distant deserts sounds the Tartar gong.

I hear the Florentine, who from his palace
Wheels out his battle-bell with dreadful din,
And Aztec priests upon their teocallis
Beat the wild war-drums made of serpent's skin;   20

The tumult of each sacked and burning village;
The shout that every prayer for mercy drowns;
The soldiers' revels in the midst of pillage;
The wail of famine in beleaguered towns;

The bursting shell, the gateway wrenched asunder,   25
The rattling musketry, the clashing blade;
And ever and anon, in tones of thunder
The diapason of the cannonade.

Is it, O man, with such discordant noises,
With such accursed instruments as these,   30
Thou drownest Nature's sweet and kindly voices,
And jarrest the celestial harmonies?

Were half the power, that fills the world with terror,
Were half the wealth, bestowed on camps and courts,
Given to redeem the human mind from error,   35
There were no need of arsenals or forts:

The warrior's name would be a name abhorrèd!
And every nation, that should lift again
Its hand against a brother, on its forehead
Would wear forevermore the curse of Cain!   40

Down the dark future, through long generations,
The echoing sounds grow fainter and then cease;
And like a bell, with solemn, sweet vibrations,
I hear once more the voice of Christ say, "Peace! "

Peace! and no longer from its brazen portals   45
The blast of War's great organ shakes the skies!
But beautiful as songs of the immortals
The holy melodies of love arise.

1844

SEAWEED

When descends on the Atlantic
   The gigantic
Storm-wind of the equinox,
Landward in his wrath he scourges
   The toiling surges,   5
Laden with seaweed from the rocks;

From Bermuda's reefs; from edges
   Of sunken ledges,
In some far-off, bright Azore;
From Bahama, and the dashing,   10
   Silver-flashing
Surges of San Salvador;

From the tumbling surf, that buries
   The Orkneyan skerries,
Answering the hoarse Hebrides;   15
And from wrecks of ships, and drifting
   Spars, uplifting
On the desolate, rainy seas;—

Ever drifting, drifting, drifting
   On the shifting   20
Currents of the restless main;
Till in sheltered coves, and reaches
   Of sandy beaches,
All have found repose again.

So when storms of wild emotion   25
   Strike the ocean
Of the poet's soul, erelong
From each cave and rocky fastness,
   In its vastness,
Floats some fragment of a song: 30

From the far-off isles enchanted,
  Heaven has planted
With the golden fruit of Truth;
From the flashing surf, whose vision
  Gleams Elysian   35
In the tropic clime of Youth;

From the strong Will, and the Endeavor
  That forever
Wrestle with the tides of Fate;
From the wreck of Hopes far-scattered,   40
  Tempest-shattered,
Floating waste and desolate;—

Ever drifting, drifting, drifting
  On the shifting
Currents of the restless heart;   45
Till at length in books recorded,
  They, like hoarded
Household words, no more depart.

                                          1845

THE FIRE OF DRIFT-WOOD

We sat within the farm-house old,
  Whose windows, looking o'er the bay,
Gave to the sea-breeze damp and cold
  An easy entrance, night and day.

Not far away we saw the port,   5
  The strange, old-fashioned, silent town,
The lighthouse, the dismantled fort,
  The wooden houses, quaint and brown.

We sat and talked until the night,
  Descending, filled the little room;   10
Our faces faded from the sight,
  Our voices only broke the gloom.

We spake of many a vanished scene,
  Of what we once had thought and said,
Of what had been, and might have been   15
  And who was changed, and who was dead;

And all that fills the hearts of friends,
  When first they feel, with secret pain,
Their lives thenceforth have separate ends,
  And never can be one again;   20

The first slight swerving of the heart,
  That words are powerless to express,
And leave it still unsaid in part,
  Or say it in too great excess.

The very tones in which we spake   25
  Had something strange, I could but mark;
The leaves of memory seemed to make
  A mournful rustling in the dark.

Oft died the words upon our lips,
  As suddenly, from out the fire   30
Built of the wreck of stranded ships,
  The flames would leap and then expire.

And, as their splendor flashed and failed,
  We thought of wrecks upon the main,
Of ships dismasted, that were hailed   35
  And sent no answer back again.

The windows, rattling in their frames,
  The ocean, roaring up the beach,
The gusty blast, the bickering flames,
  All mingled vaguely in our speech;   40

Until they made themselves a part
  Of fancies floating through the brain,
The long-lost ventures of the heart,
  That send no answers back again.

O flames that glowed! O hearts that yearned! 45
　They were indeed too much akin,
The drift-wood fire without that burned,
　The thoughts that burned and glowed within.

1849

THE JEWISH CEMETERY AT NEWPORT

How strange it seems! These Hebrews in their graves,
　Close by the street of this fair seaport town,
Silent beside the never-silent waves,
　At rest in all this moving up and down!

The trees are white with dust, that o'er their sleep 5
　Wave their broad curtains in the southwind's breath,
While underneath these leafy tents they keep
　The long, mysterious Exodus of Death.

And these sepulchral stones, so old and brown,
　That pave with level flags their burial-place, 10
Seem like the tablets of the Law, thrown down
　And broken by Moses at the mountain's base.

The very names recorded here are strange,
　Of foreign accent, and of different climes;
Alvares and Rivera interchange 15
　With Abraham and Jacob of old times.

"Blessed be God, for he created Death!"
　The mourners said, "and Death is rest and peace";
Then added, in the certainty of faith,
　"And giveth Life that nevermore shall cease." 20

Closed are the portals of their Synagogue,
　No Psalms of David now the silence break,
No Rabbi reads the ancient Decalogue
　In the grand dialect the Prophets spake.

Gone are the living, but the dead remain,   25
   And not neglected; for a hand unseen,
Scattering its bounty, like a summer rain,
   Still keeps their graves and their remembrance green.

How came they here? What burst of Christian hate,
   What persecution, merciless and blind,   30
Drove o'er the sea—that desert desolate—
   These Ishmaels and Hagars of mankind?

They lived in narrow streets and lanes obscure,
   Ghetto and Judenstrass, in mirk and mire;
Taught in the school of patience to endure   35
   The life of anguish and the death of fire.

All their lives long, with the unleavened bread
   And bitter herbs of exile and its fears,
The wasting famine of the heart they fed,
   And slaked its thirst with marah of their tears.   40

Anathema maranatha! was the cry
   That rang from town to town, from street to street:
At every gate the accursed Mordecai
   Was mocked and jeered, and spurned by Christian feet.

Pride and humiliation hand in hand   45
   Walked with them through the world where'er they went;
Trampled and beaten were they as the sand,
   And yet unshaken as the continent.

For in the background figures vague and vast
   Of patriarchs and of prophets rose sublime,   50
And all the great traditions of the Past
   They saw reflected in the coming time,

And thus forever with reverted look
   The mystic volume of the world they read,
Spelling it backward, like a Hebrew book,   55
   Till life became a Legend of the Dead.

But ah! what once has been shall be no more!
The groaning earth in travail and in pain
Brings forth its races, but does not restore,
And the dead nations rise again.   60
                                                          1852

THE SICILIAN'S TALE

King Robert of Sicily

Robert of Sicily, brother of Pope Urbane
And Valmond, Emperor of Allemaine,
Apparelled in magnificent attire,
With retinue of many a knight and squire,
On St. John's eve, at vespers, proudly sat   5
And heard the priests chant the Magnificat.
And as he listened, o'er and o'er again
Repeated, like a burden or refrain,
He caught the words, *"Deposuit potentes
De sede, et exaltavit humiles;"*   10
And slowly lifting up his kingly head
He to a learned clerk beside him said,
"What mean these words?" The clerk made answer meet,
"He has put down the mighty from their seat,
And has exalted them of low degree."   15
Thereat King Robert muttered scornfully,
" 'T is well that such seditious words are sung
Only by priests and in the Latin tongue;
For unto priests and people be it known,
There is no power can push me from my throne!"   20
And leaning back, he yawned and fell asleep,
Lulled by the chant monotonous and deep.
When he awoke, it was already night;
The church was empty, and there was no light,
Save where the lamps, that glimmered few and faint, 25
Lighted a little space before some saint.
He started from his seat and gazed around,
But saw no living thing and heard no sound.

He groped towards the door, but it was locked;
He cried aloud, and listened, and then knocked,   30
And uttered awful threatenings and complaints,
And imprecations upon men and saints.
The sounds reëchoed from the roof and walls
As if dead priests were laughing in their stalls.

At length the sexton, hearing from without   35
The tumult of the knocking and the shout,
And thinking thieves were in the house of prayer,
Came with his lantern, asking, "Who is there?"
Half choked with rage, King Robert fiercely said,
"Open: 't is I, the King! Art thou afraid?"   40
The frightened sexton, muttering, with a curse,
"This is some drunken vagabond, or worse!"
Turned the great key and flung the portal wide;
A man rushed by him at a single stride,
Haggard, half naked, without hat or cloak,   45
Who neither turned, nor looked at him, nor spoke,
But leaped into the blackness of the night,
And vanished like a spectre from his sight.

Robert of Sicily, brother of Pope Urbane
And Valmond, Emperor of Allemaine,   50
Despoiled of his magnificent attire,
Bareheaded, breathless, and besprent with mire,
With sense of wrong and outrage desperate,
Strode on and thundered at the palace gate;
Rushed through the courtyard, thrusting in his rage   55
To right and left each seneschal and page,
And hurried up the broad and sounding stair,
His white face ghastly in the torches' glare.
From hall to hall he passed with breathless speed;
Voices and cries he heard, but did not heed,   60
Until at last he reached the banquet-room,
Blazing with light, and breathing with perfume.

There on the dais sat another king,
Wearing his robes, his crown, his signet-ring,
King Robert's self in features, form, and height,   65

But all transfigured with angelic light!
It was an Angel; and his presence there
With a divine effulgence filled the air,
An exaltation, piercing the disguise,
Though none the hidden Angel recognize. 70

A moment speechless, motionless, amazed,
The throneless monarch on the Angel gazed,
Who met his look of anger and surprise
With the divine compassion of his eyes;
Then said, "Who art thou? and why com'st thou here?" 75
To which King Robert answered with a sneer,
"I am the King, and come to claim my own
From an impostor, who usurps my throne!"
And suddenly, at these audacious words,
Up sprang the angry guests, and drew their swords; 80
The Angel answered, with unruffled brow,
"Nay, not the King, but the King's Jester, thou
Henceforth shalt wear the bells and scalloped cape,
And for thy counsellor shalt lead an ape;
Thou shalt obey my servants when they call, 85
And wait upon my henchmen in the hall!"

Deaf to King Robert's threats and cries and prayers,
They thrust him from the hall and down the stairs;
A group of tittering pages ran before,
And as they opened wide the folding-door, 90
His heart failed, for he heard, with strange alarms,
The boisterous laughter of the men-at-arms,
And all the vaulted chamber roar and ring
With the mock plaudits of "Long live the King!"

Next morning, waking with the day's first beam, 95
He said within himself, "It was a dream!"
But the straw rustled as he turned his head,
There were the cap and bells beside his bed,
Around him rose the bare, discolored walls,
Close by, the steeds were champing in their stalls, 100
And in the corner, a revolting shape,
Shivering and chattering sat the wretched ape.

It was no dream; the world he loved so much
Had turned to dust and ashes at his touch!

Days came and went; and now returned again   105
To Sicily the old Saturnian reign;
Under the Angel's governance benign
The happy island danced with corn and wine,
And deep within the mountain's burning breast
Enceladus, the giant, was at rest.   110

Meanwhile King Robert yielded to his fate,
Sullen and silent and disconsolate.
Dressed in the motley garb that Jesters wear,
With look bewildered and a vacant stare,
Close shaven above the ears, as monks are shorn,   115
By courtiers mocked, by pages laughed to scorn,
His only friend the ape, his only food
What others left,—he still was unsubdued.
And when the Angel met him on his way,
And half in earnest, half in jest, would say,   120
Sternly, though tenderly, that he might feel
The velvet scabbard held a sword of steel,
"Art thou the King?" the passion of his woe
Burst from him in resistless overflow,
And, lifting high his forehead, he would fling   125
The haughty answer back, "I am, I am the King!"

Almost three years were ended; when there came
Ambassadors of great repute and name
From Valmond, Emperor of Allemaine,
Unto King Robert, saying that Pope Urbane   130
By letter summoned them forthwith to come
On Holy Thursday to his city of Rome.
The Angel with great joy received his guests,
And gave them presents of embroidered vests,
And velvet mantles with rich ermine lined,   135
And rings and jewels of the rarest kind.
Then he departed with them o'er the sea
Into the lovely land of Italy,
Whose loveliness was more resplendent made

By the mere passing of that cavalcade,   140
With plumes, and cloaks, and housings, and the stir
Of jewelled bridle and of golden spur.
And lo! among the menials, in mock state,
Upon a piebald steed, with shambling gait,
His cloak of fox-tails flapping in the wind,   145
The solemn ape demurely perched behind,
King Robert rode, making huge merriment
In all the country towns through which they went.

The Pope received them with great pomp and blare
Of bannered trumpets, on Saint Peter's square,   150
Giving his benediction and embrace,
Fervent, and full of apostolic grace.
While with congratulations and with prayers
He entertained the Angel unawares,
Robert, the Jester, bursting through the crowd,   155
Into their presence rushed, and cried aloud,
"I am the King! Look, and behold in me
Robert, your brother, King of Sicily!
This man, who wears my semblance to your eyes,
Is an impostor in a king's disguise.   160
Do you not know me? does no voice within
Answer my cry, and say we are akin?"
The Pope in silence, but with troubled mien,
Gazed at the Angel's countenance serene;
The Emperor, laughing, said, "It is strange sport   165
To keep a madman for thy Fool at court!"
And the poor, baffled Jester in disgrace
Was hustled back among the populace.

In solemn state the Holy Week went by,
And Easter Sunday gleamed upon the sky;   170
The presence of the Angel, with its light,
Before the sun rose, made the city bright,
And with new fervor filled the hearts of men,
Who felt that Christ indeed had risen again.
Even the Jester, on his bed of straw,   175
With haggard eyes the unwonted splendor saw,
He felt within a power unfelt before,

And, kneeling humbly on his chamber floor,
He heard the rushing garments of the Lord
Sweep through the silent air, ascending heavenward.   180

And now the visit ending, and once more
Valmond returning to the Danube's shore,
Homeward the Angel journeyed, and again
The land was made resplendent with his train,
Flashing along the towns of Italy   185
Unto Salerno, and from thence by sea.
And when once more within Palermo's wall,
And, seated on the throne in his great hall,
He heard the Angelus from convent towers,
As if the better world conversed with ours,   190
He beckoned to King Robert to draw nigher,
And with a gesture bade the rest retire;
And when they were alone, the Angel said
"Art thou the King?" Then, bowing down his head,
King Robert crossed both hands upon his breast,   195
And meekly answered him: "Thou knowest best!
My sins as scarlet are; let me go hence,
And in some cloister's school of penitence,
Across those stones, that pave the way to heaven,
Walk barefoot, till my guilty soul be shriven!"   200

The Angel smiled, and from his radiant face
A holy light illumined all the place,
And through the open window, loud and clear,
They heard the monks chant in the chapel near,
Above the stir and tumult of the street: 205
"He has put down the mighty from their seat,
And has exalted them of low degree!"
And through the chant a second melody
Rose like the throbbing of a single string:
"I am an Angel, and thou art the King!"   210

King Robert, who was standing near the throne,
Lifted his eyes, and lo! he was alone!
But all apparelled as in days of old,
With ermined mantle and with cloth of gold;

And when his courtiers came, they found him there 215
Kneeling upon the floor, absorbed in silent prayer.

1863

DIVINA COMMEDIA

I

Oft have I seen at some cathedral door
  A laborer, pausing in the dust and heat,
  Lay down his burden, and with reverent feet
  Enter, and cross himself, and on the floor
Kneel to repeat his paternoster o'er; 5
  Far off the noises of the world retreat;
  The loud vociferations of the street
  Become an undistinguishable roar.
So, as I enter here from day to day,
  And leave my burden at this minster gate, 10
  Kneeling in prayer, and not ashamed to pray,
The tumult of the time disconsolate
  To inarticulate murmurs dies away,
  While the eternal ages watch and wait.

1864

II

How strange the sculptures that adorn these towers! 15
  This crowd of statues, in whose folded sleeves
  Birds build their nests; while canopied with leaves
  Parvis and portal bloom like trellised bowers,
And the vast minster seems a cross of flowers!
  But fiends and dragons on the gargoyled eaves 20
  Watch the dead Christ between the living thieves,
  And, underneath, the traitor Judas lowers!
Ah! from what agonies of heart and brain,
  What exultations trampling on despair,
  What tenderness, what tears, what hate of wrong, 25
What passionate outcry of a soul in pain,
  Uprose this poem of the earth and air,
  This medieval miracle of song!

1866

III

I enter, and I see thee in the gloom
   Of the long aisles, O poet saturnine!   30
   And strive to make my steps keep pace with thine.
   The air is filled with some unknown perfume;
The congregation of the dead make room
   For thee to pass; the votive tapers shine;
   Like rooks that haunt Ravenna's groves of pine   35
   The hovering echoes fly from tomb to tomb.
From the confessionals I hear arise
   Rehearsals of forgotten tragedies,
   And lamentations from the crypts below;
And then a voice celestial that begins   40
   With the pathetic words, "Although your sins
   As scarlet be," and end with "as the snow."

                                1866

IV

With snow-white veil and garments as of flame,
   She stands before thee, who so long ago
   Filled thy young heart with passion and the woe   45
   From which thy song and all its splendors came;
And while with stern rebuke she speaks thy name,
   The ice about thy heart melts as the snow
   On mountain heights, and in swift overflow
   Comes gushing from thy lips in sobs of shame.   50
Thou makest full confession; and a gleam,
   As of the dawn on some dark forest cast,
   Seems on thy lifted forehead to increase;
Lethe and Eunoë—the remembered dream
   And the forgotten sorrow—bring at last   55
   That perfect pardon which is perfect peace.

                                1867

V

I lift mine eyes, and all the windows blaze
   With forms of Saints and holy men who died,
   Here martyred and hereafter glorified;
   And the great Rose upon its leaves displays   60
Christ's Triumph, and the angelic roundelays,

With splendor upon splendor multiplied;
And Beatrice again at Dante's side
No more rebukes, but smiles her words of praise.
And then the organ sounds, and unseen choirs 65
   Sing the old Latin hymns of peace and love
   And benedictions of the Holy Ghost;
And the melodious bells among the spires
   O'er all the house-tops and through heaven above
Proclaim the elevation of the Host! 70

                              1866

VI

O star of morning and of liberty!
   O bringer of the light, whose splendor shines
   Above the darkness of the Apennines,
   Forerunner of the day that is to be!
The voices of the city and the sea, 75
   The voices of the mountains and the pines,
   Repeat thy song, till the familiar lines
   Are footpaths for the thought of Italy!
Thy flame is blown abroad from all the heights,
   Through all the nations, and a sound is heard, 80
   As of a mighty wind, and men devout,
Strangers of Rome, and the new proselytes,
   In their own language hear thy wondrous word,
   And many are amazed and many doubt.

                              1866

THE SOUND OF THE SEA

The sea awoke at midnight from its sleep,
   And round the pebbly beaches far and wide
   I heard the first wave of the rising tide
   Rush onward with uninterrupted sweep;
A voice out of the silence of the deep, 5
   A sound mysteriously multiplied
   As of a cataract from the mountain's side,
   Or roar of winds upon a wooded steep.
So comes to us at times, from the unknown

And inaccessible solitudes of being,   10
The rushing of the sea-tides of the soul;
And inspirations, that we deem our own,
Are some divine foreshadowing and foreseeing
Of things beyond our reason or control.

1875

NATURE

As a fond mother, when the day is o'er,
  Leads by the hand her little child to bed,
  Half willing, half reluctant to be led,
And leave his broken playthings on the floor,
Still gazing at them through the open door,   5
  Nor wholly reassured and comforted
  By promises of others in their stead,
Which, though more splendid, may not please him more;
So Nature deals with us, and takes away
  Our playthings one by one, and by the hand   10
  Leads us to rest so gently, that we go
Scarce knowing if we wish to go or stay,
  Being too full of sleep to understand
How far the unknown transcends the what we know.

1878

JUGURTHA

How cold are thy baths, Apollo!
  Cried the African monarch, the splendid,
As down to his death in the hollow
  Dark dungeons of Rome he descended,
  Uncrowned, unthroned, unattended;   5
How cold are thy baths, Apollo!

How cold are thy baths, Apollo!
  Cried the Poet, unknown, unbefriended,
As the vision, that lured him to follow,

With the mist and the darkness blended,   10
And the dream of his life was ended;
How cold are thy baths, Apollo!

                 1880

ULTIMA THULE

Dedication

With favoring winds, o'er sunlit seas,
We sailed for the Hesperides,
The land where golden apples grow;
But that, ah! that was long ago.

How far since then the ocean streams   5
Have swept us from the land of dreams,
That land of fiction and of truth,
The lost Atlantis of our youth!

Whither, ah, whither? Are not these
The tempest-haunted Orcades,   10
Where sea-gulls scream, and breakers roar,
And wreck and sea-weed line the shore?

Ultima Thule! Utmost Isle!
Here in thy harbors for awhile
We lower our sails, awhile we rest   15
From the unending endless quest.

                 1880

VICTOR AND VANQUISHED

As one who long hath fled with panting breath
Before his foe, bleeding and near to fall,
I turn and set my back against the wall,
And look thee in the face, triumphant Death.
I call for aid, and no one answereth;   5
I am alone with thee, who conquerest all;

Yet me thy threatening form doth not appall,
For thou art but a phantom and a wraith.
Wounded and weak, sword broken at the hilt,
With armor shattered, and without a shield,   10
I stand unmoved; do with me what thou wilt;
I can resist no more, but will not yield.
This is no tournament where cowards tilt;
The vanquished here is victor of the field.

1882

JOHN GREENLEAF WHITTIER

John Greenleaf Whittier (1807-1892) was born on a farm near a small Massachusetts village, one of four children in a Quaker family. The exactions of New England country life and the tenets of the Friends bred in him a sense of discipline and moral severity which marked his personal and public life. He was already thoroughly familiar with the Bible and with Quaker writings by the time he paid his own way through a private academy. His practice verses were paraphrases of the Bible, anticipating the dozens of his poems which were set to hymn music.

Still farming his father's land and practicing poetry, Whittier attracted the attention of William Lloyd Garrison, who published the young farmer's first poems in his newspaper. Then, at the age of twenty-one, Whittier began his career as an editor with a Boston political weekly, the *American Manufacturer*. This career took on special significance after Whittier's first formal antislavery pronouncement, a pamphlet entitled *Justice and Expediency* (1833). From then until the end of the Civil War, he was a vigorous abolitionist. "What an absurdity is moral action apart from political!" Whittier wrote. He lobbied against slavery as a newspaper editor, notably of the *National Era* (1847-60), as a contributor of verse essays to antislavery periodicals, and as a member of the Massachusetts legislature and a political power in his own territory.

He had already established notoriety as a partisan and a humanitarian when the first comprehensive edition of his poems was published in 1849. The death in 1864 of his sister Elizabeth, his closest companion during his life; the end of the Civil War and of the abolition crusade; and the publication of *Snow-Bound* (1866), with its immediate popular and financial success, all marked a change to the emphases in Whittier's later poems, which are retrospective, autobiographical, and, for the most part, serene. In his later life, also, he was much sought after for occasional and commemorative verse, which he generously composed.

The definitive text of his poems, which Whittier helped to prepare, is Horace E. Scudder (ed.), *The Writings of John*

Greenleaf Whittier, 7 vols. (Boston, 1888-1889). This edition
was the basis of Scudder's one-volume Cambridge edition
(1894), which preserved Whittier's notes and adds his last
poems. The poems here printed follow the text of the Cam-
bridge edition, including portions of Whittier's notes. This
selection disregards, however, the sequence of poems in the
text: a thematic grouping, irrespective of dates, under nine
presumably convenient subject headings.

THE MORAL WARFARE

When Freedom, on her natal day,
Within her war-rocked cradle lay,
An iron race around her stood,
Baptized her infant brow in blood;
And, through the storm which round her swept,   5
Their constant ward and watching kept.

Then, where our quiet herds repose,
The roar of baleful battle rose,
And brethren of a common tongue
To mortal strife as tigers sprung,   10
And every gift on Freedom's shrine
Was man for beast, and blood for wine!

Our fathers to their graves have gone;
Their strife is past, their triumph won;
But sterner trials wait the race   15
Which rises in their honored place;
A moral warfare with the crime
And folly of an evil time.

So let it be. In God's own might
We gird us for the coming fight,   20
And, strong in Him whose cause is ours
In conflict with unholy powers,
We grasp the weapons He has given,—
The Light, and Truth, and Love of Heaven.

                                                       1836

THE REFORMER

All grim and soiled and brown with tan,
  I saw a Strong One, in his wrath,
Smiting the godless shrines of man
    Along his path.

The Church, beneath her trembling dome,   5
  Essayed in vain her ghostly charm:
Wealth shook within his gilded home
    With strange alarm.

Fraud from his secret chambers fled
  Before the sunlight bursting in: 10
Sloth drew her pillow o'er her head
    To drown the din.

"Spare," Art implored, "yon holy pile;
  That grand, old, time-worn turret spare;"
Meek Reverence, kneeling in the aisle,   15
    Cried out, "Forbear!"

Gray-bearded Use, who, deaf and blind,
  Groped for his old accustomed stone,
Leaned on his staff, and wept to find
    His seat o'erthrown.   20

Young Romance raised his dreamy eyes,
  O'erhung with paly locks of gold,—
"Why smite," he asked in sad surprise,
    "The fair, the old?"

Yet louder rang the Strong One's stroke,   25
  Yet nearer flashed his axe's gleam:
Shuddering and sick of heart I woke,
    As from a dream.

I looked: aside the dust-cloud rolled,
   The Waster seemed the Builder too;   30
Up springing from the ruined Old
     I saw the New.

'Twas but the ruin of the bad,—
   The wasting of the wrong and ill;
Whate'er of good the old time had   35
     Was living still.

Calm grew the brows of him I feared;
   The frown which awed me passed away,
And left behind a smile which cheered
     Like breaking day.   40

The grain grew green on battle-plains,
   O'er swarded war-mounds grazed the cow;
The slave stood forging from his chains
     The spade and plough.

Where frowned the fort, pavilions gay   45
   And cottage windows, flower-entwined,
Looked out upon the peaceful bay
     And hills behind.

Through vine-wreathed cups with wine once red,
   The lights on brimming crystal fell,   50
Drawn, sparkling, from the rivulet head
     And mossy well.

Through prison walls, like Heaven-sent hope,
   Fresh breezes blew, and sunbeams strayed,
And with the idle gallows-rope   55
     The young child played.

Where the doomed victim in his cell
   Had counted o'er the weary hours,
Glad school-girls, answering to the bell,
     Came crowned with flowers.   60

Grown wiser for the lesson given,
  I fear no longer, for I know
That, where the share is deepest driven,
    The best fruits grow.

The outworn rite, the old abuse   65
  The pious fraud transparent grown,
The good held captive in the use
    Of wrong alone,

These wait their doom, from that great law
  Which makes the past time serve today;   70
And fresher life the world shall draw
    From their decay.

O, backward-looking son of time!
  The new is old, the old is new,
The cycle of a change sublime   75
    Still sweeping through.

So wisely taught the Indian seer;
  Destroying Seva, forming Brahm,
Who wake by turns Earth's love and fear,
    Are one, the same.   80

Idly as thou, in that old day
  Thou mournest, did thy sire repine;
So, in his time, thy child grown gray
    Shall sigh for thine.

But life shall on and upward go;   85
  Th'eternal step of Progress beats
To that great anthem, calm and slow,
    Which God repeats.

Take heart! the Waster builds again,—
  A charmèd life old Goodness hath;   90
The tares may perish, but the grain
    Is not for death.

God works in all things; all obey
    His first propulsion from the night:
Wake thou and watch! the world is gray   95
    With morning light!

                                                              1846

PROEM

[To the 1849 collection, *Poems*]

I love the old melodious lays
Which softly melt the ages through,
    The songs of Spenser's golden days,
    Arcadian Sidney's silvery phrase,
Sprinkling our noon of time with freshest morning dew.   5

Yet, vainly in my quiet hours
To breathe their marvellous notes I try;
    I feel them, as the leaves and flowers
    In silence feel the dewy showers,
And drink, with glad, still lips the blessing of the sky.   10

The rigor of a frozen clime,
The harshness of an untaught ear,
    The jarring words of one whose rhyme
    Beat often Labor's hurried time,
Or Duty's rugged march through storm and strife, are here.   15

Of mystic beauty, dreamy grace,
No rounded art the lack supplies;
    Unskilled the subtle lines to trace,
    Or softer shades of Nature's face,
I view her common forms with unanointed eyes.   20

Nor mine the seer-like power to show
The secrets of the heart and mind;
    To drop the plummet-line below
    Our common world of joy and woe,
A more intense despair or brighter hope to find.   25

Yet here at least an earnest sense
Of human right and weal is shown;
   A hate of tyranny intense,
   And hearty in its vehemence,
As if my brother's pain and sorrow were my own.   30

O Freedom! if to me belong
Nor mighty Milton's gift divine,
   Nor Marvell's wit and graceful song,
   Still with a love as deep and strong
As theirs, I lay, like them, my best gifts on thy shrine!   35

                           1849

ICHABOD

    This poem was the outcome of the surprise and grief and forecast of evil consequences which I felt on reading the seventh of March speech of Daniel Webster in support of the "compromise," and the Fugitive Slave Law. No partisan or personal enmity dictated it. On the contrary my admiration of the splendid personality and intellectual power of the great Senator was never stronger than when I laid down his speech, and, in one of the saddest moments of my life, penned my protest. . . .

    So fallen! so lost! the light withdrawn
       Which once he wore!
    The glory from his gray hairs gone
       Forevermore!

    Revile him not, the Tempter hath   5
       A snare for all;
    And pitying tears, not scorn and wrath,
       Befit his fall!

    Oh, dumb be passion's stormy rage,
       When he who might   10
    Have lighted up and led his age,
       Falls back in night.

Scorn! would the angels laugh, to mark
　A bright soul driven,
Fiend-goaded, down the endless dark,   15
　From hope and heaven!

Let not the land once proud of him
　Insult him now,
Nor brand with deeper shame his dim,
　Dishonored brow.   20

But let its humbled sons, instead,
　From sea to lake,
A long lament, as for the dead,
　In sadness make.

Of all we loved and honored, naught   25
　Save power remains;
A fallen angel's pride of thought,
　Still strong in chains.

All else is gone; from those great eyes
　The soul has fled: 30
When faith is lost, when honor dies,
　The man is dead!

Then pay the reverence of old days
　To his dead fame;
Walk backward, with averted gaze,   35
　And hide the shame!

                                            1850

SONGS OF LABOR

Dedication

I would the gift I offer here
　Might graces from thy favor take,
And, seen through Friendship's atmosphere,
On softened lines and coloring, wear
The unaccustomed light of beauty, for thy sake.   5

Few leaves of Fancy's spring remain:
  But what I have I give to thee,
The o'er-sunned bloom of summer's plain,
And paler flowers, the latter rain
Calls from the westering slope of life's autumnal lea.   10

Above the fallen groves of green,
  Where youth's enchanted forest stood,
Dry root and mossëd trunk between,
A sober after-growth is seen,
As springs the pine where falls the gay-leafed maple wood!   15

Yet birds will sing, and breezes play
  Their leaf-harps in the sombre tree;
And through the bleak and wintry day
It keeps its steady green alway,—
So, even my after-thoughts may have a charm for thee.   20

Art's perfect forms no moral need,
  And beauty is its own excuse;
But for the dull and flowerless weed
Some healing virtue still must plead,
And the rough ore must find its honors in its use.   25

So haply these, my simple lays
  Of homely toil, may serve to show
The orchard bloom and tasselled maize
That skirt and gladden duty's ways,
The unsung beauty hid life's common things below.   30

Haply from them the toiler, bent
  Above his forge or plough, may gain
A manlier spirit of content,
And feel that life is wisest spent
Where the strong working hand makes strong the working
          brain.   35

The doom which to the guilty pair
  Without the walls of Eden came,
Transforming sinless ease to care

And rugged toil, no more shall bear
The burden of old crime, or mark of primal shame.   40

A blessing now, a curse no more;
    Since He, whose name we breathe with awe,
The coarse mechanic vesture wore,
A poor man toiling with the poor,
In labor, as in prayer, fulfilling the same law.   45

                                                    1850

FIRST-DAY THOUGHTS

In calm and cool and silence, once again
    I find my old accustomed place among
    My brethren, where, perchance, no human tongue
    Shall utter words; where never hymn is sung,
    Nor deep-toned organ blown, nor censer swung,   5
Nor dim light falling through the pictured pane!
There, syllabled by silence, let me hear
The still small voice which reached the prophet's ear;
Read in my heart a still diviner law
Than Israel's leader on his tables saw!   10
There let me strive with each besetting sin,
    Recall my wandering fancies, and restrain
    The sore disquiet of a restless brain;
    And, as the path of duty is made plain,
May grace be given that I may walk therein,   15
    Not like the hireling, for his selfish gain,
With backward glances and reluctant tread,
Making a merit of his coward dread,
    But, cheerful, in the light around me thrown,
    Walking as one to pleasant service led;   20
    Doing God's will as if it were my own,
Yet trusting not in mine, but in his strength alone!

                                                    1852

FOR RIGHTEOUSNESS' SAKE

Inscribed to friends under arrest for treason against the slave power.

The age is dull and mean. Men creep,
  Not walk; with blood too pale and tame
  To pay the debt they owe to shame;
Buy cheap, sell dear; eat, drink, and sleep
  Down-pillowed, deaf to moaning want;   5
Pay tithes for soul-insurance; keep
  Six days to Mammon, one to Cant.

In such a time, give thanks to God,
  That somewhat of the holy rage
  With which the prophets in their age   10
On all its decent seemings trod,
  Has set your feet upon the lie,
That man and ox and soul and clod
  Are market stock to sell and buy!

The hot words from your lips, my own,   15
  To caution trained, might not repeat;
  But if some tares among the wheat
Of generous thought and deed were sown,
  No common wrong provoked your zeal;
The silken gauntlet that is thrown   20
  In such a quarrel rings like steel.

The brave old strife the fathers saw
  For Freedom calls for men again
  Like those who battled not in vain
For England's Charter, Alfred's law;   25
  And right of speech and trial just
Wage in your name their ancient war
  With venal courts and perjured trust.

God's ways seem dark, but, soon or late,
  They touch the shining hills of day;   30
    The evil cannot brook delay,
The good can well afford to wait.
Give ermined knaves their hour of crime;
Ye have the future grand and great,
  The safe appeal of Truth to Time!   35
                           1855

LAUS DEO!

On hearing the bells ring on the passage of the constitu-
tional amendment abolishing slavery . . . January 31, 1865
.... It wrote itself, or rather sang itself, while the bells rang,
he wrote to Lucy Larcom.

        It is done!
    Clang of bell and roar of gun
Send the tidings up and down.
    How the belfries rock and reel!
    How the great guns, peal on peal,   5
Fling the joy from town to town!

    Ring, O bells!
    Every stroke exulting tells
Of the burial hour of crime.
    Loud and long, that all may hear,   10
    Ring for every listening ear
Of eternity and Time!

    Let us kneel:
    God's own voice is in that peal,
And this spot is holy ground.   15
    Lord, forgive us! What are we,
    That our eyes this glory see,
That our ears have heard the sound!

    For the Lord
    On the whirlwind is abroad;   20

In the earthquake He has spoken;
He has smitten with His thunder
The iron walls asunder,
And the gates of brass are broken!

Loud and long   25
Lift the old exulting song;
Sing with Miriam by the sea,
He has cast the mighty down;
Horse and rider sink and drown;
"He hath triumphed gloriously!"   30

Did we dare,
In our agony of prayer,
Ask for more than He has done?
When was ever his right hand
Over any time or land   35
Stretched as now beneath the sun?

How they pale,
Ancient myth and song and tale,
In this wonder of our days,
When the cruel rod of war   40
Blossoms white with righteous law,
And the wrath of man is praise!

Blotted out!
All within and all about
Shall a fresher life begin;   45
Freer breathe the universe
As it rolls its heavy curse
On the dead and buried sin!

It is done!
In the circuit of the sun   50
Shall the sound thereof go forth.
It shall bid the sad rejoice,
It shall give the dumb a voice,
It shall belt with joy the earth!

Ring and swing,   55
Bells of joy! On morning's wing
Sound the song of praise abroad!
With a sound of broken chains
Tell the nations that He reigns,
Who alone is Lord and God!   60

                1865

THE ETERNAL GOODNESS

O Friends! with whom my feet have trod
  The quiet aisles of prayer,
Glad witness to your zeal for God
  And love of man I bear.

I trace your lines of argument;   5
  Your logic linked and strong
I weigh as one who dreads dissent,
  And fears a doubt as wrong.

But still my human hands are weak
  To hold your iron creeds: 10
Against the words ye bid me speak
  My heart within me pleads.

Who fathoms the Eternal Thought?
  Who talks of scheme and plan?
The Lord is God! He needeth not   15
  The poor device of man.

I walk with bare, hushed feet the ground
  Ye tread with boldness shod;
I dare not fix with mete and bound
  The love and power of God.   20

Ye praise his justice; even such
  His pitying love I deem:
Ye seek a king; I fain would touch
  The robe that hath no seam.

Ye see the curse which overbroods   25
  A world of pain and loss;
I hear our Lord's beatitudes
  And prayer upon the cross.

More than your schoolmen teach, within
  Myself, alas! I know: 30
Too dark ye cannot paint the sin,
  Too small the merit show.

I bow my forehead to the dust,
  I veil mine eyes for shame,
And urge, in trembling self-distrust,   35
  A prayer without a claim.

I see the wrong that round me lies,
  I feel the guilt within;
I hear, with groan and travail-cries,
  The world confess its sin.   40

Yet, in the maddening maze of things,
  And tossed by storm and flood,
To one fixed trust my spirit clings;
  I know that God is good!

Not mine to look where cherubim   45
  And seraphs may not see,
But nothing can be good in Him
  Which evil is in me.

The wrong that pains my soul below
  I dare not throne above,   50
I know not of his hate,—I know
  His goodness and his love.

I dimly guess from blessings known
  Of greater out of sight,
And, with the chastened Psalmist, own   55
  His judgments too are right.

I long for household voices gone,
  For vanished smiles I long,
But God hath led my dear ones on,
  And he can do no wrong.   60

I know not what the future hath
  Of marvel or surprise,
Assured alone that life and death
  His mercy underlies.

And if my heart and flesh are weak   65
  To bear an untried pain,
The bruisëd reed He will not break,
  But strengthen and sustain.

No offering of my own I have,
  Nor works my faith to prove;   70
I can but give the gifts He gave,
  And plead his love for love.

And so beside the Silent Sea
  I wait the muffled oar;
No harm from Him can come to me   75
  On ocean or on shore.

I know not where his islands lift
  Their fronded palms in air;
I only know I cannot drift
  Beyond his love and care.   80

O brothers! if my faith is vain,
  If hopes like these betray,
Pray for me that my feet may gain
  The sure and safer way.

And Thou, O Lord! by whom are seen   85
  Thy creatures as they be,
Forgive me if too close I lean
  My human heart on Thee!

                                    1865

ABRAHAM DAVENPORT

The famous Dark Day of New England, May 19, 1780, was a physical puzzle for many years to our ancestors, but its occurrence brought something more than philosophical speculation into the minds of those who passed through it. The incident of Colonel Abraham Davenport's sturdy protest is a matter of history.

In the old days (a custom laid aside
With breeches and cocked hats) the people sent
Their wisest men to make the public laws.
And so, from a brown homestead, where the Sound
Drinks the small tribute of the Mianas,   5
Waved over by the woods of Rippowams,
And hallowed by pure lives and tranquil deaths,
Stamford sent up to the councils of the State
Wisdom and grace in Abraham Davenport.

'Twas on a May-day of the far old year   10
Seventeen hundred eighty, that there fell
Over the bloom and sweet life of the Spring,
Over the fresh earth and the heaven of noon,
A horror of great darkness, like the night
In day of which the Norland sagas tell,—   15
The Twilight of the Gods. The low-hung sky
Was black with ominous clouds, save where its rim
Was fringed with a dull glow, like that which climbs
The crater's sides from the red hell below.
Birds ceased to sing, and all the barn-yard fowls   20
Roosted; the cattle at the pasture bars
Lowed, and looked homeward; bats on leathern wings
Flitted abroad; the sounds of labor died;
Men prayed, and women wept; all ears grew sharp
To hear the doom-blast of the trumpet shatter   25
The black sky, that the dreadful face of Christ
Might look from the rent clouds, not as he looked
A loving guest at Bethany, but stern
As Justice and inexorable Law.

Meanwhile in the old State House, dim as ghosts,   30
Sat the lawgivers of Connecticut,
Trembling beneath their legislative robes.
"It is the Lord's Great Day! Let us adjourn,"
Some said; and then, as if with one accord,
All eyes were turned to Abraham Davenport.   35
He rose, slow cleaving with his steady voice
The intolerable hush. "This well may be
The Day of Judgment which the world awaits;
But be it so or not, I only know
My present duty, and my Lord's command   40
To occupy till He come. So at the post
Where he hath set me in His providence,
I choose, for one, to meet Him face to face,—
No faithless servant frightened from my task,
But ready when the Lord of the harvest calls;   45
And therefore, with all reverence, I would say,
Let God do his work, we will see to ours.
Bring in the candles." And they brought them in.

Then by the flaring lights the Speaker read,
Albeit with husky voice and shaking hands,   50
An act to amend an act to regulate
The shad and alewive fisheries. Whereupon
Wisely and well spake Abraham Davenport,
Straight to the question, with no figures of speech
Save the ten Arab signs, yet not without   55
The shrewd dry humor natural to the man:
His awe-struck colleagues listening all the while,
Between the pauses of his argument,
To hear the thunder of the wrath of God
Break from the hollow trumpet of the cloud.   60

And there he stands in memory to this day,
Erect, self-poised, a rugged face, half seen
Against the background of unnatural dark,
A witness to the ages as they pass,
That simple duty hath no place for fear.   65

                                                  1866

EDGAR ALLAN POE

Edgar Allan Poe (1809-1849) was born in Boston, Massachusetts, orphaned at the age of two, and, after growing up in the household of his wealthy foster parents, Mr. and Mrs. John Foster Allan, in Richmond, Virginia, spent the rest of his short life in poor health and incurable poverty. Having passed five years at English schools, Poe later spent a year at the University of Virginia and, after his enlistment in the United States army, a year at the military academy at West Point. Abandoning his schooling, Poe became a free-lance writer and reviewer in New York, Philadelphia, and Baltimore. From 1835 to 1845 he worked in an editorial capacity for the *Southern Literary Messenger* (1835-37), *Burton's Gentleman's Magazine* (1839-40), *Graham's Magazine* (1841-42), the *New-York Mirror* (1844-45), and the *Broadway Journal* (1845). He was the editor of the last of these, although his contributions to *Graham's* were what primarily established his influence in contemporary letters. While Poe was never able to establish his own magazine, his prospectus for such a journal reveals his understanding of the marketing of literary wares. His polemical reviews bear out this understanding, but his polemics damaged his reputation among the literati and so delayed recognition of Poe as a critic. Consequent unemployment and long spells of drinking further demoralized him. After the death of his child-wife and his unsuccessful courtship of several women, with attendant melancholy and alcohol, he died and was buried in Baltimore, Maryland, presumably the victim of a political gang.

Both in volume and in the range of subjects, Poe's poetry is small, yet it has had its influence on subsequent American poetry—partly by means of its fashion in France at the end of the nineteenth century. Most of Poe's poems appeared in print several times, in periodicals and in book form; and nearly all of them were revised, some of them extensively, both by Poe and by his editors. In his preface to his last collection of poems, *The Raven and Other Poems* (1845), he states his preference for his own most recent revision: "These trifles are collected and republished chiefly with a view to

their redemption from the many improvements to which they
have been subjected while going 'the rounds of the press.' "
The 1845 edition is the text of the poems to that date. The
text of the poems written after 1845 is the earliest collection
following Poe's death: Rufus Wilmot Griswold (ed.), *The
Works of the Late Edgar Allan Poe*, 4 vols. (New York, 1850-
52). This choice of texts—Poe's 1845 edition and then Gris-
wold's 1850 edition—was followed by what is still the most
complete edition of Poe's writings, the Virginia edition:
James A. Harrison (ed.), *The Complete Works of Edgar
Allan Poe*, 17 vols. (New York, 1902). The first poem here
printed, attributed to Poe, was first published in *Scribner's
Magazine* (September, 1875).

ROMANCE

Romance, who loves to nod and sing,
With drowsy head and folded wing,
Among the green leaves as they shake
Far down within some shadowy lake,
To me a painted paroquet   5
Hath been—a most familiar bird—
Taught me my alphabet to say—
To lisp my very earliest word
While in the wild wood I did lie,
A child—with a most knowing eye.   10

Of late, eternal Condor years
So shake the very Heaven on high
With tumult as they thunder by,
I have no time for idle cares
Through gazing on the unquiet sky.   15
And when an hour with calmer wings
Its down upon my spirit flings—
That little time with lyre and rhyme
To while away—forbidden things!
My heart would feel to be a crime   20
Unless it trembled with the strings.

                                                        1829

ALONE

From childhood's hour I have not been
As others were—I have not seen
As others saw—I could not bring
My passions from a common spring—
From the same source I have not taken   5
My sorrow—I could not awaken
My heart to joy at the same tone—
And all I loved—*I* loved alone—
Then—in my childhood, in the dawn
Of a most stormy life—was drawn   10
From every depth of good and ill
The mystery which binds me still—
From the torrent, or the fountain—
From the red cliff of the mountain—
From the sun that round me rolled   15
In its autumn tint of gold—
From the lightning in the sky
As it pass'd me flying by—
From the thunder and the storm—
And the cloud that took the form   20
When the rest of Heaven was blue
Of a demon in my view.—

                 w. *ca.* 1829; 1875

SONNET—TO SCIENCE

Science! true daughter of Old Time thou art!
   Who alterest all things with thy peering eyes.
Why preyest thou thus upon the poet's heart,
   Vulture, whose wings are dull realities?
How should he love thee? or how deem thee wise?   5
   Who wouldst not leave him in his wandering
To seek for treasure in the jewelled skies,
   Albeit he soared with an undaunted wing?

Hast thou not dragged Diana from her car?
And driven the Hamadryad from the wood?   10
To seek a shelter in some happier star?
Hast thou not torn the Naiad from her flood,
The Elfin from the green grass, and from me
The summer dream beneath the tamarind tree?

                                                     1829

THE CITY IN THE SEA

Lo! Death has reared himself a throne
In a strange city lying alone
Far down within the dim West,
Where the good and the bad and the worst and the
          best
Have gone to their eternal rest.   5
There shrines and palaces and towers
(Time-eaten towers that tremble not!)
Resemble nothing that is ours.
Around, by lifting winds forgot,
Resignedly beneath the sky   10
The melancholy waters lie.

No rays from the holy heaven come down
On the long night-time of that town;
But light from out the lurid sea
Streams up the turrets silently—   15
Gleams up the pinnacles far and free—
Up domes—up spires—up kingly halls—
Up fanes—up Babylon-like walls—
Up shadowy long-forgotten bowers
Of sculptured ivy and stone flowers   20
Up many and many a marvellous shrine
Whose wreathéd friezes intertwine
The viol, the violet, and the vine.
Resignedly beneath the sky
The melancholy waters lie.   25
So blend the turrets and shadows there

That all seem pendulous in air,
While from a proud tower in the town
Death looks gigantically down.

There open fanes and gaping graves   30
Yawn level with the luminous waves
But not the riches there that lie
In each idol's diamond eye—
Not the gaily-jewelled dead
Tempt the waters from their bed;   35
For no ripples curl, alas!
Along that wilderness of glass—
No swellings tell that winds may be
Upon some far-off happier sea—
No heavings hint that winds have been   40
On seas less hideously serene.

But lo, a stir is in the air!
The wave—there is a movement there!
As if the towers had thrust aside,
In slightly sinking, the dull tide—   45
As if their tops had feebly given
A void within the filmy Heaven.
The waves have now a redder glow—
The hours are breathing faint and low—
And when, amid no earthly moans,   50
Down, down that town shall settle hence,
Hell, rising from a thousand thrones,
Shall do it reverence.

[First titled "The Doomed City"; later, "The City of Sin."] 1831

TO HELEN

Helen, thy beauty is to me
    Like those Nicéan barks of yore,
That gently, o'er a perfumed sea,
    The weary, way-worn wanderer bore
    To his own native shore.   5

On desperate seas long wont to roam,
  Thy hyacinth hair, thy classic face,
Thy Naiad airs have brought me home
  To the glory that was Greece,
And the grandeur that was Rome.   10

Lo! in yon brilliant window-niche
  How statue-like I see thee stand,
The agate lamp within thy hand!
  Ah, Psyche, from the regions which
Are Holy-Land!   15
                                        1831

SONNET—SILENCE

There are some qualities—some incorporate things,
  That have a double life, which thus is made
A type of that twin entity which springs
  From matter and light, evinced in solid and shade.
There is a two-fold *Silence*—sea and shore—   5
  Body and soul. One dwells in lonely places,
  Newly with grass o'ergrown; some solemn graces,
Some human memories and tearful lore,
Render him terrorless: his name's "No more."
He is the corporate Silence: dread him not!   10
  No power hath he of evil in himself;
But should some urgent fate (untimely lot!)
  Bring thee to meet his shadow (nameless elf,
That haunteth the lone regions where hath trod
No foot of man,) commend thyself to God!   15
                                        1840

DREAM-LAND

By a route obscure and lonely,
Haunted by ill angels only,
Where an Eidolon, named NIGHT,
On a black throne reigns upright,

I have reached these lands but newly   5
From an ultimate dim Thule—
From a wild weird clime that lieth, sublime,
Out of SPACE—out of TIME.

Bottomless vales and boundless floods,
And chasms, and caves, and Titan woods,   10
With forms that no man can discover
For the dews that drip all over;
Mountains toppling evermore
Into seas without a shore;
Seas that restlessly aspire,   15
Surging, unto skies of fire;
Lakes that endlessly outspread
Their lone waters—lone and dead,—
Their still waters—still and chilly
With the snows of the lolling lily.   20

By the lakes that thus outspread
Their lone waters, lone and dead,—
Their sad waters, sad and chilly
With the snows of the lolling lily,—
By the mountains—near the river   25
Murmuring lowly, murmuring ever,—
By the grey woods,—by the swamp
Where the toad and the newt encamp,—
By the dismal tarns and pools
   Where dwell the Ghouls,—   30
By each spot the most unholy—
In each nook most melancholy,—
There the traveller meets, aghast,
Sheeted Memories of the Past—
Shrouded forms that start and sigh   35
As they pass the wanderer by—
White-robed forms of friends long given,
In agony, to the Earth—and Heaven.

For the heart whose woes are legion
'Tis a peaceful, soothing region—   40
For the spirit that walks in shadow

'Tis—oh 'tis an Eldorado!
But the traveller, travelling through it,
May not—dare not openly view it;
Never its mysteries are exposed   45
To the weak human eye unclosed;
So wills its King, who hath forbid
The uplifting of the fringéd lid;
And thus the sad Soul that here passes
Beholds it but through darkened glasses.   50

By a route obscure and lonely,
Haunted by ill angels only,
Where an Eidolon, named NIGHT,
On a black throne reigns upright,
I have wandered home but newly   55
From this ultimate dim Thule.

                                                  1844

ULALUME

The skies they were ashen and sober;
   The leaves they were crisped and sere—
   The leaves they were withering and sere;
It was night in the lonesome October
   Of my most immemorial year;   5
It was hard by the dim lake of Auber,
   In the misty mid region of Weir—
It was down by the dank tarn of Auber,
   In the ghoul-haunted woodland of Weir.

Here once, through an alley Titanic,   10
   Of cypress, I roamed with my Soul—
   Of cypress, with Psyche, my Soul.
These were days when my heart was volcanic
   As the scoriac rivers that roll—
   As the lavas that restlessly roll   15
Their sulphurous currents down Yaanek
   In the ultimate climes of the pole—
That groan as they roll down Mount Yaanek
   In the realms of the boreal pole.

Our talk had been serious and sober,   20
    But our thoughts they were palsied and sere—
    Our memories were treacherous and sere—
For we knew not the month was October,
    And we marked not the night of the year—
    (Ah, night of all nights in the year!)   25
We noted not the dim lake of Auber
    (Though once we had journeyed down here)—
Remembered not the dank tarn of Auber,
    Nor the ghoul-haunted woodland of Weir.

And now, as the night was senescent   30
    And star-dials pointed to morn—
    As the star-dials hinted of morn—
At the end of our path a liquescent
    And nebulous lustre was born,
Out of which a miraculous crescent   35
    Arose, with a duplicate horn—
Astarte's bediamonded crescent
    Distinct with its duplicate horn.

And I said—"She is warmer than Dian:
    She rolls through an ether of sighs—   40
    She revels in a region of sighs:
She has seen that the tears are not dry on
    These cheeks, where the worm never dies
And has come past the stars of the Lion
    To point us the path to the skies—   45
    To the Lethean peace of the skies—
Come up, in despite of the Lion,
    To shine on us with her bright eyes—
Come up through the lair of the Lion,
    With love in her luminous eyes."   50

But Psyche, uplifting her finger,
    Said—"Sadly this star I mistrust—
    Her pallor I strangely mistrust:—
Oh, hasten!—oh, let us not linger!
    Oh, fly!—let us fly!—for we must."   55

In terror she spoke, letting sink her
    Wings till they trailed in the dust—
In agony sobbed, letting sink her
    Plumes till they trailed in the dust—
    Till they sorrowfully trailed in the dust.   60

I replied—"This is nothing but dreaming:
    Let us on by this tremulous light!
    Let us bathe in this crystalline light!
Its Sibyllic splendor is beaming
    With Hope and in Beauty to-night:—   65
    See!—it flickers up the sky through the night!
Ah, we safely may trust to its gleaming,
    And be sure it will lead us aright—
We safely may trust to a gleaming
    That cannot but guide us aright,   70
    Since it flickers up to Heaven through the night."

Thus I pacified Psyche and kissed her,
    And tempted her out of her gloom—
    And conquered her scruples and gloom;
And we passed to the end of the vista,   75
    But were stopped by the door of a tomb—
    By the door of a legended tomb;
And I said—"What is written, sweet sister,
    On the door of this legended tomb?"
    She replied—"Ulalume—Ulalume—   80
    'Tis the vault of thy lost Ulalume!"

Then my heart it grew ashen and sober
    As the leaves that were crisped and sere—
    As the leaves that were withering and sere,
And I cried—"It was surely October   85
    On *this* very night of last year
    That I journeyed—I journeyed down here—
    That I brought a dread burden down here—
    On this night of all nights in the year,
    Ah, what demon has tempted me here?   90

Well I know, now, this dim lake of Auber,
This misty mid region of Weir—
Well I know, now, this dank tarn of Auber,
This ghoul-haunted woodland of Weir."

                                            1847

TO HELEN

I saw thee once—once only—years ago:
I must not say *how* many—but *not* many.
It was a July midnight; and from out
A full-orbed moon, that, like thine own soul, soaring,
Sought a precipitate pathway up through heaven,   5
There fell a silvery-silken veil of light,
With quietude and sultriness and slumber,
Upon the upturn'd faces of a thousand
Roses that grew in an enchanted garden,
Where no wind dared to stir, unless on tiptoe—   10
Fell on the upturn'd faces of these roses
That gave out, in return for the love-light,
Their odorous souls in an ecstatic death—
Fell on the upturn'd faces of these roses
That smiled and died in this parterre, enchanted   15
By thee, and by the poetry of thy presence.

Clad all in white, upon a violet bank
I saw thee half reclining; while the moon
Fell on the upturn'd faces of the roses,
And on thine own, upturn'd—alas, in sorrow!   20

Was it not Fate, that, on this July midnight—
Was it not Fate, (whose name is also Sorrow),
That bade me pause before that garden-gate,
To breathe the incense of those slumbering roses?
No footstep stirred: the hated world all slept,   25
Save only thee and me. (Oh, heaven!—oh, God!
How my heart beats in coupling those two words!)
Save only thee and me. I paused—I looked—

And in an instant all things disappeared.
(Ah, bear in mind this garden was enchanted!)   30
The pearly lustre of the moon went out:
The mossy banks and the meandering paths,
The happy flowers and the repining trees,
Were seen no more: the very roses' odors
Died in the arms of the adoring airs.   35
All—all expired save thee—save less than thou:
Save only the divine light in thine eyes—
Save but the soul in thine uplifted eyes.
I saw but them—they were the world to me.
I saw but them—saw only them for hours—   40
Saw only them until the moon went down.
What wild heart-histories seemed to lie enwritten
Upon those crystalline, celestial spheres!
How dark a woe! yet how sublime a hope!
How silently serene a sea of pride!   45
How daring an ambition! yet how deep—
How fathomless a capacity for love!

But now, at length, dear Dian sank from sight,
Into a western couch of thunder-cloud;
And thou, a ghost, amid the entombing trees   50
Didst glide away. *Only thine eyes remained.*
    They *would not* go—they never yet have gone.
Lighting my lonely pathway home that night,
They have not left me (as my hopes have) since.
They follow me—they lead me through the years   55
They are my ministers—yet I their slave.
Their office is to illumine and enkindle—
My duty, *to be saved* by their bright light,
And purified in their electric fire,
And sanctified in their elysian fire.   60
They fill my soul with Beauty (which is Hope),
And are far up in Heaven—the stars I kneel to
In the sad, silent watches of my night;
While even in the meridian glare of day
I see them still—two sweetly scintillant   65
Venuses, unextinguished by the sun!

                                                              1848

THE BELLS

I

Hear the sledges with the bells—
Silver bells!
What a world of merriment their melody foretells!
How they tinkle, tinkle, tinkle,
In the icy air of night!   5
While the stars that oversprinkle
All the heavens, seem to twinkle
With a crystalline delight;
Keeping time, time, time,
In a sort of Runic rhyme,   10
To the tintinnabulation that so musically wells
From the bells, bells, bells, bells,
Bells, bells, bells—
From the jingling and the tinkling of the bells.

II

Hear the mellow wedding bells   15
Golden bells!
What a world of happiness their harmony foretells!
Through the balmy air of night
How they ring out their delight!—
From the molten-golden notes,   20
And all in tune,
What a liquid ditty floats
To the turtle-dove that listens, while she gloats
On the moon!
Oh, from out the sounding cells,   25
What a gush of euphony voluminously wells!
How it swells!
How it dwells
On the Future!—how it tells
Of the rapture that impels   30
To the swinging and the ringing
Of the bells, bells, bells—

Of the bells, bells, bells, bells,
Bells, bells, bells—
To the rhyming and the chiming of the bells!   35

III

Hear the loud alarum bells—
Brazen bells!
What a tale of terror, now their turbulency tells!
In the startled ear of night
How they scream out their affright!   40
Too much horrified to speak,
They can only shriek, shriek,
Out of tune,
In a clamorous appealing to the mercy of the fire,
In a mad expostulation with the deaf and frantic fire,   45
Leaping higher, higher, higher,
With a desperate desire,
And a resolute endeavour
Now—now to sit, or never,
By the side of the pale-faced moon.   50
Oh, the bells, bells, bells!
What a tale their terror tells
Of Despair!
How they clang, and clash, and roar!
What a horror they outpour   55
On the bosom of the palpitating air!
Yet the ear, it fully knows,
By the twanging,
And the clanging,
How the danger ebbs and flows;   60
Yet the ear distinctly tells,
In the jangling
And the wrangling,
How the danger sinks and swells,
By the sinking or the swelling in the anger of the bells—   65
Of the bells—
Of the bells, bells, bells, bells,
Bells, bells, bells—
In the clamor and the clanging of the bells!

IV

Hear the tolling of the bells—   70
Iron bells!
What a world of solemn thought their monody compels!
In the silence of the night,
How we shiver with affright
At the melancholy menace of their tone!   75
For every sound that floats
From the rust within their throats
Is a groan.
And the people—ah, the people—
They that dwell up in the steeple,   80
All alone,
And who, tolling, tolling, tolling,
In that muffled monotone,
Feel a glory in so rolling
On the human heart a stone—   85
They are neither man nor woman—
They are neither brute nor human—
They are Ghouls:—
And their king it is who tolls:—
And he rolls, rolls, rolls,   90
Rolls
A paean from the bells!
And his merry bosom swells
With the paean of the bells!
And he dances, and he yells;   95
Keeping time, time, time,
In a sort of Runic rhyme,
To the paean of the bells:—
Of the bells:
Keeping time, time, time   100
In a sort of Runic rhyme,
To the throbbing of the bells—
Of the bells, bells, bells—
To the sobbing of the bells:—
Keeping time, time, time,   105
As he knells, knells, knells,
In a happy Runic rhyme,

To the rolling of the bells—
Of the bells, bells, bells:—
To the tolling of the bells—   110
Of the bells, bells, bells, bells,
Bells, bells, bells—
To the moaning and the groaning of the bells.

1849

HENRY DAVID THOREAU

Henry David Thoreau (1817-1862) was born in Concord, Massachusetts, where he spent most of his life. Schooled in Boston and at the Concord Academy, he was graduated from Harvard College (1837) and returned to Concord to teach school for a while, to lecture, and to employ himself at odd jobs. From 1841 to 1843 he lived in Emerson's house and consequently associated with a group of intellectuals who met there informally and called themselves the Symposium, and who included in their number Bronson Alcott, the younger W. E. Channing, Theodore Parker, Orestes Brownson, Jones Very, Margaret Fuller, and Elizabeth Peabody. This group gave form and impetus to the religious, philosophic, and literary ideas collectively known as Transcendentalism, which prospered in New England during the twenty-five years before the Civil War.

Thoreau made occasional excursions during his life: a voyage on the Concord and Merrimack rivers (1839) with his brother John; a journey to Staten Island, N. Y. (1843) as a tutor to William Emerson's children; to Walden Pond (1845-47) "to live deliberately, to front only the essential facts of life"; to the Concord jail for one night for his refusal to pay taxes; to the Maine woods on several occasions (1846, 1853, and 1857); to Cape Cod (1846); to Canada (1850); and to Minnesota, the year before his death, in search of a climate to help cure his tuberculosis. These excursions punctuated his accustomed wanderings. As Thoreau himself wrote, "I have travelled a good deal in Concord."

He published accounts of nearly all of these journeys, although only two of them, *A Week on the Concord and Merrimack Rivers* (1849) and *Walden* (1854) appeared as books during his lifetime. The rest of his essays were gathered from magazines, and, with his lectures on slavery and governmental reform and his letters, were published piecemeal after his death. Thoreau also kept a journal which he began as a college student, selections from which were published from 1881 to 1892. The first collection of his writings was the Riverside edition: Harrison G. O. Blake (ed.), *The Writings of Henry*

David Thoreau, with Bibliographical Introductions and Full Indexes, 10 vols. (Cambridge, 1894), to which a volume, *Familiar Letters* (1894), edited by Frank B. Sanborn, was added.

Thoreau was a young man when he wrote most of his poetry, and he gradually abandoned verse for prose. He published only a few of his poems, and most of these in a few magazines—particularly in *The Dial,* which was the organ of the New England "Transcendentalist movement." A few of his poems he included in his two books, mostly as illustrations of the point he happened to be making. His poems pay small heed to the conventional fashions of verse in the middle of the nineteenth century. Primarily, they avoid the insistent didacticism of Thoreau's popular contemporaries. This man was an accomplished student of Greek and Latin. He had read widely in the English poets of the sixteenth and seventeenth centuries and in German literature, all of which helped him to a perspective of the times in which he lived. The first published selection of his verse, *Poems of Nature* (1895), was edited by H. S. Salt and F. B. Sanborn. The definitive edition is: Carl Bode (ed.), *Collected Poems of Henry Thoreau* (Chicago, 1943). Each of the poems here printed follows the text which Bode has selected. Since most of them were written within a few years, dates are relatively unimportant.

WALDEN

—True, our converse a stranger is to speech,
Only the practised ear can catch the surging words,
That break and die upon thy pebbled lips.
Thy flow of thought is noiseless as the lapse of thy own
    waters,
Wafted as is the morning mist up from thy surface,   5
So that the passive Soul doth breathe it in,
And is infected with the truth thou wouldst express.

E'en the remotest stars have come in troops
And stooped low to catch the benediction
Of thy countenance. Oft as the day came round,   10

Impartial has the sun exhibited himself
Before thy narrow skylight—nor has the moon
For cycles failed to roll this way
As oft as elsewhither, and tell thee of the night.
No cloud so rare but hitherward it stalked,   15
And in thy face looked doubly beautiful.
O! tell me what the winds have writ within these thousand
          years,
On the blue vault that spans thy flood—
Or sun transferred and delicately reprinted
For thy own private reading. Somewhat   20
Within these latter days I've read,
But surely there was much that would have thrilled the
          Soul,
Which human eye saw not
I would give much to read that first bright page,
Wet from a virgin press, when Eurus—Boreas—   25
And the host of airy quill-drivers
First dipped their pens in mist.

                                                      1838

IN THE BUSY STREETS, DOMAINS OF TRADE

In the busy streets, domains of trade,
Man is a surly porter, or a vain and hectoring bully,
Who can claim no nearer kindredship with me
Than brotherhood by law.

                                                      1838

I AM A PARCEL OF VAIN STRIVINGS TIED

          I am a parcel of vain strivings tied
               By a chance bond together,
          Dangling this way and that, their links
               Were made so loose and wide,
                    Methinks,   5
               For milder weather.

A bunch of violets without their roots,
  And sorrel intermixed,
Encircled by a wisp of straw
  Once coiled about their shoots,
    The law
    By which I'm fixed.
                10

A nosegay which Time clutched from out
  Those fair Elysian fields,
With weeds and broken stems, in haste,   15
  Doth make the rabble rout
    That waste
    The day he yields.

And here I bloom for a short hour unseen,
  Drinking my juices up,   20
With no root in the land
  To keep my branches green,
    But stand
    In a bare cup.

Some tender buds were left upon my stem   25
  In mimicry of life,
But ah! the children will not know,
  Till time has withered them,
    The woe
    With which they're rife.   30

But now I see I was not plucked for naught,
  And after in life's vase
Of glass set while I might survive,
  But by a kind hand brought
    Alive   35
    To a strange place.

That stock thus thinned will soon redeem its hours,
  And by another year,
Such as God knows, with freer air,
  More fruits and fairer flowers   40
    Will bear,
    While I droop here.

                1841

WITHIN THE CIRCUIT OF THIS PLODDING LIFE

Within the circuit of this plodding life
There enter moments of an azure hue,
Untarnished fair as is the violet
Or anemone, when the spring strews them
By some meandering rivulet, which make   5
The best philosophy untrue that aims
But to console man for his grievances.
I have remembered when the winter came,
High in my chamber in the frosty nights,
When in the still light of the cheerful moon,   10
On every twig and rail and jutting spout,
The icy spears were adding to their length
Against the arrows of the coming sun,
How in the shimmering noon of summer past
Some unrecorded beam slanted across   15
The upland pastures where the Johnswort grew;
Or heard, amid the verdure of my mind,
The bee's long smothered hum, on the blue flag
Loitering amidst the mead; or busy rill,
Which now through all its course stands still and dumb   20
Its own memorial,—purling at its play
Along the slopes, and through the meadows next,
Until its youthful sound was hushed at last
In the staid current of the lowland stream;
Or seen the furrows shine but late upturned,   25
And where the fieldfare followed in the rear,
When all the fields around lay bound and hoar
Beneath a thick integument of snow.
So by God's cheap economy made rich
To go upon my winter's task again.   30

1842

GREAT GOD, I ASK THEE FOR NO MEANER PELF

Great God, I ask thee for no meaner pelf
Than that I may not disappoint myself,
That in my action I may soar as high,
As I can now discern with this clear eye.

And next in value, which thy kindness lends,   5
That I may greatly disappoint my friends,
Howe'er they think or hope that it may be,
They may not dream how thou'st distinguished me.

That my weak hand may equal my firm faith,
And my life practice more than my tongue saith;   10
That my low conduct may not show,
Nor my relenting lines,
That I thy purpose did not know,
Or overrated thy designs.

                                                      1842

MY BOOKS I'D FAIN CAST OFF, I CANNOT READ

My books I'd fain cast off, I cannot read,
'Twixt every page my thoughts go stray at large
Down in the meadow, where is richer feed,
And will not mind to hit their proper targe.

Plutarch was good, and so was Homer too,   5
Our Shakespeare's life were rich to live again,
What Plutarch read, that was not good nor true,
Nor Shakespeare's books, unless his books were men.

Here while I lie beneath this walnut bough,
What care I for the Greeks or for Troy town,   10
If juster battles are enacted now
Between the ants upon this hummock's crown?

Bid Homer wait till I the issue learn,
If red or black the gods will favor most,
Or yonder Ajax will the phalanx turn,   15
Struggling to heave some rock against the host.

Tell Shakespeare to attend some leisure hour,
For now I've business with this drop of dew,
And see you not, the clouds prepare a shower,—
I'll meet him shortly when the sky is blue.   20

This bed of herd's-grass and wild oats was spread
Last year with nicer skill than monarchs use,
A clover tuft is pillow for my head,
And violets quite overtop my shoes.

And now the cordial clouds have shut all in,   25
And gently swells the wind to say all's well,
The scattered drops are falling fast and thin,
Some in the pool, some in the flower-bell.

I am well drenched upon my bed of oats;
But see that globe come rolling down its stem,   30
Now like a lonely planet there it floats,
And now it sinks into my garment's hem.

Drip drip the trees for all the country round,
And richness rare distils from every bough,
The wind alone it is makes every sound,   35
Shaking down crystals on the leaves below.

For shame the sun will never show himself,
Who could not with his beams e'er melt me so,
My dripping locks,—they would become an elf,
Who in a beaded coat does gayly go.   40

                                                    1842

TRAVELLING

How little curious is man
He has not searched his mystery a span
But dreams of mines of treasure
Which he neglects to measure.

For three score years and ten   5
Walks to and fro amid his fellow men
O'er this small tract of continental land
And never uses a divining wand.

Our uninquiring corpses lie more low
Than our life's curiosity doth go   10
Our ambitious steps ne'er climb so high
As in their daily sport the sparrows fly

And yonder cloud's borne farther in a day
Than our most vagrant steps may ever stray.
Surely, O Lord, he has not greatly erred,   15
Who has so little from his threshold stirred.

He wanders through this low and shallow world
Scarcely his loftier thoughts and hopes unfurled,
Through this low walled world, where his huge sin
Has hardly room to rest and harbor in.   20

He wanders round until his end draws nigh
And then lays down his aged head to die
And this is life, this is that famous strife.

1842

GREAT FRIEND

I walk in nature still alone
   And know no one
Discern no lineament nor feature
   Of any creature.

Though all the firmament   5
  Is o'er me bent,
Yet still I miss the grace
  Of an intelligent and kindred face.

I still must seek the friend
Who does with nature blend,   10
Who is the person in her mask,
He is the man I ask.

Who is the expression of her meaning,
Who is the uprightness of her leaning,
Who is the grown child of her weaning   15

The center of this world,
The face of nature,
The site of human life,
Some sure foundation
And nucleus of a nation—   20
At least a private station.

We twain would walk together
Through every weather,
And see this aged nature,
Go with a bending stature.   25
                                  1842

LIGHT-WINGED SMOKE, ICARIAN BIRD

Light-winged Smoke, Icarian bird,
Melting thy pinions in thy upward flight,
Lark without song, and messenger of dawn,
Circling above the hamlets as thy nest;
Or else, departing dream, and shadowy form   5
Of midnight vision, gathering up thy skirts;
By night star-veiling, and by day
Darkening the light and blotting out the sun;
Go thou my incense upward from this hearth,
And ask the gods to pardon this clear flame. 10
                                  1843

PRAY TO WHAT EARTH DOES THIS
SWEET COLD BELONG

Pray to what earth does this sweet cold belong,
Which asks no duties and no conscience?
The moon goes up by leaps her cheerful path
In some far summer stratum of the sky,
While stars with their cold shine bedot her way.   5
The fields gleam mildly back upon the sky,
And far and near upon the leafless shrubs
The snow dust still emits a silvery light.
Under the hedge, where drift banks are their screen,
The titmice now pursue their downy dreams,   10
As often in the sweltering summer nights
The bee doth drop asleep in the flower cup,
When evening overtakes him with his load.
By the brooksides, in the still genial night,
The more adventurous wanderer may hear   15
The crystals shoot and form, and winter slow
Increase his rule by gentlest summer means.

                                              1843

IT IS NO DREAM OF MINE

It is no dream of mine,
To ornament a line;
I cannot come nearer to God and Heaven
Than I live to Walden even.
I am its stony shore,   5
And the breeze that passes o'er;
In the hollow of my hand
Are its water and its sand,
And its deepest resort
Lies high in my thought.   10

                                              1854

THE THAW

I saw the civil sun drying earth's tears—
Her tears of joy that only faster flowed,

Fain would I stretch me by the hig(h)way side,
To thaw and trickle with the melting snow,
That mingled soul and body with the tide,   5
I too may through the pores of nature flow.

But I alas nor trickle can nor fume,
One jot to forward the great work of Time,
'Tis mine to hearken while these ply the loom,
So shall my silence with their music chime.   10

               1863

WALT WHITMAN

Walt Whitman (1819-1892) built himself into a legend which he spent most of his life proclaiming. Born at West Hills, Long Island, into a Quaker family, Whitman attended public schools until he was thirteen, then found employment in a law office and in a doctor's office before becoming a printer and an itinerant schoolteacher. He wrote for several newspapers and edited (1846-48) the Brooklyn *Eagle,* a Democratic paper which nourished his own convictions about an immediate and practicing democracy in the United States, but which could not tolerate Whitman's notions about immigration and the Free Soil movement. Discharged as editor, Whitman traveled for several months to New Orleans, then back to Manhattan via the Middle West. He began to read extensively in Hegel, Goethe, Emerson, Carlyle, the Bible, and Shakespeare. Most of his poetry after 1848 was an attempt to assimilate and literally reproduce his own cumulated experiences.

Both individualism and the democratic ideal found a place in his personal mysticism. Whitman never developed a logical system of ideas: he believed at the same time in the fullness of creation and in its progress; he acknowledged evil merely by asserting value in any state of being; and matter, to him, was both alive and spiritual. Out of these rationalizations of his own experiences grew his concept of the poet, the great ethical and social teacher unconfined by any mere social program. His prosody was symptomatic of his declaration of thematic independence.

Whitman himself subsidized the first edition of the *Leaves of Grass* (1855), and during his lifetime he prepared eight more editions, incorporating, as he wrote them, the poems which he published under four separate titles: *Walt Whitman's Drum Taps* (1865), with its *Sequel to Drum Taps* (1865), *Two Rivulets* (1876), and *November Boughs* (1888), which included poems collectively entitled "Sands at Seventy." Meanwhile, there were pamphlet publications of other poems. A tenth edition of the *Leaves* (1897) includes "Posthumous Additions."

Five editions of the *Leaves* (the second, 1856; third, 1860-61; fourth, 1867; fifth, 1871-72; and seventh, 1881) represent major additions to, and revisions of, the editions they each followed into print. The other four editions (the sixth, 1876; eighth, 1889; ninth, 1892; and tenth, 1897) are primarily reprints.

By the fifth edition of the *Leaves* (1871-72), the volume included most—and most of his best—poems. In fact, Whitman encouraged the impression that he had already completed the *Leaves* in a preface to a commemorative poem published in 1872: "New World songs, and an epic of Democracy, having already had their published expression, as well as I can expect to give it, in *Leaves of Grass,* the present and any future pieces from me are really but the surplusage forming after that Volume, or the wake eddying behind it." Although Whitman did not begin a new and cumulative volume of poems, his intention to do so suggests his estimate of the scope of *Leaves of Grass.* In the remaining significant edition (the seventh, 1881-82), Whitman made his final revisions of text, titles, and sequence of poems in the volume. He continued to write poems which appeared as "annexes" in later editions, but many of these were revisions of much earlier fragments.

The poems in this selection, consequently, are chosen from the first five editions of the *Leaves.* Their dates signify their first publication in the *Leaves* or in one of the titles mentioned above. Their sequence and their titles correspond to Whitman's scheme in the seventh and following editions; and the text of each poem follows the text of the ninth edition, the last one which Whitman supervised: *Leaves of Grass* (Philadelphia, 1892).

ONE'S-SELF I SING

One's-self I sing, a simple separate person,
Yet utter the word Democratic, the word En-Masse.

Of physiology from top to toe I sing,
Not physiognomy alone nor brain alone is worthy for
    the Muse,
    I say the Form complete is worthier far,   5
The Female equally with the Male I sing.

Of Life immense in passion, pulse, and power,
Cheerful, for freest action form'd under the laws divine,
The Modern Man I sing.

                                              1867

from SONG OF MYSELF

1

I celebrate myself, and sing myself,
And what I assume you shall assume,
For every atom belonging to me as good belongs to you.

I loafe and invite my soul,
I lean and loafe at my ease observing a spear of summer grass.   5

My tongue, every atom of my blood, form'd from this soil, this
    air,
Born here of parents born here from parents the same, and
    their parents the same,
I, now thirty-seven years old in perfect health begin,
Hoping to cease not till death.

Creeds and schools in abeyance,   10
Retiring back a while sufficed at what they are, but never for-
    gotten,

I harbor for good or bad, I permit to speak at every hazard,
Nature without check with original energy.

2

Houses and rooms are full of perfumes, the shelves are crowded
    with perfumes,
I breathe the fragrance myself and know it and like it,
The distillation would intoxicate me also, but I shall not let
    it.

The atmosphere is not a perfume, it has no taste of the distil-
    lation, it is odorless,
It is for my mouth forever, I am in love with it,   5
I will go to the bank by the wood and become undisguised
    and naked,
I am mad for it to be in contact with me.

The smoke of my own breath,
Echoes, ripples, buzz'd whispers, love-root, silk-thread, crotch
    and vine,
My respiration and inspiration, the beating of my heart, the
    passing of blood and air through my lungs,   10
The sniff of green leaves and dry leaves, and of the shore and
    dark-color'd sea-rocks, and of hay in the barn,
The sound of the belch'd words of my voice loos'd to the eddies
    of the wind,
A few light kisses, a few embraces, a reaching around of arms,
The play of shine and shade on the trees as the supple boughs
    wag,
The delight alone or in the rush of the streets, or along the fields
    and hill-sides,   15
The feeling of health, the full-noon trill, the song of me rising
    from bed and meeting the sun.

Have you reckon'd a thousand acres much? have you reckon'd
    the earth much?
Have you practis'd so long to learn to read?
Have you felt so proud to get at the meaning of poems?

Stop this day and night with me and you shall possess the origin
    of all poems,   20
You shall possess the good of the earth and sun, (there are
    millions of suns left,)
You shall no longer take things at second or third hand, nor
    look through the eyes of the dead, nor feed on the
    spectres in books,
You shall not look through my eyes either, nor take things from
    me,
You shall listen to all sides and filter them your self.

3

I have heard what the talkers were talking, the talk of the be-
    ginning and the end,
But I do not talk of the beginning or the end.

There was never any more inception than there is now,
Nor any more youth or age than there is now,
And will never be any more perfection than there is now,   5
Nor any more heaven or hell than there is now.

Urge and urge and urge,
Always the procreant urge of the world.
Out of the dimness opposite equals advance, always substance
    and increase, always sex,
Always a knit of identity, always distinction, always a breed of
    life.   10

To elaborate is no avail, learn'd and unlearn'd feel that it is so.

Sure as the most certain sure, plumb in the uprights, well en-
    tretied, braced in the beams,
Stout as a horse, affectionate, haughty, electrical,
I and this mystery here we stand.

Clear and sweet is my soul, and clear and sweet is all that is not
    my soul.   15

Lack one lacks both, and the unseen is proved by the seen,
Till that becomes unseen and receives proof in its turn.

Showing the best and dividing it from the worst age vexes age,
Knowing the perfect fitness and equanimity of things, while
they discuss I am silent, and go bathe and admire myself.

Welcome is every organ and attribute of me, and of any man
hearty and clean,   20
Not an inch nor a particle of an inch is vile, and none shall be
less familiar than the rest.

I am satisfied—I see, dance, laugh, sing;
As the hugging and loving bed-fellow sleeps at my side through
the night, and withdraws at the peep of the day with
stealthy tread,
Leaving me baskets cover'd with white towels swelling the house
with their plenty,
Shall I postpone my acceptation and realization and scream
at my eyes,   25
That they turn from gazing after and down the road,
And forthwith cipher and show me to a cent,
Exactly the value of one and exactly the value of two, and which
is ahead?

5

I believe in you my soul, the other I am must not abase itself to
you,
And you must not be abased to the other.

Loafe with me on the grass, loose the stop from your throat,
Not words, not music or rhyme I want, not custom or lecture,
not even the best,
Only the lull I like, the hum of your valvèd voice.   5

I mind how once we lay such a transparent summer morning,
How you settled your head athwart my hips and gently turn'd
over upon me,
And parted the shirt from my bosom-bone, and plunged your
tongue to my bare-stript heart,
And reach'd till you felt my beard, and reach'd till you held
my feet.

Swiftly rose and spread around me the peace and knowledge
    that pass all the argument of the earth,   10
And I know that the hand of God is the promise of my own,
And I know that the spirit of God is the brother of my own,
And that all the men ever born are also my brothers, and the
    women my sisters and lovers,
And that a kelson of the creation is love,
And limitless are leaves stiff or drooping in the fields,   15
And brown ants in the little wells beneath them,
And mossy scabs of the worm fence, heap'd stones, elder,
    mullein and poke-weed.

6

A child said *What is the grass?* fetching it to me with full hands,
How could I answer the child? I do not know what it is any
    more than he.

I guess it must be the flag of my disposition, out of hopeful
    green stuff woven.

Or I guess it is the handkerchief of the Lord,
A scented gift and remembrancer designedly dropt,   5
Bearing the owner's name someway in the corners, that we may
    see and remark, and say *Whose?*

Or I guess the grass is itself a child, the produced babe of the
    vegetation.

Or I guess it is a uniform hieroglyphic,
And it means, Sprouting alike in broad zones and narrow zones,
Growing among black folks as among white,   10
Kanuck, Tuckahoe, Congressman, Cuff, I give them the same,
    I receive them the same.

And now it seems to me the beautiful uncut hair of graves.

Tenderly will I use you curling grass,
It may be you transpire from the breasts of young men,
It may be if I had known them I would have loved them,   15

It may be you are from old people, or from offspring taken soon
     out of their mothers' laps,
And here you are the mothers' laps.

This grass is very dark to be from the white heads of old
     mothers,
Darker than the colorless beards of old men,
Dark to come from under the faint red roofs of mouths.   20
O I perceive after all so many uttering tongues,
And I perceive they do not come from the roofs of mouths for
     nothing.

I wish I could translate the hints about the dead young men
     and women,
And the hints about old men and mothers, and the offspring
     taken soon out of their laps.

What do you think has become of the young and old men?   25
And what do you think has become of the women and children?

They are alive and well somewhere,
The smallest sprout shows there is really no death,
And if ever there was it led forward life, and does not wait at
     the end to arrest it,
And ceas'd the moment life appear'd.   30

All goes onward and outward, nothing collapses,
And to die is different from what any one supposed, and luckier.

9

The big doors of the country barn stand open and ready,
The dried grass of the harvest-time loads the slow-drawn wagon,
The clear light plays on the brown and gray and green
     intertinged,
The armfuls are pack'd to the sagging mow.

I am there, I help, I came stretch'd atop of the load,   5
I felt its soft jolts, one leg reclined on the other,
I jump from the cross-beams and seize the clover and timothy,
And roll head over heels and tangle my hair full of wisps.

11

Twenty-eight young men bathe by the shore,
Twenty-eight young men and all so friendly;
Twenty-eight years of womanly life and all so lonesome.

She owns the fine house by the rise of the bank,
She hides handsome and richly drest aft the blinds of the
        window.   5

Which of the young men does she like the best?
Ah the homeliest of them is beautiful to her.

Where are you off to, lady? for I see you,
You splash in the water there, yet stay stock still in your room.

Dancing and laughing along the beach came the twenty-ninth
        bather,   10
The rest did not see her, but she saw them and loved them.

The beards of the young men glisten'd with wet, it ran from
        their long hair,
Little streams pass'd all over their bodies.

An unseen hand also pass'd over their bodies,
It descended tremblingly from their temples and ribs.   15

The young men float on their backs, their white bellies bulge to
        the sun, they do not ask who seizes fast to them,
They do not know who puffs and declines with pendant and
        bending arch,
They do not think whom they souse with spray.

15

The pure contralto sings in the organ loft,
The carpenter dresses his plank, the tongue of his foreplane
        whistles its wild ascending lisp,
The married and unmarried children ride home to their
        Thanksgiving dinner,

The pilot seizes the king-pin, he heaves down with a strong arm,
The mate stands braced in the whale-boat, lance and harpoon
  are ready, 5
The duck-shooter walks by silent and cautious stretches,
The deacons are ordain'd with cross'd hands at the altar,
The spinning-girl retreats and advances to the hum of the big
  wheel,
The farmer stops by the bars as he walks on a First-day loafe
  and looks at the oats and rye,
The lunatic is carried at last to the asylum a confirm'd case, 10
(He will never sleep any more as he did in the cot in his
  mother's bedroom;)
The jour printer with gray head and gaunt jaws works at his
  case,
He turns his quid of tobacco while his eyes blurr with the manu-
  script;
The malform'd limbs are tied to the surgeon's table,
What is removed drops horribly in a pail; 15
The quadroon girl is sold at the auction-stand, the drunkard
  nods by the bar-room stove,
The machinist rolls up his sleeves, the policeman travels his
  beat, the gate-keeper marks who pass,
The young fellow drives the express-wagon, (I love him, though
  I do not know him;)
The half-breed straps on his light boots to compete in the race,
The western turkey-shooting draws old and young, some lean
  on their rifles, some sit on logs, 20
Out from the crowd steps the marksman, takes his position,
  levels his piece;
The groups of newly-come immigrants cover the wharf or levee,
As the wooly-pates hoe in the sugar-field, the overseer views
  them from his saddle,
The bugle calls in the ball-room, the gentlemen run for their
  partners, the dancers bow to each other,
The youth lies awake in the cedar-roof'd garret and harks to the
  musical rain, 25
The Wolverine sets traps on the creek that helps fill the Huron,
The squaw wrapt in her yellow-hemm'd cloth is offering mocca-
  sins and bead-bags for sale,

The connoisseur peers along the exhibition-gallery with half-
   shut eyes bent sideways,
As the deck-hands make fast the steamboat the plank is thrown
   for the shore-going passengers,
The young sister holds out the skein while the elder sister
   winds it off in a ball, and stops now and then for the
   knots,   30
The one-year wife is recovering and happy having a week ago
   borne her first child.
The clean-hair'd Yankee girl works with her sewing-machine
   or in the factory or mill,
The paving-man leans on his two-handed rammer, the reporter's
   lead flies swiftly over the note-book, the sign-painter is
   lettering with blue and gold,
The canal boy trots on the tow-path, the book-keeper counts at
   his desk, the shoemaker waxes his thread,
The conductor beats time for the band and all the performers
   follow him,   35
The child is baptized, the convert is making his first professions,
The regatta is spread on the bay, the race is begun, (how the
   white sails sparkle!)
The drover watching his drove sings out to them that would
   stray,
The pedler sweats with his pack on his back, (the purchaser
   higgling about the odd cent;)
The bride unrumples her white dress, the minute-hand of the
   clock moves slowly,   40
The opium-eater reclines with rigid head and just-open'd lips,
The prostitute draggles her shawl, her bonnet bobs on her
   tipsy and pimpled neck,
The crowd laugh at her blackguard oaths, the men jeer and
   wink to each other,
(Miserable! I do not laugh at your oaths nor jeer you;)
The President holding a cabinet council is surrounded by the
   great Secretaries,   45
On the piazza walk three matrons stately and friendly with
   twined arms,
The crew of the fish-smack pack repeated layers of halibut in
   the hold,

The Missourian crosses the plains toting his wares and his
  cattle,
As the fare-collector goes through the train he gives notice by
  the jingling of loose change,
The floor-men are laying the floor, the tinners are tinning the
  roof, the masons are calling for mortar,   50
In single file each shouldering his hod pass onward the laborers;
Seasons pursuing each other the indescribable crowd is gather'd,
  it is the fourth of Seventh-month, (what salutes of
  cannon and small arms!)
Seasons pursuing each other the plougher ploughs, the mower
  mows, and the winter-grain falls in the ground;
Off on the lakes the pike-fisher watches and waits by the hole
  in the frozen surface,
The stumps stand thick round the clearing, the squatter
  strikes deep with his axe,   55
Flatboatmen make fast towards dusk near the cotton-wood or
  pecan-trees,
Coon-seekers go through the regions of the Red river or through
  those drain'd by the Tennessee, or through those of the
  Arkansas,
Torches shine in the dark that hangs on the Chattahooche or
  Altamahaw,
Patriarchs sit at supper with sons and grandsons and great-
  grandsons around them,
In walls of adobie, in canvas tents, rest hunters, and trappers
  after their day's sport,   60
The city sleeps and the country sleeps,
The living sleep for their time, the dead sleep for their time,
The old husband sleeps by his wife and the young husband
  sleeps by his wife;
And these tend inward to me, and I tend outward to them,
And such as it is to be of these more or less I am,   65
And of these one and all I weave the song of myself.

17

These are really the thoughts of all men in all ages and lands,
  they are not original with me,

If they are not yours as much as mine they are nothing, or next
   to nothing,
If they are not the riddle and the untying of the riddle they
   are nothing,
If they are not just as close as they are distant they are nothing.

This is the grass·that grows wherever the land is and the water
   is,   5
This is the common air that bathes the globe.

20

Who goes there? hankering, gross, mystical, nude;
How is it I extract strength from the beef I eat?

What is a man anyhow? what am I? what are you?

All I mark as my own you shall offset it with your own,
Else it were time lost listening to me.   5

I do not snivel that snivel the world over,
That months are vacuums and the ground but wallow and filth.

Whimpering and truckling fold with powders for invalids,
   conformity goes to the fourth-remov'd,
I wear my hat as I please indoors or out.

Why should I pray? why should I venerate and be ceremonious?   10

Having pried through the strata, analyzed to a hair, counsel'd
   with doctors and calculated close,
I find no sweeter fat than sticks to my own bones.

In all people I see myself, none more and not one a barley-corn
   less,
And the good or bad I say of myself I say of them.

I know I am solid and sound,   15
To me the converging objects of the universe perpetually flow,
All are written to me, and I must get what the writing means.

I know I am deathless,
I know this orbit of mine cannot be swept by a carpenter's
    compass,
I know I shall not pass like a child's carlacue cut with a burnt
    stick at night.   20

I know I am august,
I do not trouble my spirit to vindicate itself or be understood,
I see that the elementary laws never apologize,
(I reckon I behave no prouder than the level I plant my house
    by, after all.)

I exist as I am, that is enough,   25
If no other in the world be aware I sit content,
And if each and all be aware I sit content.

One world is aware and by far the largest to me, and that is
    myself,
And whether I come to my own to-day or in ten thousand or
    ten million years,
I can cheerfully take it now, or with equal cheerfulness I can
    wait.   30
My foothold is tenon'd and mortis'd in granite,
I laugh at what you call dissolution,
And I know the amplitude of time.

21

I am the poet of the Body and I am the poet of the Soul,
The pleasures of heaven are with me and the pains of hell are
    with me,
The first I graft and increase upon myself, the latter I translate
    into a new tongue.

I am the poet of the woman the same as the man,
And I say it is as great to be a woman as to be a man,   5
And I say there is nothing greater than the mother of men.

I chant the chant of dilation or pride,
We have had ducking and deprecating about enough,
I show that size is only development.

Have you outstript the rest? are you the President?   10
It is a trifle, they will more than arrive there every one, and still
      pass on.

I am he that walks with the tender and growing night,
I call to the earth and sea half-held by the night.

Press close bare-bosom'd night—press close magnetic nourishing
      night!
Night of south winds—night of the large few stars!   15
Still nodding night—mad naked summer night.

Smile O voluptuous cool-breath'd earth!
Earth of the slumbering and liquid trees!
Earth of the departed sunset—earth of the mountains misty-
      topt!
Earth of the vitreous pour of the full moon just tinged with
      blue!   20
Earth of shine and dark mottling the tide of the river!
Earth of the limpid gray of clouds brighter and clearer for my
      sake!
Far swooping elbow'd earth—rich apple-blossom'd earth!
Smile, for your lover comes.

Prodigal, you have given me love—therefore to you I give love!   25
O unspeakable passionate love.

                              27

To be in any form, what is that?
(Round and round we go, all of us, and ever come back thither,)
If nothing lay more develop'd the quahaug in its callous shell
      were enough.

Mine is no callous shell,
I have instant conductors all over me whether I pass or stop,   5
They seize every object and lead it harmlessly through me.

I merely stir, press, feel with my fingers, and am happy,
To touch my person to some one else's is about as much as I can
      stand.

31

I believe a leaf of grass is no less than the journey-work of the
  stars,
And the pismire is equally perfect, and a grain of sand, and the
  egg of the wren,
And the tree-toad is a chef-d'oeuvre for the highest,
And the running blackberry would adorn the parlors of heaven,
And the narrowest hinge in my hand puts to scorn all
  machinery,   5
And the cow crunching with depress'd head surpasses any
  statue,
And a mouse is miracle enough to stagger sextillions of infidels.

I find I incorporate gneiss, coal, long-threaded moss, fruits,
  grains, esculent roots,
And am stucco'd with quadrupeds and birds all over,
And have distanced what is behind me for good reasons,   10
But call any thing back again when I desire it.

In vain the speeding or shyness,
In vain the plutonic rocks send their old heat against my
  approach,
In vain the mastodon retreats beneath its own powder'd bones,
In vain objects stand leagues off and assume manifold shapes,   15
In vain the ocean settling in hollows and the great monsters
  lying low,
In vain the buzzard houses herself with the sky,
In vain the snake slides through the creepers and logs,
In vain the elk takes to the inner passes of the woods,
In vain the razor-bill'd auk sails far north to Labrador,   20
I follow quickly, I ascend to the nest in the fissure of the cliff.

33

Space and Time! now I see it is true, what I guess'd at,
What I guess'd when I loaf'd on the grass,
What I guess'd while I lay alone in my bed,
And again as I walk'd the beach under the paling stars of the
  morning.

My ties and ballasts leave me, my elbows rest in sea-gaps,   5
I skirt sierras, my palms cover continents,
I am afoot with my vision.

By the city's quadrangular houses—in log huts, camping with
          lumbermen,
Along the ruts of the turnpike, along the dry gulch and rivulet
          bed,
Weeding my onion-patch or hoeing rows of carrots and pars-
          nips, crossing savannas, trailing in forests,   10
Prospecting, gold-digging, girdling the trees of a new purchase,
Scorch'd ankle-deep by the hot sand, hauling my boat down the
          shallow river,
Where the panther walks to and fro on a limb overhead, where
          the buck turns furiously at the hunter,
Where the rattlesnake suns his flabby length on a rock, where
          the otter is feeding on fish,
Where the alligator in his tough pimples sleeps by the bayou,   15
Where the black bear is searching for roots or honey, where the
          beaver pats the mud with his paddle-shaped tail;
Over the growing sugar, over the yellow-flower'd cotton plant,
          over the rice in its low moist field,
Over the sharp-peak'd farmhouse, with its scallop'd scum and
          slender shoots from the gutters,
Over the western persimmon, over the long-leav'd corn, over
          the delicate blue-flower flax,
Over the white and brown buckwheat, a hummer and buzzer
          there with the rest,   20
Over the dusky green of the rye as it ripples and shades in the
          breeze;
Scaling mountains, pulling myself cautiously up, holding on
          by low scragged limbs,
Walking the path worn in the grass and beat through the leaves
          of the brush,
Where the quail is whistling betwixt the woods and the wheat-
          lot,
Where the bat flies in the Seventh-month eve, where the great
          gold-bug drops through the dark,   25
Where the brook puts out of the roots of the old tree and flows
          to the meadow,

Where cattle stand and shake away flies with the tremulous shuddering of their hides,

Where the cheese-cloth hangs in the kitchen, where andirons straddle the hearth-slab, where cobwebs fall in festoons from the rafters;

Where trip-hammers crash, where the press is whirling its cylinders,

Where the human heart beats with terrible throes under its ribs,   30

Where the pear-shaped balloon is floating aloft, (floating in it myself and looking composedly down,)

Where the life-car is drawn on the slip-noose, where the heat hatches pale-green eggs in the dented sand,

Where the she-whale swims with her calf and never forsakes it,

Where the steam-ship trails hind-ways its long pennant of smoke,

Where the fin of the shark cuts like a black chip out of the water,   35

Where the half-burn'd brig is riding on unknown currents,

Where shells grow to her slimy deck, where the dead are corrupting below;

Where the dense-starr'd flag is borne at the head of the regiments,

Approaching Manhattan up by the long-stretching island,

Under Niagara, the cataract falling like a veil over my countenance,   40

Upon a door-step, upon the horse-block of hard wood outside,

Upon the race-course, or enjoying picnics or jigs or a good game of base-ball,

At he-festivals, with blackguard gibes, ironical license, bull-dances, drinking, laughter,

At the cider-mill tasting the sweets of the brown mash, sucking the juice through a straw,

At apple-peelings wanting kisses for all the red fruit I find,   45

At musters, beach-parties, friendly bees, huskings, house-raisings;

Where the mocking-bird sounds his delicious gurgles, cackles, screams, weeps,

Where the hay-rick stands in the barn-yard, where the dry-stalks are scatter'd, where the brood-cow waits in the hovel,

Where the bull advances to do his masculine work, where the
    stud to the mare, where the cock is treading the hen,
Where the heifers browse, where geese nip their food with short
    jerks,   50
Where sun-down shadows lengthen over the limitless and lone-
    some prairie,
Where herds of buffalo make a crawling spread of the square
    miles far and near,
Where the humming-bird shimmers, where the neck of the long-
    lived swan is curving and winding,
Where the laughing-gull scoots by the shore, where she laughs
    her near-human laugh,
Where bee-hives range on a gray bench in the garden half hid
    by the high weeds,   55
Where band-neck'd partridges roost in a ring on the ground
    with their heads out,
Where burial coaches enter the arch'd gates of a cemetery,
Where winter wolves bark amid wastes of snow and icicled trees,
Where the yellow-crown'd heron comes to the edge of the marsh
    at night and feeds upon small crabs,
Where the splash of swimmers and divers cools the warm noon,   60
Where the katy-did works her chromatic reed on the walnut-
    tree over the well,
Through patches of citrons and cucumbers with silver-wired
    leaves,
Through the salt-lick or orange glade, or under conical firs,
Through the gymnasium, through the curtain'd saloon, through
    the office or public hall;
Pleas'd with the native and pleas'd with the foreign, pleas'd
    with the new and old,   65
Pleas'd with the homely woman as well as the handsome,
Pleas'd with the quakeress as she puts off her bonnet and talks
    melodiously,
Pleas'd with the tune of the choir of the whitewash'd church,
Pleas'd with the earnest words of the sweating Methodist
    preacher, impress'd seriously at the camp-meeting;
Looking in at the shop-windows of Broadway the whole fore-
    noon, flatting the flesh of my nose on the thick plate
    glass,   70

Wandering the same afternoon with my face turn'd up to the
    clouds, or down a lane or along the beach,
My right and left arms round the sides of two friends, and I
    in the middle;
Coming home with the silent and dark-cheek'd bush-boy,
    (behind me he rides at the drape of the day,)
Far from the settlements studying the print of animals' feet, or
    the moccasin print,
By the cot in the hospital reaching lemonade to a feverish
    patient,   75
Nigh the coffin'd corpse when all is still, examining with a
    candle;
Voyaging to every port to dicker and adventure,
Hurrying with the modern crowd as eager and fickle as any,
Hot toward one I hate, ready in my madness to knife him,
Solitary at midnight in my back yard, my thoughts gone from
    me a long while,   80
Walking the old hills of Judaea with the beautiful gentle God
    by my side,
Speeding through space, speeding through heaven and the stars,
Speeding amid the seven satellites and the broad ring, and
    the diameter of eighty thousand miles,
Speeding with tail'd meteors, throwing fire-balls like the rest,
Carrying the crescent child that carries its own full mother
    in its belly,   85
Storming, enjoying, planning, loving, cautioning,
Backing and filling, appearing and disappearing,
I tread day and night such roads.

I visit the orchards of spheres and look at the product,
And look at quintillions ripen'd and look at quintillions green.   90

I fly those flights of a fluid and swallowing soul,
My course runs below the soundings of plummets.

I help myself to material and immaterial,
No guard can shut me off, no law prevent me.

I anchor my ship for a little while only,   95
My messengers continually cruise away or bring their returns
    to me.

I go hunting polar furs and the seal, leaping chasms with a pike-
    pointed staff, clinging to topples of brittle and blue.

I ascend to the foretruck,
I take my place late at night in the crow's-nest,
We sail the arctic sea, it is plenty light enough,   100
Through the clear atmosphere I stretch around on the wonder-
    ful beauty,
The enormous masses of ice pass me and I pass them, the
    scenery is plain in all directions,
The white-topt mountains show in the distance, I fling out my
    fancies toward them,
We are approaching some great battle-field in which we are
    soon to be engaged,
We pass the colossal outposts of the encampment, we pass with
    still feet and caution,   105
Or we are entering by the suburbs some vast and ruin'd city,
The blocks and fallen architecture more than all the living
    cities of the globe.

I am a free companion, I bivouac by invading watchfires,
I turn the bridegroom out of bed and stay with the bride myself,
I tighten her all night to my thighs and lips.   110

My voice is the wife's voice, the screech by the rail of the stairs,
They fetch my man's body up dripping and drown'd.

I understand the large hearts of heroes,
The courage of present times and all times,
How the skipper saw the crowded and rudderless wreck of the
    steamship, and Death chasing it up and down the storm,   115
How he knuckled tight and gave not back an inch, and was
    faithful of days and faithful of nights,
And chalk'd in large letters on a board, *Be of good cheer, we
    will not desert you;*
How he follow'd with them and tack'd with them three days
    and would not give it up,
How he saved the drifting company at last,
How the lank loose-gown'd women look'd when boated from
    the side of their prepared graves,   120

How the silent old-faced infants and the lifted sick, and the
    sharp-lipp'd unshaved men;
All this I swallow, it tastes good, I like it well, it becomes
    mine,
I am the man, I suffer'd, I was there.

The disdain and calmness of martyrs,
The mother of old, condemn'd for a witch, burnt with dry
    wood, her children gazing on,   125
The hounded slave that flags in the race, leans by the fence,
    blowing, cover'd with sweat,
The twinges that sting like needles his legs and neck, the
    murderous buckshot and the bullets,
All these I feel or am.

I am the hounded slave, I wince at the bite of the dogs,
Hell and despair are upon me, crack and again crack the
    marksmen,   130
I clutch the rails of the fence, my gored ribs, thinn'd with the
    ooze of my skin,
I fall on the weeds and stones,
The riders spur their unwilling horses, haul close,
Taunt my dizzy ears and beat me violently over the head with
    whipstocks.

Agonies are one of my changes of garments.   135
I do not ask the wounded person how he feels, I myself become
    the wounded person,
My hurts turn livid upon me as I lean on a cane and observe.

I am the mash'd fireman with breast-bone broken,
Tumbling walls buried me in their debris,
Heat and smoke I inspired, I heard the yelling shouts of my
    comrades,   140
I heard the distant click of their picks and shovels,
They have clear'd the beams away, they tenderly lift me forth.

I lie in the night air in my red shirt, the pervading hush is
    for my sake,
Painless after all I lie exhausted but not so unhappy,

White and beautiful are the faces around me, the heads are
    bared of their fire-caps,   145
The kneeling crowd fades with the light of the torches.

Distant and dead resuscitate,
They show as the dial or move as the hands of me, I am the
    clock myself.
I am an old artillerist, I tell of my fort's bombardment,
I am there again.   150

Again the long roll of the drummers,
Again the attacking cannon, mortars,
Again to my listening ears the cannon responsive.

I take part, I see and hear the whole,
The cries, curses, roar, the plaudits for well-aim'd shots,   155
The ambulanza slowly passing trailing its red drip,
Workmen searching after damages, making indispensable re-
    pairs,
The fall of grenades through the rent roof, the fan-shaped
    explosion,
The whizz of limbs, heads, stone, wood, iron, high in the air.

Again gurgles the mouth of my dying general, he furiously
    waves with his hand,   160
He gasps through the clot *Mind not me—mind—the entrench-
ments.*

38

Enough! enough! enough!
Somehow I have been stunn'd. Stand back!
Give me a little time beyond my cuff'd head, slumbers, dreams,
    gaping,
I discover myself on the verge of a usual mistake.

That I could forget the mockers and insults!   5
That I could forget the trickling tears and the blows of the
    bludgeons and hammers!
That I could look with a separate look on my own crucifixion
    and bloody crowning!

I remember now,
I resume the overstaid fraction,
The grave of rock multiplies what has been confided to it, or
    to any graves,   10
Corpses rise, gashes heal, fastenings roll from me.

I troop forth replenish'd with supreme power, one of an average
    unending procession,
Inland and sea-coast we go, and pass all boundary lines,
Our swift ordinances on their way over the whole earth,
The blossoms we wear in our hats the growth of thousands of
    years.   15

Eleves, I salute you! come forward!
Continue your annotations, continue your questionings.

48

I have said that the soul is not more than the body,
And I have said that the body is not more than the soul,
And nothing, not God, is greater to one than one's self is,
And whoever walks a furlong without sympathy walks to his
    own funeral drest in his shroud,
And I or you pocketless of a dime may purchase the pick of the
    earth,   5
And to glance with an eye or show a bean in its pod confounds
    the learning of all times,
And there is no trade or employment but the young man fol-
    lowing it may become a hero,
And there is no object so soft but it makes a hub for the
    wheel'd universe,
And I say to any man or woman, Let your soul stand cool and
    composed before a million universes.

And I say to mankind, Be not curious about God,   10
For I who am curious about each am not curious about God,
(No array of terms can say how much I am at peace about God
    and about death.)

I hear and behold God in every object, yet understand God not
   in the least,
Nor do I understand who there can be more wonderful than
   myself.
Why should I wish to see God better than this day?   15
I see something of God each hour of the twenty-four, and each
   moment then,
In the faces of men and women I see God, and in my own face
   in the glass,
I find letters from God dropt in the street, and every one is
   sign'd by God's name,
And I leave them where they are, for I know that wheresoe'er
   I go
Others will punctually come for ever and ever.   20

                              51

The past and present wilt—I have fill'd them, emptied them,
And proceed to fill my next fold of the future.

Listener up there! what have you to confide to me?
Look in my face while I snuff the sidle of evening,
(Talk honestly, no one else hears you, and I stay only a minute
   longer.)   5

Do I contradict myself?
Very well then I contradict myself,
(I am large, I contain multitudes.)

I concentrate toward them that are nigh, I wait on the door-
   slab.

Who has done his day's work? who will soonest be through
   with his supper?   10
Who wishes to walk with me?

Will you speak before I am gone? will you prove already too
   late?

52

The spotted hawk swoops by and accuses me, he complains of
    my gab and my loitering.

I too am not a bit tamed, I too am untranslatable,
I sound my barbaric yawp over the roofs of the world.

The last scud of day holds back for me,
It flings my likeness after the rest and true as any on the
    shadow'd wilds,   5
It coaxes me to the vapor and the dusk.

I depart as air, I shake my white locks at the runaway sun,
I effuse my flesh in eddies, and drift it in lacy jags.

I bequeath myself to the dirt to grow from the grass I love,
If you want me again look for me under your boot-soles.   10

You will hardly know who I am or what I mean,
But I shall be good health to you nevertheless,
And filter and fibre your blood.

Failing to fetch me at first keep encouraged,
Missing me one place search another,   15
I stop somewhere waiting for you.

                           1855

CROSSING BROOKLYN FERRY

1

Flood-tide below me! I see you face to face!
Clouds of the west—sun there half an hour high—I see you also
    face to face.

Crowds of men and women attired in the usual costumes, how
    curious you are to me!

On the ferry-boats the hundreds and hundreds that cross, re-
    turning home, are more curious to me than you suppose,
And you that shall cross from shore to shore years hence are
    more to me, and more in my meditations, than you
    might suppose.   5

                                2

The impalpable sustenance of me from all things at all hours
    of the day,
The simple, compact, well-join'd scheme, myself disintegrated,
    every one disintegrated yet part of the scheme,
The similitudes of the past and those of the future,
The glories strung like beads on my smallest sights and hear-
    ings, on the walk in the street and the passage over the
    river,
The current rushing so swiftly and swimming with me far
    away,   10
The others that are to follow me, the ties between me and them,
The certainty of others, the life, love, sight, hearing of others.

Others will enter the gates of the ferry and cross from shore to
    shore,
Others will watch the run of the flood-tide,
Others will see the shipping of Manhattan north and west, and
    the heights of Brooklyn to the south and east,   15
Others will see the islands large and small;
Fifty years hence, others will see them as they cross, the sun
    half an hour high,
A hundred years hence, or ever so many hundred years hence,
    others will see them,
Will enjoy the sunset, the pouring-in of the flood-tide, the fall-
    ing-back to the sea of the ebb-tide.

                                3

It avails not, time nor place—distance avails not,   20
I am with you, you men and women of a generation, or ever so
    many generations hence,
Just as you feel when you look on the river and sky, so I felt,

Just as any of you is one of a living crowd, I was one of a crowd,
Just as you are refresh'd by the gladness of the river and the
      bright flow, I was refresh'd,
Just as you stand and lean on the rail, yet hurry with the swift
      current, I stood yet was hurried,   25
Just as you look on the numberless masts of ships and the thick-
      stemm'd pipes of steamboats, I look'd.

I too many and many a time cross'd the river of old,
Watched the Twelfth-month sea-gulls, saw them high in the air
      floating with motionless wings, oscillating their bodies,
Saw how the glistening yellow lit up parts of their bodies and
      left the rest in strong shadow,
Saw the slow-wheeling circles and the gradual edging toward
      the south,   30
Saw the reflection of the summer sky in the water,
Had my eyes dazzled by the shimmering track of beams,
Look'd at the fine centrifugal spokes of light round the shape of
      my head in the sunlit water,
Look'd on the haze on the hills southward and south-westward,
Look'd on the vapor as it flew in fleeces tinged with violet,   35
Look'd toward the lower bay to notice the vessels arriving,
Saw their approach, saw aboard those that were near me,
Saw the white sails of schooners and sloops, saw the ships at
      anchor,
The sailors at work in the rigging or out astride the spars,
The round masts, the swinging motion of the hulls, the slender
      serpentine pennants,   40
The large and small steamers in motion, the pilots in their
      pilot-houses,
The white wake left by the passage, the quick tremulous whirl
      of the wheels,
The flags of all nations, the falling of them at sunset,
The scallop-edged waves in the twilight, the ladled cups, the
      frolicsome crests and glistening,
The stretch afar growing dimmer and dimmer, the gray walls
      of the granite storehouses by the docks,   45
On the river the shadowy group, the big steam-tug closely
      flank'd on each side by the barges, the hay-boat, the be-
      lated lighter,

On the neighboring shore the fires from the foundry chimneys
   burning high and glaringly into the night,
Casting their flicker of black contrasted with wild red and yel-
   low light over the tops of houses, and down into the
   clefts of streets.

4

These and all else were to me the same as they are to you,
I loved well those cities, loved well the stately and rapid river,   50
The men and women I saw were all near to me,
Others the same—others who look back on me because I look'd
   forward to them,
(The time will come, though I stop here to-day and to-night.)

5

What is it then between us?
What is the count of the scores or hundreds of years be-
   tween us?   55

Whatever it is, it avails not—distance avails not, and place
   avails not,
I too lived, Brooklyn of ample hills was mine,
I too walk'd the streets of Manhattan island, and bathed in the
   waters around it,
I too felt the curious abrupt questionings stir within me,
In the day among crowds of people sometimes they came upon
   me,   60
In my walks home late at night or as I lay in my bed they came
   upon me,
I too had been struck from the float forever held in solution,
I too had receiv'd identity by my body,
That I was I knew was of my body, and what I should be I
   knew I should be of my body.

6

It is not upon you alone the dark patches fall,   65
The dark threw its patches down upon me also,

The best I had done seem'd to me blank and suspicious,
My great thoughts as I supposed them, were they not in reality
    meagre?
Nor is it you alone who know what it is to be evil,
I am he who knew what it was to be evil, 70
I too knitted the old knot of contrariety,
Blabb'd, blush'd, resented, lied, stole, grudg'd,
Had guile, anger, lust, hot wishes I dared not speak,
Was wayward, vain, greedy, shallow, sly, cowardly, malignant
The wolf, the snake, the hog, not wanting in me, 75
The cheating look, the frivolous word, the adulterous wish, not
    wanting,
Refusals, hates, postponements, meanness, laziness, none of
    these wanting,
Was one with the rest, the days and haps of the rest,
Was call'd by my nighest name by clear loud voices of young
    men as they saw me approaching or passing,
Felt their arms on my neck as I stood, or the negligent leaning
    of their flesh against me as I sat, 80
Saw many I loved in the street or ferry-boat or public assembly,
    yet never told them a word,
Lived the same life with the rest, the same old laughing,
    gnawing, sleeping,
Play'd the part that still looks back on the actor or actress,
The same old role, the role that is what we make it, as great as
    we like,
Or as small as we like, or both great and small. 85

7

Closer yet I approach you,
What thought you have of me now, I had as much of you—I laid
    in my stores in advance,
I consider'd long and seriously of you before you were born.

Who was to know what should come home to me?
Who knows but I am enjoying this? 90
Who knows, for all the distance, but I am as good as looking
    at you now, for all you cannot see me?

8

Ah, what can ever be more stately and admirable to me than
    mast-hemm'd Manhattan?
River and sunset and scallop-edg'd waves of flood-tide?
The sea-gulls oscillating their bodies, the hay-boat in the twi-
    light, and the belated lighter?
What gods can exceed these that clasp me by the hand, and
    with voices I love call me promptly and loudly by my
    nighest name as I approach?   95

What is more subtle than this which ties me to the woman or
    man that looks in my face?
Which fuses me into you now, and pours my meaning into you?
We understand then do we not?
What I promis'd without mentioning it, have you not accepted?
What the study could not teach—what the preaching could not
    accomplish is accomplish'd, is it not?   100

9

Flow on, river! flow with the flood-tide, and ebb with the ebb-
    tide!
Frolic on, crested and scallop-edg'd waves!
Gorgeous clouds of the sunset! drench with your splendor me,
    or the men and women generations after me!
Cross from shore to shore, countless crowds of passengers!
Stand up, tall masts of Mannahatta! stand up, beautiful hills
    of Brooklyn!   105
Throb, baffled and curious brain! throw out questions and
    answers!
Suspend here and everywhere, eternal float of solution!
Gaze, loving and thirsting eyes, in the house or street or public
    assembly!
Sound out, voices of young men! loudly and musically call me
    by my nighest name!
Live, old life! play the part that looks back on the actor or the
    actress!   110
Play the old role, the role that is great or small according as
    one makes it!

Consider, you who peruse me, whether I may not in unknown
    ways be looking upon you;
Be firm, rail over the river, to support those who lean idly,
    yet haste with the hasting current;
Fly on, sea-birds! fly sideways, or wheel in large circles high in
    the air;
Receive the summer sky, you water, and faithfully hold it till
    all downcast eyes have time to take it from you!   115
Diverge, fine spokes of light, from the shape of my head, or any
    one's head, in the sunlit water!
Come on, ships from the lower bay! pass up or down, white-
    sail'd schooners, sloops, lighters!
Flaunt away, flags of all nations! be duly lower'd at sunset!
Burn high your fires, foundry chimneys! cast black shadows at
    night-fall! cast red and yellow light over the tops of the
    houses!
Appearances, now or henceforth, indicate what you are,   120
You necessary film, continue to envelop the soul,
About my body for me, and your body for you, be hung our
    divinest aromas,
Thrive, cities—bring your freight, bring your shows, ample
    and sufficient rivers,
Expand, being than which none else is perhaps more spiritual,
Keep your places, objects than which none else is more lasting.   125

You have waited, you always wait, you dumb, beautiful
    ministers,
We receive you with free sense at last, and are insatiate hence-
    forward,
Not you any more shall be able to foil us, or withold yourselves
    from us,
We use you, and do not cast you aside—we plant you perma-
    nently within us,
We fathom you not—we love you—there is perfection in you
    also,   130
You furnish your parts toward eternity,
Great or small, you furnish your parts toward the soul.

                1856

OUT OF THE CRADLE ENDLESSLY ROCKING

Out of the cradle endlessly rocking,
Out of the mocking-bird's throat, the musical shuttle,
Out of the Ninth-month midnight,
Over the sterile sands and the fields beyond, where the child
    leaving his bed wander'd alone, bareheaded, barefoot,
Down from the shower'd halo,   5
Up from the mystic play of shadows twining and twisting as if
    they were alive,
Out from the patches of briers and blackberries,
From the memories of the bird that chanted to me,
From your memories sad brother, from the fitful risings and
    fallings I heard,
From under that yellow half-moon late-risen and swollen as if
    with tears,   10
From those beginning notes of yearning and love there in the
    mist,
From the thousand responses of my heart never to cease,
From the myriad thence-arous'd words,
From the word stronger and more delicious than any,
From such as now they start the scene revisiting,   15
As a flock, twittering, rising, or overhead passing,
Borne hither, ere all eludes me, hurriedly,
A man, yet by these tears a little boy again,
Throwing myself on the sand, confronting the waves,
I, chanter of pains and joys, uniter of here and hereafter,   20
Taking all hints to use them, but swiftly leaping beyond them,
A reminiscence sing.

Once Paumanok,
When the lilac-scent was in the air and Fifth-month grass
    was growing,
Up this seashore in some briers,   25
Two feather'd guests from Alabama, two together,
And their nest, and four light-green eggs spotted with brown,
And every day the he-bird to and fro near at hand,

And every day the she-bird crouch'd on her nest, silent, with
    bright eyes,
And every day I, a curious boy, never too close, never disturb-
    ing them,   30
Cautiously peering, absorbing, translating.

Shine! shine! shine!
Pour down your warmth, great sun!
While we bask, we two together.

Two together!   35
Winds blow south, or winds blow north,
Day come white, or night come black,
Home, or rivers and mountains from home,
Singing all time, minding no time,
While we two keep together.   40

Till of a sudden,
May-be kill'd, unknown to her mate,
One forenoon the she-bird crouch'd not on the nest,
Nor return'd that afternoon, nor the next,
Nor ever appear'd again.   45

And thenceforward all summer in the sound of the sea,
And at night under the full of the moon in calmer weather,
Over the hoarse surging of the sea,
Or flitting from brier to brier by day,
I saw, I heard at intervals the remaining one, the he-bird,   50
The solitary guest from Alabama.

Blow! blow! blow!
Blow up sea-winds along Paumanok's shore;
I wait and I wait till you blow my mate to me.

Yes, when the stars glisten'd,   55
All night long on the prong of a moss-scallop'd stake,
Down almost amid the slapping waves,
Sat the lone singer wonderful causing tears.

He call'd on his mate,
He pour'd forth the meanings which I of all men know.   60

Yes my brother I know,
The rest might not, but I have treasur'd every note,
For more than once dimly down to the beach gliding,
Silent, avoiding the moonbeams, blending myself with the
    shadows,
Recalling now the obscure shapes, the echoes, the sounds and
    sights after their sorts,   65
The white arms out in the breakers tirelessly tossing,
I, with bare feet, a child, the wind wafting my hair,
Listen'd long and long.

Listen'd to keep, to sing, now translating the notes,
Following you my brother.   70

Soothe! soothe! soothe!
Close on its wave soothes the wave behind,
And again another behind embracing and lapping, every one
    close,
But my love soothes not me, not me.

Low hangs the moon, it rose late,   75
It is lagging—O I think it is heavy with love, with love.

O madly the sea pushes upon the land,
With love, with love.

O night! do I not see my love fluttering out among the
    breakers?
What is that little black thing I see there in the white?   80

Loud! loud! loud!
Loud I call to you, my love!
High and clear I shoot my voice over the waves,
Surely you must know who is here, is here,
You must know who I am, my love.   85

Low-hanging moon!
What is that dusky spot in your brown yellow?

O it is the shape, the shape of my mate!
O moon do not keep her from me any longer.

Land! Land! O land! 90
Whichever way I turn, O I think you could give me my mate
        back again if you only would,
For I am almost sure I see her dimly whichever way I look.

O rising stars!
Perhaps the one I want so much will rise, will rise with some
        of you.

O throat! O trembling throat! 95
Sound clearer through the atmosphere!
Pierce the woods, the earth,
Somewhere listening to catch you must be the one I want.

Shake out carols!
Solitary here, the night's carols! 100
Carols of lonesome love! death's carols!
Carols under that lagging, yellow, waning moon!
O under that moon where she droops almost down into the sea!
O reckless despairing carols.

But soft! sink low! 105
Soft! let me just murmur,
And do you wait a moment you husky-nois'd sea,
For somewhere I believe I heard my mate responding to me,
So faint, I must be still, be still to listen,
But not altogether still, for then she might not come immedi-
        ately to me. 110

Hither my love!
Here I am! here!
With this just-sustain'd note I announce myself to you,
This gentle call is for you my love, for you.

Do not be decoy'd elsewhere, 115
That is the whistle of the wind, it is not my voice,
That is the fluttering, the fluttering of the spray,
Those are the shadows of leaves.

O darkness! O in vain!
O I am very sick and sorrowful.   120

O brown halo in the sky near the moon, drooping upon the sea!
O troubled reflection in the sea!
O throat! O throbbing heart!
And I singing uselessly, uselessly all the night.

O past! O happy life! O songs of joy!   125
In the air, in the woods, over fields,
Loved! loved! loved! loved! loved!
But my mate no more, no more with me!
We two together no more.

The aria sinking,   130
All else continuing, the stars shining,
The winds blowing, the notes of the bird continuous echoing,
With angry moans the fierce old mother incessantly moaning,
On the sands of Paumanok's shore gray and rustling,
The yellow half-moon enlarged, sagging down, drooping, the
          face of the sea almost touching,   135
The boy ecstatic, with his bare feet the waves, with his hair the
          atmosphere dallying,
The love in the heart long pent, now loose, now at last tumultu-
          ously bursting,
The aria's meaning, the ears, the soul, swiftly depositing,
The strange tears down the cheeks coursing,
The colloquy there, the trio, each uttering,   140
The undertone, the savage old mother incessantly crying,
To the boy's soul's questions sullenly timing, some drown'd
          secret hissing,
To the outsetting bard.

Demon or bird! (said the boy's soul,)
Is it indeed toward your mate you sing? or is it really to me?   145
For I, that was a child, my tongue's use sleeping, now I have
          heard you,
Now in a moment I know what I am for, I awake,
And already a thousand singers, a thousand songs, clearer,
          louder and more sorrowful than yours,

A thousand warbling echoes have started to life within me,
    never to die.

O you singer solitary, singing by yourself, projecting me,   150
O solitary me listening, never more shall I cease perpetuating
    you,
Never more shall I escape, never more the reverberations,
Never more the cries of unsatisfied love be absent from me,
Never again leave me to be the peaceful child I was before
    what there in the night,
By the sea under the yellow and sagging moon,   155
The messenger there arous'd, the fire, the sweet, hell within,
The unknown want, the destiny of me.

O give me the clew! (it lurks in the night here somewhere,)
O if I am to have so much, let me have more!

A word then, (for I will conquer it,)   160
The word final, superior to all,
Subtle, sent up—what is it?—I listen;
Are you whispering it, and have been all the time, you sea
    waves?
Is that it from your liquid rims and wet sands?

Whereto answering, the sea,   165
Delaying not, hurrying not,
Whisper'd me through the night, and very plainly before day-
    break,
Lisp'd to me the low and delicious word death,
And again death, death, death, death,
Hissing melodious, neither like the bird nor like my arous'd
    child's heart,   170
But edging near as privately for me rustling at my feet,
Creeping thence steadily up to my ears and laving me softly all
    over,
Death, death, death, death, death.

Which I do not forget,
But fuse the song of my dusky demon and brother,   **175**

That he sang to me in the moonlight on Paumanok's gray
    beach,
With the thousand responsive songs at random,
My own songs awaked from that hour,
And with them the key, the word up from the waves,
The word of the sweetest song and all songs,   180
That strong and delicious word which, creeping to my feet,
(Or like some old crone rocking the cradle, swathed in sweet
    garments, bending aside,)
The sea whisper'd me.

                                            1860

EIGHTEEN SIXTY-ONE

Arm'd year—year of the struggle,
No dainty rhymes or sentimental love verses for you terrible
    year,
Not you as some pale poetling seated at a desk lisping cadenzas
    piano,
But as a strong man erect, clothed in blue clothes, advancing,
    carrying a rifle on your shoulder,
With well-gristled body and sunburnt face and hands, with a
    knife in the belt at your side,   5
As I heard you shouting loud, your sonorous voice ringing
    across the continent,
Your masculine voice O year, as rising amid the great cities,
Amid the men of Manhattan I saw you as one of the workmen,
    the dwellers in Manhattan,
Or with large steps crossing the prairies out of Illinois and
    Indiana,
Rapidly crossing the West with springy gait and descending
    the Alleghanies,   10
Or down from the great lakes or in Pennsylvania, or on deck
    along the Ohio river,
Or southward along the Tennessee or Cumberland rivers, or at
    Chattanooga on the mountain top,
Saw I your gait and saw I your sinewy limbs clothed in blue,
    bearing weapons, robust year,

Heard your determin'd voice launch'd forth again and again,
Year that suddenly sang by the mouths of the round-lipp'd
    cannon,   15
I repeat you, hurrying, crashing, sad, distracted year.

                                          1865

BIVOUAC ON A MOUNTAIN SIDE

I see before me now a traveling army halting,
Below a fertile valley spread, with barns and the orchards of
    summer,
Behind, the terraced sides of a mountain, abrupt, in places
    rising high,
Broken, with rocks, with clinging cedars, with tall shapes
    dingily seen,
The numerous camp-fires scatter'd near and far, some away up
    on the mountain,   5
The shadowy forms of men and horses, looming, large-sized
    flickering,
And over all the sky—the sky! far, far out of reach, studded,
    breaking out, the eternal stars.

                                          1865

NOT THE PILOT

Not the pilot has charged himself to bring his ship into port,
    though beaten back and many times baffled;
Not the pathfinder penetrating inland weary and long,
By deserts parch'd, snows chill'd, rivers wet, perseveres till he
    reaches his destination,
More than I have charged myself, heeded or unheeded, to
    compose a march for these States,
For a battle-call, rousing to arms if need be, years, centuries
    hence.   5

                                        1867

YEAR THAT TREMBLED AND REEL'D
BENEATH ME

Year that trembled and reel'd beneath me!
Your summer wind was warm enough, yet the air I breathed
    froze me,
A thick gloom fell through the sunshine and darken'd me,
Must I change my triumphant songs? said I to myself,
Must I indeed learn to chant the cold dirges of the baffled?   5
And sullen hymns of defeat?

                                              1865

LONG, TOO LONG AMERICA

Long, too long America,
Traveling roads all even and peaceful you learn'd from joys
    and prosperity only,
But now, ah now, to learn from crises of anguish, advancing,
    grappling with direst fate and recoiling not,
And now to conceive and show to the world what your children
    en-masse really are,
(For who except myself has yet conceiv'd what your children
    en-masse really are?)   5

                                              1865

RACE OF VETERANS

Race of veterans—race of victors!
Race of the soil, ready for conflict—race of the conquering
    march!
(No more credulity's race, abiding-temper'd race,)
Race henceforth owning no law but the law of itself,
Race of passion and the storm.   5

                                              1865

WORLD TAKE GOOD NOTICE

World take good notice, silver stars fading,
Milky hue ript, weft of white detaching,
Coals thirty-eight, baleful and burning,
Scarlet, significant, hands off warning,
Now and henceforth flaunt from these shores.   5

1865

LOOK DOWN FAIR MOON

Look down fair moon and bathe this scene,
Pour softly down night's nimbus floods on faces ghastly,
    swollen, purple,
On the dead on their backs with arms toss'd wide,
Pour down your unstinted nimbus sacred moon.

1865

RECONCILIATION

Word over all, beautiful as the sky,
Beautiful that war and all its deeds of carnage must in time
    be utterly lost,
That the hands of the sisters Death and Night incessantly
    softly wash again, and ever again, this soil'd world;
For my enemy is dead, a man divine as myself is dead,
I look where he lies white-faced and still in the coffin—I draw
    near,   5
Bend down and touch lightly with my lips the white face in
    the coffin.

1865

LO, VICTRESS ON THE PEAKS

Lo, Victress on the peaks,
Where thou with mighty brow regarding the world,
(The world O Libertad, that vainly conspired against thee,)
Out of its countless beleaguering toils, after thwarting them
    all,
Dominant, with the dazzling sun around thee,   5
Flauntest now unharm'd in immortal soundness and bloom—
    lo, in these hours supreme,
No poem proud, I chanting bring to thee, nor mastery's rap-
    turous verse,
But a cluster containing night's darkness and blood-dripping
    wounds,
And psalms of the dead.

                                                              1865

SPIRIT WHOSE WORK IS DONE

Spirit whose work is done—spirit of dreadful hours!
Ere departing fade from my eyes your forests of bayonets;
Spirit of gloomiest fears and doubts, (yet onward ever unfal-
    tering pressing,)
Spirit of many a solemn day and many a savage scene—electric
    spirit,
That with muttering voice through the war now closed, like
    a tireless phantom flitted,   5
Rousing the land with breath of flame, while you beat and beat
    the drum,
Now as the sound of the drum, hollow and harsh to the last,
    reverberates round me,
As your ranks, your immortal ranks, return, return from the
    battles,
As the muskets of the young men yet lean over their shoulders,
As I look on the bayonets bristling over their shoulders,   10
As those slanted bayonets, whole forests of them appearing in
    the distance, approach and pass on, returning home-
    ward,

Moving with steady motion, swaying to and fro to the right and
    left,
Evenly, lightly rising and falling while the steps keep time;
Spirit of hours I knew, all hectic red one day, but pale as death
    next day,
Touch my mouth ere you depart, press my lips close,   15
Leave me your pulses of rage—bequeath them to me—fill me
    with currents convulsive,
Let them scorch and blister out of my chants when you are
    gone,
Let them identify you to the future in these songs.

                                                1865

WHEN LILACS LAST IN THE DOORYARD BLOOM'D

1

When lilacs last in the dooryard bloom'd
And the great star early droop'd in the western sky in the night,
I mourn'd, and yet shall mourn with ever-returning spring.

Ever-returning spring, trinity sure to me you bring,
Lilac blooming perennial and drooping star in the west,   5
And thought of him I love.

2

O powerful western fallen star!
O shades of night—O moody, tearful night!
O great star disappear'd—O the black murk that hides the star!
O cruel hands that hold me powerless—O helpless soul of me!   10
O harsh surrounding cloud that will not free my soul.

3

In the dooryard fronting an old farm-house near the white-
    wash'd palings,
Stands the lilac-bush tall-growing with heart-shaped leaves of
    rich green,
With many a pointed blossom rising delicate, with the perfume
    strong I love,

With every leaf a miracle—and from this bush in the dooryard,   15
With delicate-color'd blossoms and heart-shaped leaves of rich
    green,
A sprig with its flower I break.

4

In the swamp in secluded recesses,
A shy and hidden bird is warbling a song.

Solitary the thrush,   20
The hermit withdrawn to himself, avoiding the settlements,
Sings by himself a song.

Song of the bleeding throat,
Death's outlet song of life, (for well dear brother I know,
If thou wast not granted to sing thou wouldst surely die.)   25

5

Over the breast of the spring, the land, amid cities,
Amid lanes and through old woods, where lately the violets
    peep'd from the ground, spotting the gray debris,
Amid the grass in the fields each side of the lanes, passing the
    endless grass,
Passing the yellow-spear'd wheat, every grain from its shroud in
    the dark-blown fields uprisen,
Passing the apple-tree blows of white and pink in the orchards,   30
Carrying a corpse to where it shall rest in the grave,
Night and day journeys a coffin.

6

Coffin that passes through lanes and streets,
Through day and night with the great cloud darkening the
    land,
With the pomp of the inloop'd flags with the cities draped in
    black,   35
With the show of the States themselves as of crape-veil'd women
    standing,
With processions long and winding and the flambeaus of the
    night,

With the countless torches lit, with the silent sea of faces and
    the unbared heads,
With the waiting depot, the arriving coffin, and the sombre
    faces,
With dirges through the night, with the thousand voices rising
    strong and solemn,   40
With all the mournful voices of the dirges pour'd around the
    coffin,
The dim-lit churches and the shuddering organs—where amid
    these you journey,
With the tolling tolling bells' perpetual clang,
Here, coffin that slowly passes,
I give you my sprig of lilac.   45

7

(Nor for you, for one alone,
Blossoms and branches green to coffins all I bring,
For fresh as the morning, thus would I chant a song for you
    O sane and sacred death.
All over bouquets of roses,
O death, I cover you over with roses and early lilies,   50
But mostly and now the lilac that blooms the first,
Copious I break, I break the sprigs from the bushes,
With loaded arms I come, pouring for you,
For you and the coffins all of you O death.)

8

O western orb sailing the heaven,   55
Now I know what you must have meant as a month since I
    walk'd,
As I walk'd in silence the transparent shadowy night,
As I saw you had something to tell as you bent to me night
    after night,
As you droop'd from the sky low down as if to my side, (while
    the other stars all look'd on,)
As we wander'd together the solemn night, (for something I
    know not what kept me from sleep,)   60
As the night advanced, and I saw on the rim of the west how
    full you were of woe,

As I stood on the rising ground in the breeze in the cool trans-
        parent night,
As I watch'd where you pass'd and was lost in the netherward
        black of the night,
As my soul in its trouble dissatisfied sank, as where you sad orb,
Concluded, dropt in the night, and was gone.   65

9

Sing on there in the swamp,
O singer bashful and tender, I hear your notes, I hear your call,
I hear, I come presently, I understand you,
But a moment I linger, for the lustrous star has detain'd me,
The star my departing comrade holds and detains me.   70

10

O how shall I warble myself for the dead one there I loved?
And how shall I deck my song for the large sweet soul that
        has gone?
And what shall my perfume be for the grave of him I love?
Sea-winds blown from east and west,
Blown from the Eastern sea and blown from the Western sea,
        till there on the prairies meeting,   75
These and with these and the breath of my chant,
I'll perfume the grave of him I love.

11

O what shall I hang on the chamber walls?
And what shall the pictures be that hang on the walls,
To adorn the burial-house of him I love?   80

Pictures of growing spring and farms and homes,
With the Fourth-month eve at sundown, and the gray smoke
        lucid and bright,
With floods of the yellow gold of the gorgeous, indolent, sinking
        sun, burning, expanding the air,
With the fresh sweet herbage under foot, and the pale green
        leaves of the trees prolific,
In the distance the flowing glaze, the breast of the river, with
        a wind-dapple here and there,   85

With ranging hills on the banks, with many a line against the
    sky, and shadows,
And the city at hand with dwellings so dense, and stacks of
    chimneys,
And all the scenes of life and the workshops, and the workmen
    homeward returning.

12

Lo, body and soul—this land,
My own Manhattan with spires, and the sparkling and hurrying
    tides, and the ships,   90
The varied and ample land, the South and the North in the
    light, Ohio's shores and flashing Missouri,
And ever the far-spreading prairies cover'd with grass and corn.

Lo, the most excellent sun so calm and haughty,
The violet and purple morn with just-felt breezes,
The gentle soft-born measureless light,   95
The miracle spreading bathing all, the fulfill'd noon,
The coming eve delicious, the welcome night and the stars,
Over my cities shining all, enveloping man and land.

13

Sing on, sing on you gray-brown bird,
Sing from the swamps, the recesses, pour your chant from the
    bushes,   100
Limitless out of the dusk, out of the cedars and pines.

Sing on dearest brother, warble your reedy song,
Loud human song, with voice of uttermost woe,

O liquid and free and tender!
O wild and loose to my soul—O wondrous singer!   105
You only I hear—yet the star holds me, (but will soon depart,)
Yet the lilac with mastering odor holds me.

14

Now while I sat in the day and look'd forth,
In the close of the day with its light and the fields of spring,
    and the farmers preparing their crops,

In the large unconscious scenery of my land with its lakes and
    forests,   110
In the heavenly aerial beauty, (after the perturb'd winds and
    the storms,)
Under the arching heavens of the afternoon swift passing, and
    the voices of children and women,
The many-moving sea-tides, and I saw the ships how they sail'd,
And the summer approaching with richness, and the fields all
    busy with labor,
And the infinite separate houses, how they all went on, each
    with its meals and minutia of daily usages,   115
And the streets how their throbbings throbb'd, and the cities
    pent—lo, then and there,
Falling upon them all and among them all, enveloping me with
    the rest,
Appear'd the cloud, appear'd the long black trail,
And I knew death, its thought, and the sacred knowledge of
    death.

Then with the knowledge of death as walking one side of me,   120
And the thought of death close-walking the other side of me,
And I in the middle as with companions, and as holding the
    hands of companions,
I fled forth to the hiding receiving night that talks not,
Down to the shores of the water, the path by the swamp in the
    dimness,
To the solemn shadowy cedars and ghostly pines so still.   125

And the singer so shy to the rest receiv'd me,
The gray-brown bird I know receiv'd us comrades three,
And he sang the carol of death, and a verse for him I love.

From deep secluded recesses,
From the fragrant cedars and the ghostly pines so still,   130
Came the carol of the bird.

And the charm of the carol rapt me,
As I held as if by their hands my comrades in the night,
And the voice of my spirit tallied the song of the bird.

Come lovely and soothing death, 135
Undulate round the world, serenely arriving, arriving,
In the day, in the night, to all, to each,
Sooner or later delicate death.

Prais'd be the fathomless universe,
For life and joy, and for objects and knowledge curious, 140
And for love, sweet love—but praise! praise! praise!
For the sure-enwinding arms of cool-enfolding death.

Dark mother always gliding near with soft feet,
Have none chanted for thee a chant of fullest welcome?
Then I chant it for thee, I glorify thee above all, 145
I bring thee a song that when thou must indeed come, come
        unfalteringly.

Approach strong deliveress,
When it is so, when thou hast taken them I joyously sing the
        dead,
Lost in the loving floating ocean of thee,
Laved in the flood of thy bliss O death. 150

From me to thee glad serenades,
Dances for thee I propose saluting thee, adornments and feast-
        ings for thee,
And the sights of the open landscape and the high-spread sky
        are fitting,
And life and the fields, and the huge and thoughtful night.

The night in silence under many a star, 155
The ocean shore and the husky whispering wave whose voice
        I know,
And the soul turning to thee O vast and well-veil'd death,
And the body gratefully nestling close to thee.

Over the tree-tops I float thee a song,
Over the rising and sinking waves, over the myriad fields and
        the prairies wide, 160
Over the dense-pack'd cities all and the teeming wharves and
        ways,
I float this carol with joy, with joy to thee O death.

15

To the tally of my soul,
Loud and strong kept up the gray-brown bird,
With pure deliberate notes spreading filling the night.   165

Loud in the pines and cedars dim,
Clear in the freshness moist and the swamp-perfume,
And I with my comrades there in the night.

While my sight that was bound in my eyes unclosed,
As to long panoramas of visions.   170

And I saw askant the armies,
I saw as in noiseless dreams hundreds of battle-flags,
Borne through the smoke of the battles and pierc'd with mis-
          siles I saw them,
And carried hither and yon through the smoke, and torn and
          bloody,
And at last but a few shreds left on the staffs, (and all in
          silence,)   175
And the staffs all splinter'd and broken.

I saw battle-corpses, myriads of them,
And the white skeletons of young men, I saw them,
I saw the debris and debris of all the slain soldiers of the war,
But I saw they were not as was thought,   180
They themselves were fully at rest, they suffer'd not,
The living remain'd and suffer'd, the mother suffer'd,
And the wife and the child and the musing comrade suffer'd,
And the armies that remain'd suffer'd.

16

Passing the visions, passing the night,   185
Passing, unloosing the hold of my comrades' hands,
Passing the song of the hermit bird and the tallying song of
          my soul,
Victorious song, death's outlet song, yet varying ever-altering
          song,
As low and wailing, yet clear the notes, rising and falling,
          flooding the night,

Sadly sinking and fainting, as warning and warning, and yet
    again bursting with joy, 190
Covering the earth and filling the spread of the heaven,
As that powerful psalm in the night I heard from recesses,
Passing, I leave thee lilac with heart-shaped leaves,
I leave thee there in the door-yard, blooming, returning with
    spring.

I cease from my song for thee, 195
From my gaze on thee in the west, fronting the west, com-
    muning with thee,
O comrade lustrous with silver face in the night.

Yet each to keep and all, retrievements out of the night,
The song, the wondrous chant of the gray-brown bird,
And the tallying chant, the echo arous'd in my soul, 200
With the lustrous and drooping star with the countenance full
    of woe,
With the holders holding my hand nearing the call of the bird,
Comrades mine and I in the midst, and their memory ever to
    keep, for the dead I loved so well,
For the sweetest, wisest soul of all my days and lands—and this
    for his dear sake,
Lilac and star and bird twined with the chant of my soul, 205
There in the fragrant pines and the cedars dusk and dim.

                                      1865

THERE WAS A CHILD WENT FORTH

There was a child went forth every day,
And the first object he look'd upon, that object he became,
And that object became part of him for the day or a certain part
    of the day,
Or for many years or stretching cycles of years.

The early lilacs became part of this child, 5
And grass and white and red morning-glories, and white and
    red clover, and the song of the phoebe-bird,

And the Third-month lambs and the sow's pink-faint litter, and the mare's foal and the cow's calf,

And the noisy brood of the barnyard or by the mire of the pond-side,

And the fish suspending themselves so curiously below there, and the beautiful curious liquid,

And the water-plants with their graceful flat heads, all became part of him.   10

The field-sprouts of Fourth-month and Fifth-month became part of him,

Winter-grain sprouts and those of the light-yellow corn, and the esculent roots of the garden,

And the apple-trees cover'd with blossoms and the fruit after-ward, and wood-berries, and the commonest weeds by the road,

And the old drunkard staggering home from the outhouse of the tavern whence he had lately risen,

And the schoolmistress that pass'd on her way to the school,   15

And the friendly boys that pass'd, and the quarrelsome boys,

And the tidy and fresh-cheek'd girls, and the barefoot negro boy and girl,

And all the changes of city and country wherever he went.

His own parents, he that had father'd him and she that had con-ceiv'd him in her womb and birth'd him,

They gave this child more of themselves than that,   20

They gave him afterward every day, they became part of him.

The mother at home quietly placing the dishes on the supper-table,

The mother with mild words, clean her cap and gown, a whole-some odor falling off her person and clothes as she walks by,

The father, strong, self-sufficient, manly, mean, anger'd unjust,

The blow, the quick loud word, the tight bargain, the crafty lure,   25

The family usages, the language, the company, the furniture, the yearning and swelling heart,

Affection that will not be gainsay'd, the sense of what is real, the thought if after all it should prove unreal,

The doubts of day-time and the doubts of night-time, the curi-
ous whether and how,
Whether that which appears so is so, or is it all flashes and
specks?
Men and women crowding fast in the streets, if they are not
flashes and specks what are they?   30
The streets themselves and the facades of houses, and goods in
the windows,
Vehicles, teams, the heavy-plank'd wharves, the huge crossing at
the ferries,
The village on the highland seen from afar at sunset, the river
between,
Shadows, aureola and mist, the light falling on roofs and gables
of white or brown two miles off,
The schooner near by sleepily dropping down the tide, the little
boat slack-tow'd astern,   35
The hurrying tumbling waves, quick-broken crests, slapping,
The strata of color'd clouds, the long bar of maroon-tint away
solitary by itself, the spread of purity it lies motionless in,
The horizon's edge, the flying sea-crow, the fragrance of salt
marsh and shore mud,
These became part of that child who went forth every day, and
who now goes, and will always go forth every day.

1855

PASSAGE TO INDIA

1

Singing my days,
Singing the great achievements of the present,
Singing the strong light works of engineers,
Our modern wonders, (the antique ponderous Seven outvied,)
In the Old World the east the Suez canal,   5
The New by its mighty railroad spann'd,
The seas inlaid with eloquent gentle wires;
Yet first to sound, and ever sound, the cry with thee O soul,
The Past! the Past! the Past!

The Past—the dark unfathom'd retrospect!   10
The teeming gulf—the sleepers and the shadows!
The past—the infinite greatness of the past!
For what is the present after all but a growth out of the past?
(As a projectile form'd, impell'd, passing a certain line, still
      keeps on,
So the present, utterly form'd, impell'd by the past.)   15

2

Passage O soul to India!
Eclaircise the myths Asiatic, the primitive fables.

Not you alone proud truths of the world,
Nor you alone ye facts of modern science,
But myths and fables of eld, Asia's, Africa's fables,   20
The far-darting beams of the spirit, the unloos'd dreams,
The deep diving bibles and legends,
The daring plots of the poets, the elder religions;
O you temples fairer than lilies pour'd over by the rising sun!
O you fables spurning the know, eluding the hold of the
      known, mounting to heaven!   25
You lofty and dazzling towers, pinnacled, red as roses, bur-
      nish'd with gold!
Towers of fables immortal fashion'd from mortal dreams!
You too I welcome and fully the same as the rest!
You too with joy I sing.

Passage to India!   30
Lo, soul, seest thou not God's purpose from the first?
The earth to be spann'd, connected by network,
The races, neighbors, to marry and be given in marriage,
The oceans to be cross'd, the distant brought near,
The lands to be welded together.   35

A worship new I sing.
You captains, voyagers, explorers, yours,
You engineers, you architects, machinists, yours,
You, not for trade or transportation only,
But in God's name, and for thy sake O soul.   40

3

Passage to India!
Lo soul for thee of tableaus twain.
I see in one the Suez canal initiated, open'd,
I see the procession of steamships, the Empress Eugenie's lead-
  ing the van,
I mark from on deck the strange landscape, the pure sky, the
  level sand in the distance,   45
I pass swiftly the picturesque groups, the workmen gather'd,
The gigantic dredging machines.

In one again, different, (yet thine, all thine, O soul, the same,)
I see over my own continent the Pacific railroad surmounting
  every barrier,
I see continual trains of cars winding along the Platte carrying
  freight and passengers,   50
I hear the locomotives rushing and roaring, and the shrill
  steam-whistle,
I hear the echoes reverberate through the grandest scenery in
  the world,
I cross the Laramie plains, I note the rocks in grotesque shapes,
  the buttes,
I see the plentiful larkspur and wild onions, the barren, color-
  less, sage-deserts,
I see in glimpses afar or towering immediately above me the
  great mountains, I see the Wind river and the Wahsatch
  mountains,   55
I see the Monument mountain and the Eagle's Nest, I pass the
  Promontory, I-ascend the Nevadas,
I scan the noble Elk mountain and wind around its base,
I see the Humboldt range, I thread the valley and cross the
  river,
I see the clear waters of lake Tahoe, I see forests of majestic
  pines,
Or crossing the great desert, the alkaline plains, I behold en-
  chanting mirages of waters and meadows,   60
Marking through these and after all, in duplicate slender lines,
Bridging the three or four thousand miles of land travel,
Tying the Eastern to the Western sea,
The road between Europe and Asia.

(Ah Genoese thy dream! thy dream!   65
Centuries after thou art laid in thy grave,
The shore thou foundest verifies thy dream.)

4

Passage to India!
Struggles of many a captain, tales of many a sailor dead,
Over my mood stealing, and spreading they come,   70
Like clouds and cloudlets in the unreach'd sky.

Along all history, down the slopes,
As a rivulet running, sinking now, and now again to the surface
    rising,
A ceaseless thought, a varied train—lo, soul, to thee, thy sight,
    they rise,
The plans, the voyages again, the expeditions;   75
Again Vasco de Gama sails forth,
Again the knowledge gain'd, the mariner's compass,
Lands found and nations born, thou born America,
For purpose vast, man's long probation fill'd,
Thou rondure of the world at last accomplish'd.   80

5

O vast Rondure, swimming in space,
Cover'd all over with visible power and beauty,
Alternate light and day and the teeming spiritual darkness,
Unspeakable high processions of sun and moon and countless
    stars above,
Below, the manifold grass and waters, animals, mountains,
    trees,   85
With inscrutable purpose, some hidden prophetic intention,
Now first it seems my thought begins to span thee.

Down from the gardens of Asia descending radiating,
Adam and Eve appear, then their myriad progeny after them,
Wandering, yearning, curious, with restless explorations,   90
With questionings, baffled, formless, feverish, with never-happy
    hearts,
With that sad incessant refrain, *Wherefore unsatisfied soul?*
    and *Whither O mocking life?*

Ah who shall soothe these feverish children?
Who justify these restless explorations?
Who speak the secret of impassive earth?   95
Who bind it to us? what is this separate Nature so unnatural?
What is this earth to our affections? (unloving earth, without
    a throb to answer ours,
Cold earth, the place of graves.)

Yet soul be sure the first intent remains, and shall be carried
    out,
Perhaps even now the time has arrived.   100

After the seas are all cross'd, (as they seem already cross'd,)
After the great captains and engineers have accomplish'd their
    work,
After the noble inventors, after the scientists, the chemist,
    the geologist, ethnologist,
Finally shall come the poet worthy of that name,
The true son of God shall come singing his songs.   105

Then not your deeds only O voyagers, O scientists and inven-
    tors, shall be justified,
All these hearts as of fretted children shall be sooth'd,
All affection shall be fully responded to, the secret shall be
    told,
All these separations and gaps shall be taken up and hook'd
    and link'd together,
The whole earth, this cold, impassive, voiceless earth, shall
    be completely justified,   110
Trinitas divine shall be gloriously accomplish'd and compacted
    by the true son of God, the poet,
(He shall indeed pass the straits and conquer the mountains,
He shall double the cape of Good Hope to some purpose,)
Nature and Man shall be disjoin'd and diffused no more,
The true son of God shall absolutely fuse them.   115

6

Year at whose wide-flung door I sing!
Year of the purpose accomplish'd!
Year of the marriage of continents, climates and oceans!

(No mere doge of Venice now wedding the Adriatic,)
I see O year in you the vast terraqueous globe given and giving
    all,   120
Europe to Asia, Africa join'd, and they to the New World,
The lands, geographies, dancing before you, holding a festival
    garland,
As brides and bridegrooms hand in hand.

Passage to India!
Cooling airs from Caucasus, far, soothing cradle of man,   125
The river Euphrates flowing, the past lit up again.

Lo soul, the retrospect brought forward,
The old, most populous, wealthiest of earth's lands,
The streams of the Indus and the Ganges and their many
    affluents,
(I my shores of America walking to-day behold, resuming all,)   130
The tale of Alexander on his warlike marches suddenly dying,
On one side China and on the other Persia and Arabia,
To the south the great seas and the bay of Bengal,
The flowing literatures, tremendous epics, religions, castes,
Old occult Brahma interminably far back, the tender and
    junior Buddha,   135
Central and southern empires and all their belongings,
    possessors,
The wars of Tamerlane, the reign of Aurungzebe,
The traders, rulers, explorers, Moslems, Venetians, Byzantium,
    the Arabs, Portuguese,
The first traveler famous yet, Marco Polo, Patouta, the Moor,
Doubts to be solv'd, the map incognita, blanks to be fill'd   140
The foot of man unstay'd, the hands never at rest,
Thyself O soul that will not brook a challenge.
The medieval navigators rise before me,
The world of 1492, with its awaken'd enterprise,
Something swelling in humanity now like the sap of the earth
    in spring,   145
The sunset splendor of chivalry declining.

And who art thou sad shade?
Gigantic, visionary, thyself a visionary,

With majestic limbs and pious beaming eyes,
Spreading around with every look of thine a golden world,   150
Enhuing it with gorgeous hues.

As the chief histrion,
Down to the footlights walks in some great scena,
Dominating the rest I see the Admiral himself,
(History's type of courage, action, faith,)   155
Behold him sail from Palos leading his little fleet,
His voyage behold, his return, his great fame,
His misfortunes, calumniators, behold him a prisoner, chain'd,
Behold his dejection, poverty, death.

(Curious in time I stand, noting the efforts of heroes,   160
Is the deferment long? bitter the slander, poverty, death?
Lies the seed unreck'd for centuries in the ground? lo, to God's
      due occasion,
Uprising in the night, it sprouts, blooms,
And fills the earth with use and beauty.)

7

Passage indeed O soul to primal thought,   165
Not lands and seas alone, thy own clear freshness,
The young maturity of brood and bloom,
To realms of budding bibles.

O soul, repressless, I with thee and thou with me,
Thy circumnavigation of the world begin,   170
Of man, the voyage of his mind's return.
To reason's early paradise,
Back, back to wisdom's birth, to innocent intuitions,
Again with fair creation.

8

O we can wait no longer,   175
We too take ship O soul,
Joyous we too launch out on trackless seas,
Fearless for unknown shores on waves of ecstasy to sail,
Amid the wafting winds, (thou pressing me to thee, I thee to
      me, O soul,)

Caroling free, singing our song of God,   180
Chanting our chant of pleasant exploration.

With laugh and many a kiss,
(Let others deprecate, let others weep for sin, remorse, humilia-
          tion,)
O soul thou pleasest me, I thee.

Ah more than any priest O soul we too believe in God,   185
But with the mystery of God we dare not dally.

O soul thou pleasest me, I thee,
Sailing these seas or on the hills, or waking in the night,
Thoughts, silent thoughts, of Time and Space and Death, like
          waters flowing,
Bear me indeed as through the regions infinite,   190
Whose air I breathe, whose ripples hear, lave me all over,
Bathe me O God in thee, mounting to thee,
I and my soul to range in range of thee.

O Thou transcendent,
Nameless, the fibre and the breath,   195
Light of the light, shedding forth universes, thou centre of
          them,
Thou mightier centre of the true, the good, the loving,
Thou moral, spiritual fountain—affection's source—thou res-
          ervoir,
(O pensive soul of me—O thirst unsatisfied—waitest not there?
Waitest not haply for us somewhere there the Comrade
          perfect?)   200
Thou pulse—thou motive of the stars, suns, systems,
That, circling, move in order, safe, harmonious,
Athwart the shapeless vastnesses of space,
How should I think, how breathe a single breath, how speak,
          if out of myself,
I could not launch, to those, superior universes?   205
Swiftly I shrivel at the thought of God,
At Nature and its wonders, Time and Space and Death,
But that I, turning, call to thee O soul, thou actual Me,

And lo, thou gently masterest the orbs,
Thou matest Time, smilest content at Death, 210
And fillest, swellest full the vastnesses of Space.

Greater than stars or suns,
Bounding O soul thou journeyest forth;
What love than thine and ours could wider amplify?
What aspirations, wishes, outvie thine and ours O soul? 215
What dreams of the ideal? what plans of purity, perfection,
   strength,
What cheerful willingness for others' sake to give up all?
For others' sake to suffer all?

Reckoning ahead O soul, when thou, the time achiev'd,
The seas all cross'd, weather'd the capes, the voyage done, 220
Surrounded, copest, frontest God, yieldest, the aim attain'd,
As fill'd with friendship, love complete, the Elder Brother
   found,
The Younger melts in fondness in his arms.

9

Passage to more than India!
Are thy wings plumed indeed for such far flights? 225
O soul, voyagest thou indeed on voyages like those?
Disportest thou on waters such as those?
Soundest below the Sanscrit and the Vedas?
Then have thy bent unleash'd.

Passage to you, your shores, ye aged fierce enigmas! 230
Passage to you, to mastership of you, ye strangling problems!
You, strew'd with the wrecks of skeletons, that, living, never
   reach'd you.

Passage to more than India!
O secret of the earth and sky!
Of you O waters of the sea! O winding creeks and rivers! 235
Of you O woods and fields! of you strong mountains of my
   land!
Of you O prairies! of you gray rocks!

O morning red! O clouds! O rain and snows!
O day and night, passage to you!

O sun and moon and all you stars! Sirius and Jupiter!   240
Passage to you!

Passage, immediate passage! the blood burns in my veins!
Away O soul! hoist instantly the anchor!
Cut the hawsers—haul out—shake out every sail!
Have we not stood here like trees in the ground long enough?   245
Have we not grovel'd here long enough, eating and drinking
        like mere brutes?
Have we not darken'd and dazed ourselves with books long
        enough?

Sail forth—steer for the deep waters only,
Reckless O soul, exploring, I with thee, and thou with me,
For we are bound where mariner has not yet dared to go,   250
And we will risk the ship, ourselves and all.

O my brave soul!
O farther farther sail!
O daring joy, but safe! are they not all the seas of God?
O farther, farther, farther sail!   255

                                                    1872

EMILY DICKINSON

Emily Elizabeth Dickinson (1830-1886) was born in Amherst, Massachusetts, where she spent her life. After attending the Amherst Academy and Mount Holyoke Female Seminary, she lived in her father's house, unmarried and, for nearly the last half of her life, secluded from all but a small circle of friends. One of these was her sister-in-law and neighbor, Susan Dickinson; another, also a neighbor, was Mabel Loomis Todd. To both these women she sent copies of many of her poems. By Miss Dickinson's own claim, three other people significantly influenced her life: Benjamin F. Newton, a law student in her father's office, who excited her about reading and encouraged her to write poetry; the Reverend Charles Wadsworth, a Presbyterian minister; and Thomas Wentworth Higginson, lecturer, writer, and Unitarian minister. Although Miss Dickinson met Wadsworth only several times, she considered him her "dearest earthly friend," and a significant crisis in her life occurred in 1862 when he accepted a call to a church in San Francisco. She wrote prodigiously, for about three years, intense, explosive poems. In 1862 she wrote to Higginson, sending him copies of her verse and asking for criticism and advice. Although he generously responded and continued, throughout her life, to encourage her, Higginson tended to measure the poems by conventional standards of rhyme and metaphor. She realized this, and, discouraged by editors who insisted on "smoothing" the vital eccentricities, she abandoned the idea of publishing her poems.

Scarcely a half-dozen poems were published during her lifetime, most of those without her consent. Compare this with the number of poems she wrote: seventeen hundred and seventy-five. Nearly all of her poems survive in manuscript, most of them in but a single draft. Two-thirds of them she herself preserved: fair copies or semifinal drafts sewn together in packets. Others she sent to friends, and still others remain in rough form on odd scraps of paper. Shortly after the poet's death, the discovery of the packets by Miss Dickinson's sister, Lavinia, began a curious and confused publishing history. No one group of persons had all the poems, and, in time, animosities between the manuscript holders encouraged competition and hostility, preventing anything like a consistent or complete edition. Moreover, in addition to making errors arising from difficulty in reading the manuscripts, the editors variously changed words and whole lines in order to produce metrical regularity and more conventional metaphors. Precisely what the poet had written and what the editors wrote was for many years unknown.

The publishing history records the discovery of the poet. Lavinia Dickinson prevailed upon Mrs. Todd and Mr. Higginson to edit and publish *Poems* (1890) and *Poems, Second Series* (1891). *Poems, Third Series* (1896) was edited by Mrs. Todd. The first two titles were continuously reissued through the 1890s; they were also collected in one volume (1893); and the poems in all three series, together with one hundred and two additional poems, appeared in *Letters of Emily Dickinson,* 2 vols. (1894), edited by Mrs. Todd. This constituted the Dickinson canon until 1914, when the poet's niece, Martha Dickinson Bianchi, drawing on the poems which Emily Dickinson had sent her mother, edited *The Single Hound,* and with Alfred L. Hampson edited four more collections (1929, 1930, 1936, 1937), of which the second and fourth included all poems previously published. From a new source, six hundred and eighty-eight more poems and fragments were edited by Mabel Loomis Todd and Millicent Todd Bingham as *Bolts of Melody* (1945); and Mrs. Bingham edited further poems, which appeared in the *New England Quarterly,* XX (1947). By this time, piecemeal publication had accounted for all but about forty of the poems, but there was still no consistent editing, correction of previous editorial errors, or ordering of the text. This was the state of the poems until Thomas H. Johnson edited *The Poems of Emily Dickinson,* 3 vols. (Cambridge, 1955), the definitive edition of all her known poems, based on the best manuscript copies, and including variations suggested by the poet as well as the alterations made by the editors of the first three series.

The poems here printed represent still another text, based on the manuscripts published by Johnson but modified in several ways. When the poet has indicated variants, we have exercised the privilege extended to us, choosing wherever possible the New England colloquialism instead of the conventional nineteenth-century diction. We have regularized spelling and capitalization and eliminated quotation marks and italics. In the several cases where we believe previous editorial alterations have improved the poem, we have used the published text and indicated it by the date of the edition in parentheses. Also, when the published alterations of a manuscript are significant, we have indicated those alterations in brackets. The dates of composition and sequence of the poems are established in Johnson's text. Most of the dates are approximate, and the last two poems are undated.

I

Some things that fly there be—
Birds, hours, the bumble-bee:
Of these no elegy.

Some things that stay there be—
Grief, hills, eternity: 5
Nor this behooveth me.

There are, that resting, rise.
Can I expound the skies?
How still the riddle lies!

c. 1859

II

These are the days when birds come back,
A very few, a bird or two,
To take a backward look.

These are the days when skies resume
The old, old sophistries of June—   5
A blue and gold mistake.

Oh fraud that cannot cheat the bee,
Almost thy plausibility
Induces my belief.

Till ranks of seeds their witness bear,   10
And softly through the altered air
Hurries a timid leaf!

Oh sacrament of summer days,
Oh last communion in the haze,
Permit a child to join,   15

Thy sacred emblems to partake,
Thy consecrated bread to take
And thine immortal wine!

                                                    c. 1859

III

Faith is a fine invention
For gentlemen who see;
But microscopes are prudent
In an emergency.

                                                    c. 1860

IV

The thought beneath so slight a film
Is more distinctly seen—
As laces just reveal the surge,
Or mists the Apennine.

                                                    c. 1860

V

I taste a liquor never brewed,
From tankards scooped in pearl;
Not all the Frankfort berries
Yield such an alcohol!

Inebriate of air am I,   5
And debauchee of dew,
Reeling, through endless summer days,
From inns of molten blue.

When landlords turn the drunken bee
Out of the foxglove's door,   10
When butterflies renounce their drams,
I shall but drink the more!

Till seraphs swing their snowy hats,
And saints to windows run,
To see the little tippler   15
From Manzanilla come! [1]

                        c. 1860

VI

There's a certain slant of light,
On winter afternoons,
That oppresses, like the weight
Of cathedral tunes.

Heavenly hurt it gives us;   5
We can find no scar,
But internal difference
Where the meanings are.

None may teach it anything,
'Tis the seal, despair—   10
An imperial affliction
Sent us of the air.

When it comes, the landscape listens,
Shadows hold their breath;
When it goes, 'tis like the distance   15
On the look of death.

                  c. 1861 (1890)

VII

I felt a funeral in my brain,
And mourners to and fro
Kept treading, treading, till it seemed
That sense was breaking through.

And when they all were seated,   5
A service like a drum

---

[1] [Come staggering toward the sun. (1861)]
[Leaning against the sun! (1890)]

Kept beating, beating, till I thought
My mind was going numb.

And then I heard them lift a box,
And creak across my grain   10
With those same boots of lead, again;
Then space began to toll

As all the heavens were a bell,
And being but an ear,
And I and silence some strange race,   15
Wrecked, solitary, here.

And then a plank in reason broke,
And I dropped down, and down—
And hit a world at every plunge,
And finished knowing then.   20

                                   c. 1861

VIII

The soul selects her own society,
Then shuts the door;
To her divine majority
Present no more.

Unmoved, she notes the chariot's pausing   5
At her low gate;
Unmoved, an emperor be kneeling
Upon her mat.

I've known her from an ample nation
Choose one;   10
Then close the valves of her attention
Like stone.

                                   c. 1862

IX

I know that He exists.
Somewhere, in silence,

He has hid his rare life
From our gross eyes.

'Tis an instant's play.   5
'Tis a fond ambush,
Just to make bliss
Earn her own surprise!

But should the play
Prove piercing earnest,   10
Should the glee glaze
In death's stiff stare,

Would not the fun
Look too expensive!
Would not the jest   15
Have crawled too far!

                                              c. 1862

X

After great pain a formal feeling comes—
The nerves sit ceremonious like tombs;
The stiff heart questions—was it He that bore?
And yesterday—or centuries before?

The feet, mechanical, go round—   5
Of ground, or air, or ought—
A wooden way,
Regardless grown,
A quartz contentment, like a stone—

This is the hour of lead,   10
Remembered if outlived,
As freezing persons recollect the snow—
First chill, then stupor, then the letting go.

                                              1862

XI

I dreaded that first robin, so,
But he is mastered, now,

I'm some accustomed to him grown,
He hurts a little, though.

I thought if I could only live   5
Till that first shout got by,
Not all pianos in the woods
Had power to mangle me.

I dared not meet the daffodils,
For fear their yellow gown   10
Would pierce me with a fashion
So foreign to my own.

I wished the grass would hurry,
So, when 'twas time to see,
He'd be too tall, the tallest one   15
Could stretch, to look at me.

I could not bear the bees should come,
I wished they'd stay away
In those dim countries where they go:
What word had they for me?   20

They're here, though; not a creature failed,
No blossom stayed away
In gentle deference to me,
The Queen of Calvary.

Each one salutes me as he goes,   25
And I my childish plumes
Lift, in bereaved acknowledgment
Of their unthinking drums.

                                               1862

XII

Much madness is divinest sense
To a discerning eye;
Much sense, the starkest madness.
'Tis the majority

In this, as all, prevails.   5
Assent, and you are sane;
Demur, you're straightway dangerous,
And handled with a chain.

                                          c. 1862

XIII

A wife at daybreak I shall be;
Sunrise, hast thou a flag for me?
At midnight I am yet a maid—
How short it takes to make it bride!
Then, midnight, I have passed from thee   5
Unto the east and victory.

Midnight, "Good night!"
I hear them call.
The angels bustle in the hall,
Softly my future climbs the stair,   10
I fumble at my childhood's prayer—
So soon to be a child no more!
Eternity, I'm coming, Sir,—
Master, I've seen the face before.

                                          c. 1862

XIV

I would not paint a picture.
I'd rather be the one
Its bright impossibility
To dwell delicious on,
And wonder how the fingers feel   5
Whose rare celestial stir
Provokes so sweet a torment,
Such sumptuous despair.

I would not talk like cornets.
I'd rather be the one   10
Raised softly to the ceilings
And out, and easy on
Through villages of ether,

Myself, upborn balloon,
By but a lip of metal,   15
The pier to my pontoon.

Nor would I be a poet.
It's finer own the ear,
Enamored, impotent, content
The license to revere—   20
A privilege so awful
What would the dower be
Had I the art to stun myself
With bolts of melody!
                                        1862

XV

'Twas warm at first like us,
Until there crept thereon
A chill, like frost upon a glass,
Till all the scene be gone.

The forehead copied stone,   5
The fingers grew too cold
To ache, and like a skater's brook
The busy eyes congealed.

It straightened—that was all—
It crowded cold to cold;   10
It multiplied indifference
As pride were all it could.

And even when with cords
'Twas lowered like a freight,
It made no signal, nor demurred,   15
But dropped like adamant.
                               c. 1862

XVI

I've seen a dying eye
Run round and round a room

In search of something, as it seemed,
Then cloudier become;

And then, obscure with fog,   5
And then be soldered down,
Without disclosing what it be,
'Twere blessed to have seen.

                                                    c. 1862

XVII

The brain is wider than the sky,
For, put them side by side,
The one the other will include
With ease, and you beside.

The brain is deeper than the sea,   5
For, hold them, blue to blue,
The one the other will absorb,
As sponges, buckets do.

The brain is just the weight of God,
For, heft them, pound for pound,   10
And they will differ, if they do,
As syllable from sound.

                                                    c. 1862

XVIII

I cannot live with you,
It would be life,
And life is over there
Behind the shelf

The sexton keeps the key to,   5
Putting up
Our life—his porcelain—
Like a cup

Discarded of the housewife,
Quaint or broke;   10

A newer Sevres pleases,
Old ones crack.

I could not die with you,
For one must wait
To shut the other's gaze down.   15
You could not,

And I—could I stand by
And see you freeze
Without my right of frost,
Death's privilege?   20

Nor could I rise with you,
Because your face
Would put out Jesus'.
That new grace

Glow plain and foreign   25
On my homesick eye,
Except that you than he
Shone closer by.

They'd judge us—how?
For you served Heaven, you know,   30
Or sought to;
I could not,

Because you saturated sight,
And I had no more eyes
For sordid consequence   35
As Paradise.

And were you lost, I would be,
Though my name
Rang loudest
On the heavenly fame.   40

And were you saved,
And I condemned to be

Where you were not,
That self were hell to me.

So we must meet apart,   45
You there, I here,
With just the door ajar
That oceans are,
And prayer,
And that white privilege   50
Despair.

                                        c. 1862

XIX

Pain has an element of blank;
It cannot recollect
When it began, or if there were
A day when it was not.

It has no future but itself,   5
Its infinite realms contain
Its past, enlightened to perceive
New periods of pain.

                              c. 1862 (1890)

XX

Because I could not stop for death,
He kindly stopped for me;
The carriage held but just ourselves
And immortality.

We slowly drove, he knew no haste,   5
And I had put away
My labor, and my leisure too,
For his civility.

We passed the school where children strove
At recess, in the ring.
We passed the fields of gazing grain,
We passed the setting sun.

Or rather he passed us.
The dews drew quivering and chill,
For only gossamer my gown—   15
My tippet only tulle.

We paused before a house that seemed
A swelling of the ground;
The roof was scarcely visible,
The cornice but a mound.   20

Since then 'tis centuries; but each
Feels shorter than the day
I first surmised the horses' heads
Were toward eternity.

                                        c. 1863

XXI

Presentiment is that long shadow on the lawn
Indicative that suns go down;
The notice to the startled grass
That darkness is about to pass.

                                    c. 1863 (1890)

XXII

The sky is low, the clouds are mean.
A travelling flake of snow
Across a barn or through a rut
Debates if it will go.

A narrow wind complains all day   5
How some one treated him;
Nature, like us, is sometimes caught
Without her diadem.

                                        c. 1866

XXIII

The last night that she lived,
It was a common night,
Except the dying; this to us
Made nature different.

We noticed smallest things,   5
Things overlooked before,
By this great light upon our minds
Italicized, as 'twere.

As we went out and in
Between her final room   10
And rooms where those to be alive
Tomorrow were, a blame

That others could exist
While she must finish quite,
A jealousy for her arose   15
So nearly infinite.

We waited while she passed;
It was a narrow time,
Too jostled were our souls to speak,
At length the notice came.   20

She mentioned, and forgot;
Then lightly as a reed
Bent to the water, shivered scarce,
Consented and was dead.

And we, we placed the hair,   25
And drew the head erect;
And then an awful leisure was,
Our faith to regulate.

c. 1866

XXIV

To make a prairie it takes a clover and one bee,
One clover, and a bee,
And revery.
The revery alone will do
If bees are few.   5

(1896)

XXV

Elysium is as far as to
The very nearest room,
If in that room a friend await
Felicity or doom.

What fortitude the soul contains,   5
That it can so endure
The accent of a coming foot,
The opening of a door!

c. 1882

SIDNEY LANIER

Sidney Lanier (1842-1881) was born in Macon, Georgia, into an aristocratic family. He attended Oglethorpe College and studied music. Later, he became a private in the Confederate Army, where his exploits as a mounted scout were cut short by capture and imprisonment. He returned to Georgia in 1865 with a few poems, the manuscript of a novel, which was later published as *Tiger-Lilies* (1867), a determination to be an artist of some sort, and a body stricken with tuberculosis. After avid reading among the English and German Romantics and the writings of the English Victorians, he embarked on the several careers which lasted out his short life. He published poetry and literary criticism; he was a musician—a flutist in the Peabody Orchestra at Baltimore; and he became a lecturer in English literature at Johns Hopkins in 1879, two years before he died of tuberculosis. His lectures within this short period comprised the posthumously published *The English Novel* (1883) and the two volumes of *Shakespeare and His Forerunners* (1902). He published one volume of *Poems* (1877); and all his verse was posthumously collected, in *Poems* (1884). He also published a book on prosody, *The Science of English Verse* (1880).

Certain emphases are evident in Lanier's poems: an acute social consciousness and virtuosity in meter and sound. These singular emphases were not always consistent with each other or, in fact, with themselves. On the one hand, he celebrated the rural life and indicted the national economic system for its damage to agrarianism. He propagandized for better living and educational conditions in the South, for small and independent farms, and for a new and bold emphasis on art.

He believed in man's perfectibility by a kind of evolutionary process which he called "etherealizing." He wrote in an early essay, "Retrospects and Prospects": "For as time flows on, man and nature steadily etherealize. As time flows on, the *sense* kingdom continually decreases and the *soul* kingdom continually increases." In his poems he characteristically evangelized these convictions in terms of large emotional abstractions. On the other hand, he concentrated on a pre-

213

cise and sometimes limiting metrical expression. Lanier occasionally attempted to model his verse on Anglo-Saxon poetry, which measured line length by time rather than by stress. He also attempted to illustrate, in his poetry, the affinity of music and verse language, which was part of his prosodic theory in *The Science of English Verse*. In this respect some of his poems anticipated later experiments in quantitative verse—Ezra Pound's, for instance.

A full critical edition of Lanier's works was published in ten volumes (Baltimore: Johns Hopkins, 1946) of which Volume I—Charles R. Anderson (ed.), Sidney Lanier: *Poems and Poem Outlines*—is the text of these present selections.

CORN

To-day the woods are trembling through and through
With shimmering forms, that flash before my view,
Then melt in green as dawn-stars melt in blue.
    The leaves that wave against my cheek caress
    Like women's hands; the embracing boughs express   5
        A subtlety of mighty tenderness;
The copse-depths into little noises start,
That sound anon like beatings of a heart,
Anon like talk 'twixt lips not far apart.
    The beech dreams balm, as a dreamer hums a song;   10
    Through that vague wafture, expirations strong
    Throb from young hickories breathing deep and long
With stress and urgence bold of prisoned spring
      And ecstasy of burgeoning.
    Now, since the dew-plashed road of morn is dry,   15
    Forth venture odors of more quality
    And heavenlier giving. Like Jove's locks awry,
      Long muscadines
Rich-wreathe the spacious foreheads of great pines,
And breathe ambrosial passion from their vines.   20
    I pray with mosses, ferns and flowers shy
    That hide like gentle nuns from human eye
    To lift adoring perfumes to the sky.
I hear faint bridal-sighs of brown and green

Dying to silent hints of kisses keen   25
As far lights fringe into a pleasant sheen.
  I start at fragmentary whispers, blown
  From undertalks of leafy souls unknown,
  Vague purports sweet, of inarticulate tone.

Dreaming of gods, men, nuns and brides, between   30
Old companies of oaks that inward lean
To join their radiant amplitudes of green
  I slowly move, with ranging looks that pass
  Up from the matted miracles of grass
Into yon veined complex of space   35
Where sky and leafage interlace
  So close, the heaven of blue is seen
  Inwoven with a heaven of green.

I wander to the zigzag-cornered fence
Where sassafras, intrenched in brambles dense,   40
Contests with stolid vehemence
  The march of culture, setting limb and thorn
  As pikes against the army of the corn.

There, while I pause, my fieldward-faring eyes
Take harvests, where the stately corn-ranks rise,   45
        Of inward dignities
And large benignities and insights wise,
        Graces and modest majesties.
Thus, without theft, I reap another's field;
Thus, without tilth, I house a wondrous yield,   50
And heap my heart with quintuple crops concealed.

Look, out of line one tall corn-captain stands
Advanced beyond the foremost of his bands,
  And waves his blades upon the very edge
  And hottest thicket of the battling hedge.   55
Thou lustrous stalk, that ne'er mayst walk nor talk,
  Still shalt thou type the poet-soul sublime
  That leads the vanward of his timid time
  And sings up cowards with commanding rhyme—

Soul calm, like thee, yet fain, like thee, to grow   60
By double increment, above, below;
   Soul homely, as thou art, yet rich in grace like thee,
   Teaching the yeomen selfless chivalry
     That moves in gentle curves of courtesy;
Soul filled like thy long veins with sweetness tense,   65
     By every godlike sense
Transmuted from the four wild elements.
     Drawn to high plans,
     Thou lift'st more stature than a mortal man's,
Yet ever piercest downward in the mould   70
     And keepest hold
   Upon the reverend and steadfast earth
     That gave thee birth;
   Yea, standest smiling in thy future grave,
     Serene and brave,   75
   With unremitting breath
   Inhaling life from death,
Thine epitaph writ fair in fruitage eloquent,
     Thyself thy monument.
     As poets should,   80
Thou hast built up thy hardihood
With universal food,
   Drawn in select proportion fair
   From honest mould and vagabond air;
From darkness of the dreadful night,   85
     And joyful light;
   From antique ashes, whose departed flame
   In thee has finer life and longer fame;
From wounds and balms,
From storms and calms,   90
From potsherds and dry bones
     And ruin-stones.
Into thy vigorous substance thou hast wrought
Whate'er the hand of Circumstance hath brought;
   Yea, into cool solacing green hast spun   95
   White radiance hot from out the sun.
So thou dost mutually leaven
Strength of earth with grace of heaven;
   So thou dost marry new and old

Into a one of higher mould; 100
So thou dost reconcile the hot and cold,
    The dark and bright,
And many a heart-perplexing opposite,
      And so,
    Akin by blood to high and low, 105
Fitly thou playest out thy poet's part,
Richly expending thy much-bruisèd heart
    In equal care to nourish lord in hall
      Or beast in stall:
    Thou took'st from all that thou might'st give to all. 110

O steadfast dweller on the selfsame spot
Where thou wast born, that still repinest not—
Type of the home-fond heart, the happy lot!—
    Deeply thy mild content rebukes the land
    Whose flimsy homes, built on the shifting sand 115
Of trade, for ever rise and fall
With alternation whimsical,
    Enduring scarce a day,
    Then swept away
By swift engulfments of incalculable tides 120
Whereon capricious Commerce rides.

Look, thou substantial spirit of content!
Across this little vale, thy continent,
    To where, beyond the mouldering mill,
    Yon old deserted Georgian hill 125
Bares to the sun his piteous aged crest
      And seamy breast,
    By restless-hearted children left to lie
    Untended there beneath the heedless sky,
    As barbarous folk expose their old to die. 130

Upon that generous-rounding side,
    With gullies scarified
Where keen Neglect his lash hath plied,
Dwelt one I knew of old, who played at toil,
And gave to coquette Cotton soul and soil. 135
    Scorning the slow reward of patient grain,

He sowed his heart with hopes of swifter gain,
Then sat him down and waited for the rain.
He sailed in borrowed ships of usury—
A foolish Jason on a treacherous sea,   140
Seeking the Fleece and finding misery.
Lulled by smooth-rippling loans, in idle trance
He lay, content that unthrift Circumstance
Should plough for him the stony field of Chance.
Yea, gathering crops whose worth no man might tell,   145
He staked his life on games of Buy-and-Sell,
And turned each field into a gambler's hell.
    Aye, as each year began,
    My farmer to the neighboring city ran;
Passed with a mournful anxious face   150
Into the banker's inner place;
Parleyed, excused, pleaded for longer grace;
    Railed at the drought, the worm, the rust, the grass;
    Protested ne'er again 'twould come to pass;
    With many an *oh* and *if* and *but alas*   155
Parried or swallowed searching questions rude,
And kissed the dust to soften Dives's mood.
At last, small loans by pledges great renewed,
    He issues smiling from the fatal door,
    And buys with lavish hand his yearly store   160
    Till his small borrowings will yield no more.
Aye, as each year declined,
With bitter heart and ever-brooding mind
He mourned his fate unkind.
    In dust, in rain, with might and main,   165
    He nursed his cotton, cursed his grain,
    Fretted for news that made him fret again,
Snatched at each telegram of Future Sale,
And thrilled with Bulls' or Bears' alternate wail—
In hope or fear alike for ever pale.   170
    And thus from year to year, through hope and fear,
    With many a curse and many a secret tear,
    Striving in vain his cloud of debt to clear,
        At last
He woke to find his foolish dreaming past,   175
    And all his best-of-life the easy prey

Of squandering scamps and quacks that lined his way
      With vile array,
From rascal statesman down to petty knave;
Himself, at best, for all his bragging brave,   180
A gamester's catspaw and a banker's slave.
   Then, worn and gray, and sick with deep unrest,
   He fled away into the oblivious West,
         Unmourned, unblest.

Old hill! old hill! thou gashed and hairy Lear   185
Whom the divine Cordelia of the year,
E'en pitying Spring, will vainly strive to cheer—
   King, that no subject man nor beast may own,
   Discrowned, undaughtered and alone—
Yet shall the great God turn thy fate,   190
And bring thee back into thy monarch state
         And majesty immaculate.
Lo, through hot waverings of the August morn,
   Thou givest from thy vasty sides forlorn
   Visions of golden treasuries of corn—   195
Ripe largesse lingering for some bolder heart
That manfully shall take thy part,
         And tend thee,
         And defend thee,
With antique sinew and with modern art.   200
                                                         1875

THE SYMPHONY

"O Trade! O Trade! would thou wert dead!
The Time needs heart—'tis tired of head:
We're all for love," the violins said.
"Of what avail the rigorous tale
Of bill for coin and box for bale?   5
Grant thee, O Trade! thine uttermost hope:
Level red gold with blue sky-slope,
And base it deep as devils grope:
When all's done, what hast thou won
Of the only sweet that's under the sun?   10

Ay, canst thou buy a single sigh
Of true love's least, least ecstasy?"
Then, with a bridegroom's heart-beats trembling,
All the mightier strings assembling
Ranged them on the violins' side   15
As when the bridegroom leads the bride,
And, heart in voice, together cried:
"Yea, what avail the endless tale
Of gain by cunning and plus by sale?
Look up the land, look down the land—   20
The poor, the poor, the poor, they stand
Wedged by the pressing of Trade's hand
Against an inward-opening door
That pressure tightens evermore:
They sigh a monstrous foul-air sigh   25
For the outside leagues of liberty,
Where Art, sweet lark, translates the sky
Into a heavenly melody.
'Each day, all day' (these poor folks say),
'In the same old year-long, drear-long way,   ɩ   30
We weave in the mills and heave in the kilns,
We sieve mine-meshes under the hills,
And thieve much gold from the Devil's bank tills,
To relieve, O God, what manner of ills?—
The beasts, they hunger, and eat, and die;   35
And so do we, and the world's a sty;
Hush, fellow-swine: why nuzzle and cry?
Swinehood hath no remedy
Say many men, and hasten by,
Clamping the nose and blinking the eye.   40
But who said once, in the lordly tone,
Man shall not live by bread alone
But all that cometh from the Throne?
    Hath God said so?
    But Trade saith *No:*   45
And the kilns and the curt-tongued mills say *Go:*
There's plenty that can, if you can't: we know.
Move out, if you think you're underpaid.
The poor are prolific; we're not afraid;
    Trade is trade.' "   50

Thereat this passionate protesting
  Meekly changed, and softened till
It sank to sad requesting
  And suggesting sadder still:
"And oh, if men might some time see   55
How piteous-false the poor decree
That trade no more than trade must be!
Does business mean, *Die, you—live, I?*
Then 'Trade is trade' but sings a lie:
'Tis only war grown miserly.   60
If business is battle, name it so:
War-crimes less will shame it so,
And widows less will blame it so.
Alas: for the poor to have some part
In yon sweet living lands of Art,   65
Makes problem not for head, but heart.
Vainly might Plato's brain revolve it:
Plainly the heart of a child could solve it."

And then, as when from words that seem but rude
We pass to silent pain that sits abroad   70
Back in our heart's great dark and solitude,
So sank the strings to gentle throbbing
Of long chords change-marked with sobbing—
Motherly sobbing, not distinctlier heard
Than half wing-openings of the sleeping bird,   75
Some dream of danger to her young hath stirred.

Then stirring and demurring ceased, and lo!
Every least ripple of the strings' song-flow
Died to a level with each level bow
And made a great chord tranquil-surfaced so,   80
As a brook beneath his curving bank doth go
To linger in the sacred dark and green
Where many boughs the still pool overlean
And many leaves make shadow with their sheen.
    But presently   85
A velvet flute-note fell down pleasantly
Upon the bosom of that harmony,
And sailed and sailed incessantly,

As if a petal from a wild-rose blown
Had fluttered down upon that pool of tone   90
And boatwise dropped o' the convex side
And floated down the glassy tide
And clarified and glorified
The solemn spaces where the shadows bide.
From the warm concave of that fluted note   95
Somewhat, half song, half odor, forth did float,
As if a rose might somehow be a throat:
"When Nature from her far-off glen
Flutes her soft messages to men,
The flute can say them o'er again;   100
Yea, Nature, singing sweet and lone,
Breathes through life's strident polyphone
The flute-voice in the world of tone.
  Sweet friends,
  Man's love ascends   105
To finer and diviner ends
Than man's mere thought e'er comprehends.
  For I, e'en I,
  As here I lie,
A petal on a harmony,   110
Demand of Science whence and why
Man's tender pain, man's inward cry,
When he doth gaze on earth and sky?
I am not overbold:
  I hold   115
Full powers from Nature manifold.
I speak for each no-tonguèd tree
That, spring by spring, doth nobler be,
And dumbly and most wistfully
His mighty prayerful arms outspreads   120
Above men's oft-unheeding heads,
And his big blessing downward sheds.
I speak for all-shaped blooms and leaves,
Lichens on stones and moss on eaves,
Grasses and grains in ranks and sheaves;   125
Broad-fronded ferns and keen-leaved canes,
And briery mazes bounding lanes,

And marsh-plants, thirsty-cupped for rains,
And milky stems and sugary veins;
For every long-armed woman-vine   130
That round a piteous tree doth twine;
For passionate odors, and divine
Pistils, and petals crystalline;
All purities of shady springs,
All shynesses of film-winged things   135
That fly from tree-trunks and bark-rings;
All modesties of mountain-fawns
That leap to covert from wild lawns,
And tremble if the day but dawns;
All sparklings of small beady eyes   140
Of birds, and sidelong glances wise
Wherewith the jay hints tragedies;
All piquancies of prickly burs,
And smoothnesses of downs and furs
Of eiders and of minevers;   145
All limpid honeys that do lie
At stamen-bases, nor deny
The humming-birds' fine roguery,
Bee-thighs, nor any butterfly;
All gracious curves of slender wings,   150
Bark-mottlings, fibre-spiralings,
Fern-wavings and leaf-flickerings;
Each dial-marked leaf and flower-bell
Wherewith in every lonesome dell
Time to himself his hours doth tell;   155
All tree-sounds, rustlings of pine-cones,
Wind-sighings, doves' melodious moans,
And night's unearthly under-tones;
All placid lakes and waveless deeps,
All cool reposing mountain-steeps,   160
Vale-calms and tranquil lotos-sleeps;—
Yea, all fair forms, and sounds, and lights,
And warmths, and mysteries, and mights,
Of Nature's utmost depths and heights,
—These doth my timid tongue present,   165
Their mouthpiece and leal instrument

And servant, all love-eloquent.
I heard, when '*All for love*' the violins cried:
So, Nature calls through all her system wide,
Give me thy love, O man, so long denied.   170
Much time is run, and man hath changed his ways,
Since Nature, in the antique fable-days,
Was hid from man's true love by proxy fays,
False fauns and rascal gods that stole her praise.
The nymphs, cold creatures of man's colder brain,   175
Chilled Nature's streams till man's warm heart was fain
Never to lave its love in them again.
Later, a sweet Voice *Love thy neighbor* said;
Then first the bounds of neighborhood outspread
Beyond all confines of old ethnic dread.   180
Vainly the Jew might wag his covenant head:
'*All men are neighbors,*' so the sweet Voice said.
So, when man's arms had circled all man's race,
The liberal compass of his warm embrace
Stretched bigger yet in the dark bounds of space;   185
With hands a-grope he felt smooth Nature's grace,
Drew her to breast and kissed her sweetheart face:
Yea man found neighbors in great hills and trees
And streams and clouds and suns and birds and bees,
And throbbed with neighbor-loves in loving these.   190
But oh, the poor! the poor! the poor!
That stand by the inward-opening door
Trade's hand doth tighten ever more,
And sigh their monstrous foul-air sigh
For the outside hills of liberty,   195
Where Nature spreads her wild blue sky
For Art to make into melody!
Thou Trade! thou king of the modern days!
   Change thy ways,
   Change thy ways;   200
Let the sweaty laborers file
   A little while,
   A little while,
Where Art and Nature sing and smile.
Trade! is thy heart all dead, all dead?   205

And hast thou nothing but a head?
I'm all for heart," the flute-voice said,
And into sudden silence fled,
Like as a blush that while 'tis red
Dies to a still, still white instead.   210

Thereto a thrilling calm succeeds,
Till presently the silence breeds
A little breeze among the reeds
That seems to blow by sea-marsh weeds:
Then from the gentle stir and fret   215
Sings out the melting clarionet,
Like as a lady sings while yet
Her eyes with salty tears are wet.
"O Trade! O Trade!" the Lady said,
"I too will wish thee utterly dead   220
If all thy heart is in thy head.
For O my God! and O my God!
What shameful ways have women trod
At beckoning of Trade's golden rod!
Alas when sighs are traders' lies,   225
And heart's-ease eyes and violet eyes
    Are merchandise!
O purchased lips that kiss with pain!
O cheeks coin-spotted with smirch and stain!
O trafficked hearts that break in twain!   230
—And yet what wonder at my sisters' crime?
So hath Trade withered up Love's sinewy prime,
Men love not women as in olden time.
Ah, not in these cold merchantable days
Deem men their life an opal gray, where plays   235
The one red Sweet of gracious ladies'-praise.
Now, comes a suitor with sharp prying eye—
Says, *Here, you Lady, if you'll sell, I'll buy:
Come, heart for heart—a trade? What! weeping? why?*
Shame on such wooers' dapper mercery!   240
I would my lover kneeling at my feet
In humble manliness should cry, *O sweet!*
I know not if thy heart my heart will greet:

I ask not if thy love my love can meet:
Whate'er thy worshipful soft tongue shall say,   245
I'll kiss thine answer, be it yea or nay:
I do but know I love thee, and I pray
To be thy knight until my dying day.
Woe him that cunning trades in hearts contrives!
Base love good women to base loving drives.   250
If men loved larger, larger were our lives;
And wooed they nobler, won they nobler wives."

There thrust the bold straightforward horn
To battle for that lady lorn,
With heartsome voice of mellow scorn,   255
Like any knight in knighthood's morn.
   "Now comfort thee," said he,
     "Fair Lady.
For God shall right thy grievous wrong,
And man shall sing thee a true-love song,   260
Voiced in act his whole life long,
   Yea, all thy sweet life long,
     Fair Lady.
Where's he that craftily hath said,
The day of chivalry is dead?   265
I'll prove that lie upon his head,
   Or I will die instead,
     Fair Lady.
Is Honor gone into his grave?
Hath Faith become a caitiff knave,   270
And Selfhood turned into a slave
   To work in Mammon's Cave,
     Fair Lady?
Will Truth's long blade ne'er gleam again?
Hath Giant Trade in dungeons slain   275
All great contempts of mean-got gain
   And hates of inward stain,
     Fair Lady?
For aye shall name and fame be sold,
And place be hugged for the sake of gold,   280
And smirch-robed Justice feebly scold

At Crime all money-bold,
  Fair Lady?
Shall self-wrapt husbands aye forget
Kiss-pardons for the daily fret   285
Wherewith sweet wifely eyes are wet—
  Blind to lips kiss-wise set—
    Fair Lady?
Shall lovers higgle, heart for heart,
Till wooing grows a trading mart   290
Where much for little, and all for part,
  Make love a cheapening art,
    Fair Lady?
Shall woman scorch for a single sin
That her betrayer can revel in,   295
And she be burnt, and he but grin
  When that the flames begin,
    Fair Lady?
Shall ne'er prevail the woman's plea,
We maids would far, far whiter be   300
If that our eyes might sometimes see
  Men maids in purity,
    Fair Lady?
Shall Trade aye salve his conscience-aches
With jibes at Chivalry's old mistakes—   305
The wars that o'erhot knighthood makes
  For Christ's and ladies' sakes,
    Fair Lady?
Now by each knight that e'er hath prayed
To fight like a man and love like a maid,   310
Since Pembroke's life, as Pembroke's blade,
  I' the scabbard, death, was laid,
    Fair Lady,
I dare avouch my faith is bright
That God doth right and God hath might,   315
Nor time hath changed His hair to white,
  Nor His dear love to spite,
    Fair Lady.
I doubt no doubts: I strive, and shrive my clay,
And fight my fight in the patient modern way   320

For true love and for thee—ah me! and pray
    To be thy knight until my dying day,
        Fair Lady."
Made end that knightly horn, and spurred away
Into the thick of the melodious fray.   325

And then the hautboy played and smiled,
And sang like any large-eyed child,
Cool-hearted and all undefiled.
    "Huge Trade!" he said,
"Would thou wouldst lift me on thy head,   330
And run where'er my finger led!
Once said a Man—and wise was He—
Never shalt thou the heavens see,
Save as a little child thou be."
Then o'er sea-lashings of commingling tunes   335
The ancient wise bassoons,
    Like weird
    Gray-beard
Old harpers sitting on the high sea-dunes,
    Chanted runes: 340
"Bright-waved gain, gray waved loss,
The sea of all doth lash and toss,
One wave forward and one across:
But now 'twas trough, now 'tis crest,
And worst doth foam and flash to best,   345
    And curst to blest.

"Life Life! thou sea-fugue, writ from east to west,
    Love, Love alone can pore
    On thy dissolving score
    Of harsh half-phrasings,   350
        Blotted ere writ,
    And double erasings
        Of chords most fit.
Yea, Love, sole music-master blest,
May read thy weltering palimpsest.   355
To follow Time's dying melodies through,
And never to lose the old in the new,

And ever to solve the discords true—
    Love alone can do.
And ever Love hears the poor-folks' crying,   360
And ever Love hears the women's sighing,
And ever sweet knighthood's death-defying,
And ever wise childhood's deep implying,
But never a trader's glozing and lying.

"And yet shall Love himself be heard,   365
Though long deferred, though long deferred:
O'er the modern waste a dove hath whirred:
Music is Love in search of a word."

                                                               1875

THE WAVING OF THE CORN

Ploughman, whose gnarly hand yet kindly wheeled
Thy plough to ring this solitary tree
    With clover, whose round plat, reserved a-field,
In cool green radius twice my length may be—
    Scanting the corn thy furrows else might yield,   5
To pleasure August, bees, fair thoughts, and me,
        That here come oft together—daily I,
        Stretched prone in summer's mortal ecstasy,
Do stir with thanks to thee, as stirs this morn
        With waving of the corn.   10

Unseen, the farmer's boy from round the hill
Whistles a snatch that seeks his soul unsought,
    And fills some time with tune, howbeit shrill;
The cricket tells straight on his simple thought—
    Nay, 'tis the cricket's way of being still;   15
The peddler beé drones in, and gossips naught;
        Far down the wood, a one-desiring dove
        Times me the beating of the heart of love:
And these be all the sounds that mix, each morn,
        With waving of the corn.   20

From here to where the louder passions dwell,
Green leagues of hilly separation roll:
Trade ends where yon far clover ridges swell.
Ye terrible Towns, ne'er claim the trembling soul
That, craftless all to buy or hoard or sell,   25
From out your deadly complex quarrel stole
To company with large amiable trees,
Suck honey summer with unjealous bees,
And take Time's strokes as softly as this morn
Takes waving of the corn.   30

                                                        1877

THE HARLEQUIN OF DREAMS

Swift through some trap mine eyes have never found,
Dim-panelled in the painted scene of sleep,
Thou, giant Harlequin of Dreams, dost leap
Upon my spirit's stage. Then sight and sound,
Then space and time, then language, mete and bound,   5
And all familiar forms that firmly keep
Man's reason in the road, change faces, peep
Betwixt the legs, and mock the daily round.
Yet thou canst more than mock: sometimes my tears
At midnight break through bounden lids—a sign   10
Thou hast a heart; and oft thy little leaven
Of dream-taught wisdom works me bettered years.
In one night witch, saint, trickster, fool divine,
I think thou'rt Jester at the Court of Heaven!

                                                        1878

A BALLAD OF TREES AND THE MASTER

Into the woods my Master went,
Clean forspent, forspent.
Into the woods my Master came,
Forspent with love and shame.
But the olives they were not blind to Him,   5

The little gray leaves were kind to Him:
The thorn-tree had a mind to Him
   When into the woods He came.

Out of the woods my Master went,
   And He was well content.   10
Out of the woods my Master came,
   Content with death and shame.
When Death and Shame would woo Him last,
From under the trees they drew Him last:
'Twas on a tree they slew Him—last   15
   When out of the woods He came.

                        1880

BURN THE STUBBLE!

"Wind and Fire, Wind and Fire,
   —O War, kindle and rage again.
The stubble is rank, and we desire
   To burn Life off, for the coming grain.

"Who lies a-ground, that's born to fly?   5
   Who loves a grief that stings his wife?
Who laughs when his hungry children die?
   Who works in vain, and likes his life?

"Let these arise and run to the sea
   And sail over Exile's mournful main.   10
Here's work: the stubble is rank, and we
   Must burn some room for the coming grain."

—O gasping Heart, with long desire,
   Endure, endure, till the round earth turn.
O God, come Thou, and set the fire.   15
   O Heart, be calm, till God shall burn.

                 w 1868; 1945

EDWIN ARLINGTON ROBINSON

Edwin Arlington Robinson (1869-1935) was born in Head Tide, Maine, and spent most of his growing years in Gardiner, Maine. He attended Harvard College (1891-93) until he was called home because of his father's illness; by this time he had already decided to be a poet. While still in school he "became violently excited over the structure and music of English blank verse." For four years after leaving college, he wrote continuously, experimenting with his own verse and with metrical translations of other writings; and he tried without success to publish his work. He later wrote of having collected hundreds of rejection slips from editors and publishers, until he began to realize that the convictions in his poems offended traditional notions of what poems ought to say. Consequently, he published his own first volume, a selection of some forty poems entitled *The Torrent and the Night Before* (1896), which presented a series of terse portraits of small people in a small town. A second volume, *The Children of the Night* (1897), added to the selections in the first. In 1900 he moved to New York City and worked as an inspector of construction in the city subways. Two years later, a second edition of *The Children of the Night* was reviewed in a magazine by President Theodore Roosevelt; and, after Robinson had published a narrative poem, *Captain Craig* (1902), Roosevelt publicly endorsed the poet by arranging for him a convenient clerkship in the New York customs house (1905-10). Thereafter Robinson's following grew.

One first thinks of Robinson's "Tilbury Town" portraits, but the range of his work grew beyond these early writings. He tried playwriting once or twice with indifferent success, and then found the medium he wanted: blank verse narrative, varied by dialogue and dramatic monologue. This is the form of his Arthurian trilogy: *Merlin* (1917), *Lancelot* (1920), and *Tristram* (1927). This trilogy marks as well Robinson's preoccupation, in his other verse narratives, with the problems of personal and ethical responsibility. Among these dramatic narratives are *Avon's Harvest* (1921), *Roman Bartholow* (1923), *The Man Who Died Twice* (1924), *Cavender's House* (1929), and *Matthias at the Door* (1931).

232

All of these poems share a playwright's interest in characters, in the psychology of motives, and in the ethical problems of individuals.

Robinson published twenty-seven volumes of poetry; one more was posthumously published. Three times he won the Pulitzer Prize: for his first collection of poems (1922), for *The Man Who Died Twice,* and for *Tristram.*

The text of the first two of these selections is Robinson's first volume; for the next three, his second volume; and for the rest, *Collected Poems of Edwin Arlington Robinson* (New York, 1937).

LUKE HAVERGAL

Go to the western gate, Luke Havergal,
There where the vines cling crimson on the wall,
And in the twilight wait for what will come.
The leaves will whisper there of her, and some,
Like flying words, will strike you as they fall;   5
But go, and if you listen she will call.
Go to the western gate, Luke Havergal—
Luke Havergal.

No, there is not a dawn in eastern skies
To rift the fiery night that's in your eyes;   10
But there, where western glooms are gathering,
The dark will end the dark, if anything:
God slays Himself with every leaf that flies,
And hell is more than half of paradise.
No, there is not a dawn in eastern skies—   15
In eastern skies.

Out of a grave I come to tell you this,
Out of a grave I come to quench the kiss
That flames upon your forehead with a glow
That blinds you to the way that you must go.   20
Yes, there is yet one way to where she is,—
Bitter, but one that faith may never miss.
Out of a grave I come to tell you this—
To tell you this.

There is the western gate, Luke Havergal,   25
There are the crimson leaves upon the wall.
Go, for the winds are tearing them away,—
Nor think to riddle the dead words they say,
Nor any more to feel them as they fall;
But go, and if you trust her she will call.   30
There is the western gate, Luke Havergal—
Luke Havergal.

                                                        1896

ZOLA

Because he puts the compromising chart
Of hell before your eyes, you are afraid;
Because he counts the price that you have paid
For innocence, and counts it from the start,
You loathe him. But he sees the human heart   5
Of God meanwhile, and in His hand was weighed
Your squeamish and emasculate crusade
Against the grim dominion of his art.

Never until we conquer the uncouth
Connivings of our shamed indifference   10
(We call it Christian faith) are we to scan
The racked and shrieking hideousness of Truth
To find, in hate's polluted self-defence
Throbbing, the pulse, the divine heart of man.

                                                        1896

WALT WHITMAN

The master-songs are ended, and the man
That sang them is a name. And so is God
A name; and so is love, and life, and death,
And everything. But we, who are too blind
To read what we have written, or what faith   5
Has written for us, do not understand:
We only blink, and wonder.

Last night it was the song that was the man,
But now it is the man that is the song.
We do not hear him very much to-day: 10
His piercing and eternal cadence rings
Too pure for us—too powerfully pure,
Too lovingly triumphant, and too large;
But there are some that hear him, and they know
That he shall sing to-morrow for all men,   15
And that all time shall listen.

The master-songs are ended? Rather say
No songs are ended that are ever sung,
And that no names are dead names. When we write
Men's letters on proud marble or on sand,   20
We write them there forever.

                                        1896

RICHARD CORY

Whenever Richard Cory went down town,
We people on the pavement looked at him:
He was a gentleman from sole to crown,
Clean favored, and imperially slim.

And he was always quietly arrayed,   5
And he was always human when he talked;
But still he fluttered pulses when he said,
"Good-morning," and he glittered when he walked.

And he was rich—yes, richer than a king—
And admirably schooled in every grace: 10
In fine, we thought that he was everything
To make us wish that we were in his place.

So on we worked, and waited for the light,
And went without the meat, and cursed the bread;
And Richard Cory, one calm summer night,   15
Went home and put a bullet through his head.

                                        1897

REUBEN BRIGHT

Because he was a butcher and thereby
Did earn an honest living (and did right),
I would not have you think that Reuben Bright
Was any more a brute than you or I;
For when they told him that his wife must die,   5
He stared at them, and shook with grief and fright,
And cried like a great baby half that night,
And made the women cry to see him cry.

And after she was dead, and he had paid
The singers and the sexton and the rest,   10
He packed a lot of things that she had made
Most mournfully away in an old chest
Of hers, and put some chopped-up cedar boughs
In with them, and tore down the slaughter-house.

                                                        1897

OCTAVES

II

Tumultously void of a clean scheme
Whereon to build, whereof to formulate,
The legion life that riots in mankind
Goes ever plunging upward, up and down,
Most like some crazy regiment at arms,   5
Undisciplined of aught but Ignorance,
And ever led resourcelessly along
To brainles carnage by drunk trumpeters.

III

To me the groaning of world-worshippers
Rings like a lonely music played in hell
By one with art enough to cleave the walls
Of heaven with his cadence, but without

The wisdom or the will to comprehend 5
The strangeness of his own perversity,
And all without the courage to deny
The profit and the pride of his defeat.

XI

Still through the dusk of dead, blank-legended,
And unremunerative years we search
To get where life begins, and still we groan
Because we do not find the living spark
Where no spark ever was; and thus we die, 5
Still searching, like poor old astronomers
Who totter off to bed and go to sleep,
To dream of untriangulated stars.

XVIII

Like a white wall whereon forever breaks
Unsatisfied the tumult of green seas,
Man's unconjectured godliness rebukes
With its imperial silence the lost waves
Of insufficient grief. This mortal surge 5
That beats against us now is nothing else
Than plangent ignorance. Truth neither shakes
Nor wavers; but the world shakes, and we shriek.

1897

THE MAN AGAINST THE SKY

Between me and the sunset, like a dome
Against the glory of a world on fire,
Now burned a sudden hill,
Bleak, round, and high, by flame-lit height made
      higher,
With nothing on it for the flame to kill 5
Save one who moved and was alone up there
To loom before the chaos and the glare
As if he were the last god going home
Unto his last desire.

Dark, marvelous, and inscrutable he moved on   10
Till down the fiery distance he was gone,
Like one of those eternal, remote things
That range across a man's imaginings
When a sure music fills him and he knows
What he may say thereafter to few men,—   15
The touch of ages having wrought
An echo and a glimpse of what he thought
A phantom or a legend until then;
For whether lighted over ways that save,
Or lured from all repose,   20
If he go on too far to find a grave,
Mostly alone he goes.

Even he, who stood where I had found him,
On high with fire all round him,
Who moved along the molten west,   25
And over the round hill's crest,
That seemed half ready with him to go down,
Flame-bitten and flame-cleft,
As if there were to be no last thing left
Of a nameless unimaginable town,—   30
Even he who climbed and vanished may have taken
Down to the perils of a depth not known,
From death defended though by men forsaken,
The bread that every man must eat alone;
He may have walked while others hardly dared   35
Look on to see him stand where many fell;
And upward out of that, as out of hell,
He may have sung and striven
To mount where more of him shall yet be given,
Bereft of all retreat,   40
To sevenfold heat,—
As on a day when three in Dura shared
The furnace, and were spared
For glory by that king of Babylon
Who made himself so great that God, who heard,   45
Covered him with long feathers, like a bird.

Again, he may have gone down easily,
By comfortable altitudes, and found,
As always, underneath him solid ground
Whereon to be sufficient and to stand   50
Possessed already of the promised land,
Far stretched, and fair to see:
A good sight, verily,
And one to make the eyes of her who bore him
Shine glad with hidden tears.   55
Why question of his ease of who before him,
In one place or another where they left
Their names as far behind them as their bones,
And yet by dint of slaughter toil and theft,
And shrewdly sharpened stones,   60
Carved hard the way for his ascendency
Through deserts of lost years?
Why trouble him now who sees and hears
No more than what his innocence requires,
And therefore to no other height aspires   65
Than one at which he neither quails nor tires?
He may do more by seeing what he sees
Than others eager for iniquities;
He may, by seeing all things for the best,
Incite futurity to do the rest.   70

Or with an even likelihood,
He may have met with atrabilious eyes
The fires of time on equal terms and passed
Indifferently down, until at last
His only kind of grandeur would have been,   75
Apparently, in being seen.
He may have had for evil or for good
No argument; he may have had no care
For what without himself went anywhere
To failure or to glory, and least of all   80
For such a stale, flamboyant miracle;
He may have been the prophet of an art
Immovable to old idolatries;
He may have been a player without a part,

Annoyed that even the sun should have the skies   85
For such a flaming way to advertise;
He may have been a painter sick at heart
With Nature's toiling for a new surprise;
He may have been a cynic, who now, for all
Of anything divine that his effete   90
Negation may have tasted,
Saw truth in his own image, rather small,
Forbore to fever the ephemeral,
Found any barren height a good retreat
From any swarming street,   95
And in the sun saw power superbly wasted;
And when the primitive old-fashioned stars
Came out again to shine on joys and wars
More primitive, and all arrayed for doom,
He may have proved a world a sorry thing   100
In his imagining,
And life a lighted highway to the tomb.

Or, mounting with infirm unsearching tread,
His hopes to chaos led,
He may have stumbled up there from the past,   105
And with an aching strangeness viewed the last
Abysmal conflagration of his dreams,—
A flame where nothing seems
To burn but flame itself, by nothing fed;
And while it all went out,   110
Not even the faint anodyne of doubt
May then have eased a painful going down
From pictured heights of power and lost renown,
Revealed at length to his outlived endeavor
Remote and unapproachable forever;   115
And at his heart there may have gnawed
Sick memories of a dead faith foiled and flawed
And long dishonored by the living death
Assigned alike by chance
To brutes and hierophants;   120
And anguish fallen on those he loved around him
May once have dealt the last blow to confound him,
And so have left him as death leaves a child,

Who sees it all too near;
And he who knows no young way to forget   125
May struggle to the tomb unreconciled.
Whatever suns may rise or set
There may be nothing kinder for him here
Than shafts and agonies;
And under these   130
He may cry out and stay on horribly;
Or, seeing in death too small a thing to fear,
He may go forward like a stoic Roman
Where pangs and terrors in his pathway lie,—
Or, seizing the swift logic of a woman,   135
Curse God and die.

Or maybe there, like many another one
Who might have stood aloft and looked ahead,
Black-drawn against wild red,
He may have built, unawed by fiery gules   140
That in him no commotion stirred,
A living reason out of molecules
Why molecules occurred,
And one for smiling when he might have sighed
Had he seen far enough,   145
And in the same inevitable stuff
Discovered an odd reason too for pride
In being what he must have been by laws
Infrangible and for no kind of cause.
Deterred by no confusion or surprise   150
He may have seen with his mechanic eyes
A world without a meaning, and had room,
Alone amid magnificence and doom,
To build himself an airy monument
That should, or fail him in his vague intent,   155
Outlast an accidental universe—
To call it nothing worse—
Or, by the burrowing guile
Of Time disintegrated and effaced,
Like once-remembered mighty trees go down   160
To ruin, of which by man may now be traced
No part sufficient even to be rotten,

And in the book of things that are forgotten
Is entered as a .hing not quite worth while.
He may have been so great   165
That satraps would have shivered at his frown.
And all he prized alive may rule a state
No larger than a grave that holds a clown;
He may have been a master of his fate,
And of his atoms,—ready as another   170
In his emergence to exonerate
His father and his mother;
He may have been a captain of a host,
Self-eloquent and ripe for prodigies,
Doomed here to swell by dangerous degrees,   175
And then give up the ghost.
Nahum's great grasshoppers were such as these,
Sun-scattered and soon lost.

Whatever the dark road he may have taken,
This man who stood on high   180
And faced alone the sky,
Whatever drove or lured or guided him,—
A vision answering a faith unshaken,
An easy trust assumed of easy trials,
A sick negation born of weak denials,   185
A crazed abhorrence of an old condition,
A blind attendance on a brief ambition,—
Whatever stayed him or derided him,
His way was even as ours;
And we, with all our wounds and all our powers,   190
Must each await alone at his own height
Another darkness or another light;
And there, of our poor self dominion reft,
If inference and reason shun
Hell, Heaven, and Oblivion,   195
May thwarted will (perforce precarious,
But for our conservation better thus)
Have no misgiving left
Of doing yet what here we leave undone?
Or if unto the last of these we cleave,   200
Believing or protesting we believe

In such an idle and ephemeral
Florescence of the diabolical,—
If, robbed of two fond old enormities
Our being had no onward auguries,   205
What then were this great love of ours to say
For launching other lives to voyage again
A little farther into time and pain,'
A little faster in a futile chase
For a kingdom and a power and a Race   210
That would have still in sight
A manifest end of ashes and eternal night?
Is this the music of the toys we shake
So loud,—as if there might be no mistake
Somewhere in our indomitable will?   215
Are we no greater than the noise we make
Along one blind atomic pilgrimage
Whereon by crass chance billeted we go
Because our brains and bones and cartilage
Will have it so?   220
If this we say, then let us all be still
About our share in it, and live and die
More quietly thereby.

Where was he going, this man against the sky?
You know not, nor do I.   225
But this we know, if we know anything:
That we may laugh and fight and sing
And of our transience here make offering
To an orient Word that will not be erased,
Or, save in incommunicable gleams   230
Too permanent for dreams,
Be found or known.
No tonic and ambitious irritant
Of increase or of want
Has made an otherwise insensate waste   235
Of ages overthrown
A ruthless, veiled, implacable foretaste
Of other ages that are still to be
Depleted and rewarded variously
Because a few, by fate's economy,   240

Shall seem to move the world the way it goes;
No soft evangel of equality,
Safe-cradled in a communal repose
That huddles into death and may at last
Be covered well with equatorial snows—   245
And all for what, the devil only knows—
Will aggregate an inklingly to confirm
The credit of a sage or of a worm,
Or tell us why one man in five
Should have a care to stay alive   250
While in his heart he feels no violence
Laid on his humor and intelligence
When infant Science makes a pleasant face
And waves again that hollow toy, the Race;
No planetary trap where souls are wrought   255
For nothing but the sake of being caught
And sent again to nothing will attune
Itself to any key of any reason
Why man should hunger through another season
To find out why 'twere better late than soon   260
To go away and let the sun and moon
And all the silly stars illuminate
A place for creeping things,
And those that root and trumpet and have wings,
And herd and ruminate,   265
Or dive and flash and poise in rivers and seas,
Or by their loyal tails in lofty trees
Hang screeching lewd victorious derision
Of man's immortal vision.
Shall we, because Eternity records   270
Too vast an answer for the time-born words
We spell, whereof so many are dead that once
In our capricious lexicons
Were so alive and final, hear no more
The Word itself, the living word   275
That none alive has ever heard
Or ever spelt,
And few have ever felt
Without the fears and old surrenderings

And terrors that began   280
When Death let fall a feather from his wings
And humbled the first man?
Because the weight of our humility,
Wherefrom we gain
A little wisdom and much pain,   285
Falls here too sore and there too tedious,
Are we in anguish or complacency,
Not looking far enough ahead
To see by what mad couriers we are led
Along the roads of the ridiculous,   290
To pity ourselves and laugh at faith
And while we curse life bear it?
And if we see the soul's dead end in death,
Are we to fear it?
What folly is here that has not yet a name   295
Unless we say outright that we are liars?
What have we seen beyond our sunset fires
That lights again the way by which we came?
Why pay we such a price, and one we give
So clamoringly, for each racked empty day   300
That leads one more last human hope away,
As quiet fiends would lead past our crazed eyes
Our children to an unseen sacrifice?
If after all that we have lived and thought,
All comes to Nought,—   305
If there be nothing after Now,
And we be nothing anyhow,
And we know that,—why live?
'Twere sure but weaklings' vain distress
To suffer dungeons where so many doors   310
Will open on the cold eternal shores
That look sheer down
To the dark tideless floods of Nothingness
Where all who know may drown.

                                            1916

HILLCREST
(To Mrs. Edward MacDowell)

No sound of any storm that shakes
Old island walls with older seas
Comes here where now September makes
An island in a sea of trees.

Between the sunlight and the shade   5
A man may learn till he forgets
The roaring of a world remade,
And all his ruins and regrets;

And if he still remembers here
Poor fights he may have won or lost,—   10
If he be ridden with the fear
Of what some other fight may cost,—

If, eager to confuse too soon,
What he has known with what may be,
He reads a planet out of tune   15
For cause of his jarred harmony,—

If here he venture to unroll
His index of adagios,
And he be given to console
Humanity with what he knows,—   20

He may by contemplation learn
A little more than what he knew,
And even see great oaks return
To acorns out of which they grew.

He may, if he but listen well,   25
Through twilight and the silence here
Be told what there are none may tell
To vanity's impatient ear;

And he may never dare again
Say what awaits him, or be sure   30
What sunlit labyrinth of pain
He may not enter and endure.

Who knows to-day from yesterday
May learn to count no thing too strange:
Love builds of what Time takes away,   35
Till Death itself is less than Change.

Who sees enough in his duress
May go as far as dreams have gone;
Who sees a little may do less
Than many who are blind have done;   40

Who sees unchastened here the soul
Triumphant has no other sight
Than has a child who sees the whole
World radiant with his own delight.

Far journeys and hard wandering   45
Await him in whose crude surmise
Peace, like a mask, hides everything
That is and has been from his eyes;

And all his wisdom is unfound,
Or like a web that error weaves   50
On airy looms that have a sound
No louder now than falling leaves.

                                          1916

DEMOS

I

All you that are enamored of my name
    And least intent on what most I require,
    Beware; for my design and your desire,
Deplorably, are not as yet the same.

Beware, I say, the failure and the shame   5
    Of losing that for which you now aspire
    So blindly, and of hazarding entire
The gift that I was bringing when I came.

Give as I will, I cannot give you sight
    Whereby to see that with you there are some   10
    To lead you, and be led. But they are dumb
Before the wrangling and the shrill delight
    Of your deliverance that has not come,
And shall not, if I fail you—as I might.

II

So little have you seen of what awaits   15
    Your fevered glimpse of a democracy
    Confused and foiled with an equality
Not equal to the envy it creates,
That you see not how near you are the gates
    Of an old king who listens fearfully   20
    To you that are outside and are to be
The noisy lords of imminent estates.

Rather be then your prayer that you shall have
    Your kingdom undishonored. Having all,
    See not the great among you for the small,   25
But hear their silence; for the few shall save
    The many, or the many are to fall—
Still to be wrangling in a noisy grave.

                                                   1919

NEW ENGLAND

Here where the wind is always north-north-east
And children learn to walk on frozen toes,
Wonder begets an envy of all those
Who boil elsewhere with such a lyric yeast
Of love that you will hear them at a feast   5
Where demons would appeal for some repose,
Still clamoring where the chalice overflows
And crying wildest who have drunk the least.

Passion is here a soilure of the wits,
We're told, and Love a cross for them to bear;   10
Joy shivers in the corner where she knits
And Conscience always has the rocking-chair,
Cheerful as when she tortured into fits
The first cat that was ever killed by Care.

                                        1923

NOT ALWAYS

I

In surety and obscurity twice mailed,
And first achieving with initial rout
A riddance of weak fear and weaker doubt,
He strove alone. But when too long assailed
By nothing, even a stronger might have quailed   5
As he did, and so might have gazed about
Where he could see the last light going out,
Almost as if the fire of God had failed.

And so it was till out of silence crept
Invisible avengers of a name   10
Unknown, like jungle-hidden jaguars.
But there were others coming who had kept
Their watch and word; and out of silence came
A song somewhat as of the morning stars.

                                        1924

A CHRISTMAS SONNET
For One in Doubt

While you that in your sorrow disavow
Service and hope, see love and brotherhood
Far off as ever, it will do no good
For you to wear his thorns upon your brow
For doubt of him. And should you question how   5

To serve him best, he might say, if he could,
"Whether or not the cross was made of wood
Whereon you nailed me, is no matter now."

Though other saviors have in older lore
A Legend, and for older gods have died—   10
Though death may wear the crown it always wore
And ignorance be still the sword of pride—
Something is here that was not here before,
And strangely has not yet been crucified.

                                                  1928

ROBERT FROST

Robert Lee Frost (1874-   ) was born in San Francisco, California, and, at the age of ten, after the death of his father, moved with his mother to her home in Lawrence, Massachusetts. He attended Dartmouth College for a few months, and, later, Harvard for two years. Meantime, he married and worked as a mill worker, schoolteacher, newspaper reporter, and shoemaker. After leaving college—his high marks did not compensate for the irksome discipline of classes—he lived for twelve years on a farm in New Hampshire, where he wrote and taught school. Frost sold his property and moved to England (1912-15), where he established a literary reputation by publishing two volumes of poems: *A Boy's Will* (1913) and *North of Boston* (1914). Returning to New England, he became a professor of English at Amherst, and during his tenure (1916-38) published seven volumes of poems. Then, while continuing to write (several volumes of new poems, two verse plays, and editions of both selected and collected poems), he became a peripatetic teacher, poet-in-residence, or lecturer in dozens of colleges. During the past thirty years he has received honorary degrees, four Pulitzer Prizes, the gold medal of the National Institute of Arts and Letters, honorary lectureships, and other gestures of homage.

Robert Frost has never set down any systematic theory of poetry, but in his elliptical way he has said a lot about basic principles. He is concerned, for instance, with the form—he calls it the shape—of a poem; and he has chided those contemporaries who have experimented with form by imposing limitations on the verse: "Poetry, for example, was tried without punctuation. It was tried without capital letters. It was tried without any image but those to the eye. . . . It was tried without content under the trade name of poesie pure. It was tried without phrase, epigram, coherence, logic and consistency. It was tried without ability. . . . It was tried without feeling or sentiment like murder for small pay in the underworld. These many things was it tried without, and what had we left? Still something." That something, Frost suggests, is the conception of a dramatic situation: ". . . the object in writing poetry is to make all poems sound as different as possible from each other, and the resources for that of vowels, consonants, punctuation, syntax, words, sentences, meter are not enough. We need the help of context—meaning—subject matter. That is the greatest help towards variety." Theme alone, he adds, can steady us down.

The text of these selections is *Complete Poems of Robert Frost* (New York, 1949). The sequence, based on first publication, is altered for "The Pasture," the prefatory verse in all editions of the collected poems.

THE PASTURE

I'm going out to clean the pasture spring;
I'll only stop to rake the leaves away
(And wait to watch the water clear, I may):
I sha'n't be gone long.—You come too.

I'm going out to fetch the little calf   5
That's standing by the mother. It's so young
It totters when she licks it with her tongue.
I sha'n't be gone long.—You come too.

                                                    1914

MOWING

There was never a sound beside the wood but one,
And that was my long scythe whispering to the ground.
What was it it whispered? I knew not well myself;
Perhaps it was something about the heat of the sun,
Something, perhaps, about the lack of sound—   5
And that was why it whispered and did not speak.
It was no dream of the gift of idle hours,
Or easy gold at the hand of fay or elf:
Anything more than the truth would have seemed too weak
To the earnest love that laid the swale in rows,   10

Not without feeble-pointed spikes of flowers
(Pale orchises), and scared a bright green snake.
The fact is the sweetest dream that labor knows.
My long scythe whispered and left the hay to make.

                                                                    1913

THE DEATH OF THE HIRED MAN

Mary sat musing on the lamp-flame at the table
Waiting for Warren. When she heard his step,
She ran on tip-toe down the darkened passage
To meet him in the doorway with the news
And put him on his guard. 'Silas is back.'   5
She pushed him outward with her through the door
And shut it after her. 'Be kind,' she said.
She took the market things from Warren's arms
And set them on the porch, then drew him down
To sit beside her on the wooden steps.   10

'When was I ever anything but kind to him?
But I'll not have the fellow back,' he said.
'I told him so last haying, didn't I?
If he left then, I said, that ended it.
What good is he? Who else will harbor him   15
At his age for the little he can do?
What help he is there's no depending on.
Off he goes always when I need him most.
He thinks he ought to earn a little pay,
Enough at least to buy tobacco with,   20
So he won't have to beg and be beholden.
"All right," I say, "I can't afford to pay
Any fixed wages, though I wish I could."
"Someone else can." "Then someone else will have to."
I shouldn't mind his bettering himself   25
If that was what it was. You can be certain,
When he begins like that, there's someone at him
Trying to coax him off with pocket-money,—
In haying time, when any help is scarce.
In winter he comes back to us. I'm done.'   30

'Sh! not so loud: he'll hear you,' Mary said.

'I want him to: he'll have to soon or late.'

'He's worn out. He's asleep beside the stove.
When I came up from Rowe's I found him here,
Huddled against the barn-door fast asleep,   35
A miserable sight, and frightening, too—
You needn't smile—I didn't recognize him—
I wasn't looking for him—and he's changed.
Wait till you see.'

                          'Where did you say he'd been?'   40

'He didn't say. I dragged him to the house,
And gave him tea and tried to make him smoke.
I tried to make him talk about his travels.
Nothing would do: he just kept nodding off.'

'What did he say? Did he say anything?'   45

'But little.'

                  'Anything? Mary, confess
He said he'd come to ditch the meadow for me.'

'Warren!'

                  'But did he? I just want to know.'   50

'Of course he did. What would you have him say?
Surely you wouldn't grudge the poor old man
Some humble way to save his self-respect.
He added, if you really care to know,
He meant to clear the upper pasture, too.   55
That sounds like something you have heard before?
Warren, I wish you could have heard the way
He jumbled everything. I stopped to look
Two or three times—he made me feel so queer—

To see if he was talking in his sleep.   60
He ran on Harold Wilson—you remember—
The boy you had in haying four years since.
He's finished school, and teaching in his college.
Silas declares you'll have to get him back.
He says they two will make a team for work: 65
Between them they will lay this farm as smooth!
The way he mixed that in with other things.
He thinks young Wilson a likely lad, though daft
On education—you know how they fought
All through July under the blazing sun,   70
Silas up on the cart to build the load,
Harold along beside to pitch it on.'

'Yes, I took care to keep well out of earshot.'

'Well, those days trouble Silas like a dream.
You wouldn't think they would. How some things linger!   75
Harold's young college boy's assurance piqued him.
After so many years he still keeps finding
Good arguments he sees he might have used.
I sympathize. I know just how it feels
To think of the right thing to say too late.   80
Harold's associated in his mind with Latin.
He asked me what I thought of Harold's saying
He studied Latin like the violin
Because he liked it—that an argument!
He said he couldn't make the boy believe   85
He could find water with a hazel prong—
Which showed how much good school had ever done him.
He wanted to go over that. But most of all
He thinks if he could have another chance
To teach him how to build a load of hay—'   90

'I know, that's Silas' one accomplishment,
He bundles every forkful in its place,
And tags and numbers it for future reference,
So he can find and easily dislodge it
In the unloading. Silas does that well.   95

He takes it out in bunches like big birds' nests.
You never see him standing on the hay
He's trying to lift, straining to lift himself.'

'He thinks if he could teach him that, he'd be
Some good perhaps to someone in the world.   100
He hates to see a boy the fool of books.
Poor Silas, so concerned for other folk,
And nothing to look backward to with pride,
And nothing to look forward to with hope,
So now and never any different.'   105

Part of a moon was falling down the west,
Dragging the whole sky with it to the hills.
Its light poured softly in her lap. She saw it
And spread her apron to it. She put out her hand
Among the harp-like morning-glory strings,   110
Taut with the dew from garden bed to eaves,
As if she played unheard some tenderness
That wrought on him beside her in the night.
'Warren,' she said, 'he has come home to die:
You needn't be afraid he'll leave you this time.'   115

'Home,' he mocked gently.

                            'Yes, what else but home?
It all depends on what you mean by home.
Of course he's nothing to us, any more
Than was the hound that came a stranger to us   120
Out of the woods, worn out upon the trail.'

'Home is the place where, when you have to go there,
They have to take you in.'

                            'I should have called it
Something you somehow haven't to deserve.'   125

Warren leaned out and took a step or two,
Picked up a little stick, and brought it back
And broke it in his hand and tossed it by.

'Silas has better claim on us you think
Than on his brother? Thirteen little miles   130
As the road winds would bring him to his door.
Silas has walked that far no doubt today.
Why doesn't he go there? His brother's rich,
A somebody—director in the bank.'

'He never told us that.'   135

                'We know it though.'

'I think his brother ought to help, of course.
I'll see to that if there is need. He ought of right
To take him in, and might be willing to—
He may be better than appearances.   140
But have some pity on Silas. Do you think
If he had any pride in claiming kin
Or anything he looked for from his brother,
He'd keep so still about him all this time?

'I wonder what's between them.'   145

                        'I can tell you.
Silas is what he is—we wouldn't mind him—
But just the kind that kinsfolk can't abide.
He never did a thing so very bad.
He don't know why he isn't quite as good   150
As anybody. Worthless though he is,
He won't be made ashamed to please his brother.'

'*I* can't think Si ever hurt anyone.'

'No, but he hurt my heart the way he lay
And rolled his old head on that sharp-edged chair-back.   155
He wouldn't let me put him on the lounge.
You must go in and see what you can do.
I made the bed up for him there tonight.
You'll be surprised at him—how much he's broken.
His working days are done; I'm sure of it.'   160

'I'd not be in a hurry to say that.'

'I haven't been. Go, look, see for yourself.
But, Warren, please remember how it is:
He's come to help you ditch the meadow.
He has a plan. You mustn't laugh at him.   165
He may not speak of it, and then he may.
I'll sit and see if that small sailing cloud
Will hit or miss the moon.'

               It hit the moon.
Then there were three there, making a dim row,   170
The moon, the little silver cloud, and she.

Warren returned—too soon, it seemed to her,
Slipped to her side, caught up her hand and waited.

'Warren?' she questioned.

              'Dead,' was all he answered.   175

                          1913

AFTER APPLE-PICKING

My long two-pointed ladder's sticking through a tree
Toward heaven still,
And there's a barrel that I didn't fill
Beside it, and there may be two or three
Apples I didn't pick upon some bough.   5
But I am done with apple-picking now.
Essence of winter sleep is on the night,
The scent of apples: I am drowsing off.
I cannot rub the strangeness from my sight
I got from looking through a pane of glass   10
I skimmed this morning from the drinking trough
And held against the world of hoary grass.
It melted and I let it fall and break.
But I was well
Upon my way to sleep before it fell,   15

And I could tell
What form my dreaming was about to take.
Magnified apples appear and disappear,
Stem end and blossom end,
And every fleck of russet showing clear. 20
My instep arch not only keeps the ache,
It keeps the pressure of a ladder-round.
I feel the ladder sway as the boughs bend.
And I keep hearing from the cellar bin
The rumbling sound 25
Of load on load of apples coming in.
For I have had too much
Of apple-picking: I am overtired
Of the great harvest I myself desired.
There were ten thousand thousand fruit to touch, 30
Cherish in hand, lift down, and not let fall.
For all
That struck the earth,
No matter if not bruised or spiked with stubble.
Went surely to the cider-apple heap 35
As of no worth.
One can see what will trouble
This sleep of mine, whatever sleep it is.
Were he not gone,
The woodchuck could say whether it's like his 40
Long sleep, as I describe its coming on,
Or just some human sleep.

1914

BIRCHES

When I see birches bend to left and right
Across the lines of straighter darker trees,
I like to think some boy's been swinging them.
But swinging doesn't bend them down to stay
As ice-storms do. Often you must have seen them 5
Loaded with ice a sunny winter morning
After a rain. They click upon themselves
As the breeze rises, and turn many-colored

As the stir cracks and crazes their enamel.
Soon the sun's warmth makes them shed crystal shells   10
Shattering and avalanching on the snow-crust—
Such heaps of broken glass to sweep away
You'd think the inner dome of heaven had fallen.
They are dragged to the withered bracken by the load,
And they seem not to break; though once they are bowed   15
So low for long, they never right themselves:
You may see their trunks arching in the woods
Years afterwards, trailing their leaves on the ground
Like girls on hands and knees that throw their hair
Before them over their heads to dry in the sun.   20
But I was going to say when Truth broke in
With all her matter-of-fact about the ice-storm
I should prefer to have some boy bend them
As he went out and in to fetch the cows—
Some boy too far from town to learn baseball,   25
Whose only play was what he found himself,
Summer or winter, and could play alone.
One by one he subdued his father's trees
By riding them down over and over again
Until he took the stiffness out of them,   30
And not one but hung limp, not one was left
For him to conquer. He learned all there was
To learn about not launching out too soon
And so not carrying the tree away
Clear to the ground. He always kept his poise   35
To the top branches, climbing carefully
With the same pains you use to fill a cup
Up to the brim, and even above the brim.
Then he flung outward, feet first, with a swish,
Kicking his way down through the air to the ground.   40
So was I once myself a swinger of birches.
And so I dream of going back to be.
It's when I'm weary of considerations,
And life is too much like a pathless wood
Where your face burns and tickles with the cobwebs   45
Broken across it, and one eye is weeping
From a twig's having lashed across it open.
I'd like to get away from earth awhile

And then come back to it and begin over.
May no fate willfully misunderstand me 50
And half grant what I wish and snatch me away
Not to return. Earth's the right place for love:
I don't know where it's likely to go better.
I'd like to go by climbing a birch tree,
And climb black branches up a snow-white trunk 55
Toward heaven, till the tree could bear no more,
But dipped its top and set me down again.
That would be good both going and coming back.
One could do worse than be a swinger of birches.

1915

'OUT, OUT—'

The buzz saw snarled and rattled in the yard
And made dust and dropped stove-length sticks of
    wood,
Sweet-scented stuff when the breeze drew across it.
And from there those that lifted eyes could count
Five mountain ranges one behind the other 5
Under the sunset far into Vermont.
And the saw snarled and rattled, snarled and rattled,
As it ran light, or had to bear a load.
And nothing happened: day was all but done.
Call it a day, I wish they might have said 10
To please the boy by giving him the half hour
That a boy counts so much when saved from work.
His sister stood beside them in her apron
To tell them 'Supper.' At the word, the saw,
As if to prove saws knew what supper meant, 15
Leaped out at the boy's hand, or seemed to leap—
He must have given the hand. However it was,
Neither refused the meeting. But the hand!
The boy's first outcry was a rueful laugh,
As he swung toward them holding up the hand 20
Half in appeal, but half as if to keep
The life from spilling. Then the boy saw all—
Since he was old enough to know, big boy

Doing a man's work, though a child at heart—
He saw all spoiled. 'Don't let him cut my hand off—   25
The doctor, when he comes. Don't let him, sister!'
So. But the hand was gone already.
The doctor put him in the dark of ether.
He lay and puffed his lips out with his breath.
And then—the watcher at his pulse took fright.   30
No one believed. They listened at his heart.
Little—less—nothing!—and that ended it.
No more to build on there. And they, since they
Were not the one dead, turned to their affairs.

1916

MEETING AND PASSING

As I went down the hill along the wall
There was a gate I had leaned at for the view
And had just turned from when I first saw you
As you came up the hill. We met. But all
We did that day was mingle great and small   5
Footprints in summer dust as if we drew
The figure of our being less than two
But more than one as yet. Your parasol
Pointed the decimal off with one deep thrust.
And all the time we talked you seemed to see   10
Something down there to smile at in the dust.
(Oh, it was without prejudice to me!)
Afterward I went past what you had passed
Before we met and you what I had passed.

1916

THE AX-HELVE

I've known ere now an interfering branch
Of alder catch my lifted ax behind me.
But that was in the woods, to hold my hand
From striking at another alder's roots,

And that was, as I say, an alder branch.   5
This was a man, Baptiste, who stole one day
Behind me on the snow in my own yard
Where I was working at the chopping-block,
And cutting nothing not cut down already.
He caught my ax expertly on the rise,   10
When all my strength put forth was in his favor,
Held it a moment where it was, to calm me,
Then took it from me—and I let him take it.
I didn't know him well enough to know
What it was all about. There might be something   15
He had in mind to say to a bad neighbor
He might prefer to say to him disarmed.
But all he had to tell me in French-English
Was what he thought of—not me, but my ax,
Me only as I took my ax to heart.   20
It was the bad ax-helve someone had sold me—
'Made on machine,' he said, plowing the grain
With a thick thumbnail to show how it ran
Across the handle's long drawn serpentine,
Like the two strokes across a dollar sign.   25
'You give her one good crack, she's snap raght off.
Den where's your hax-ead flying t'rough de hair?'
Admitted; and yet, what was that to him?

'Come on my house and I put you one in
What's las' awhile—good hick'ry what's grow crooked.   30
De second growt' I cut myself—tough, tough!'

Something to sell? That wasn't how it sounded.

'Den when you say you come? It's cost you nothing.
Tonaght?'

        As well tonight as any night.   35

Beyond an over-warmth of kitchen stove
My welcome differed from no other welcome.
Baptiste knew best why I was where I was.
So long as he would leave enough unsaid,

I shouldn't mind his being overjoyed   40
(If overjoyed he was) at having got me
Where I must judge if what he knew about an ax
That not everybody else knew was to count
For nothing in the measure of a neighbor.
Hard if, though cast away for life with Yankees,   45
A Frenchman couldn't get his human rating!

Mrs. Baptiste came in and rocked a chair
That had as many motions as the world:
One back and forward, in and out of shadow,
That got her nowhere; one more gradual,   50
Sideways, that would have run her on the stove
In time, had she not realized her danger
And caught herself up bodily, chair and all,
And set herself back where she started from.
'She ain't spick too much Henglish—dat's too bad.'   55

I was afraid, in brightening first on me,
Then on Baptiste, as if she understood
What passed between us, she was only feigning.
Baptiste was anxious for her; but no more
Than for himself, so placed he couldn't hope   60
To keep his bargain of the morning with me
In time to keep me from suspecting him
Of really never having meant to keep it.

Needlessly soon he had his ax-helves out,
A quiverful to choose from, since he wished me   65
To have the best he had, or had to spare—
Not for me to ask which, when what he took
Had beauties he had to point me out at length
To insure their not being wasted on me.
He liked to have it slender as a whipstock,   70
Free from the least knot, equal to the strain
Of bending like a sword across the knee.
He showed me that the lines of a good helve
Were native to the grain before the knife
Expressed them, and its curves were no false curves   75

Put on it from without. And there its strength lay
For the hard work. He chafed its long white body
From end to end with his rough hand shut round it.
He tried it at the eye-hole in the ax-head.
'Hahn, hahn,' he mused, 'don't need much taking down.' 80
Baptiste knew how to make a short job long
For love of it, and yet not waste time either.

Do you know, what we talked about was knowledge?
Baptiste on his defense about the children
He kept from school, or did his best to keep— 85
Whatever school and children and our doubts
Of laid-on education had to do
With the curves of his ax-helves and his having
Used these unscrupulously to bring me
To see for once the inside of his house. 90
Was I desired in friendship, partly as someone
To leave it to, whether the right to hold
Such doubts of education should depend
Upon the education of those who held them?

But now he brushed the shavings from his knee 95
And stood the ax there on its horse's hoof,
Erect, but not without its waves, as when
The snake stood up for evil in the Garden,—
Top-heavy with a heaviness his short,
Thick hand made light of, steel-blue chin drawn down 100
And in a little—a French touch in that.
Baptiste drew back and squinted at it, pleased;
'See how she's cock her head!'

1917

FIRE AND ICE

Some say the world will end in fire,
Some say in ice.
From what I've tasted of desire
I hold with those who favor fire.

But if it had to perish twice,   5
I think I know enough of hate
To say that for destruction ice
Is also great
And would suffice

1920

STOPPING BY WOODS ON A SNOWY EVENING

Whose woods these are I think I know.
His house is in the village though;
He will not see me stopping here
To watch his woods fill up with snow.

My little horse must think it queer   5
To stop without a farmhouse near
Between the woods and frozen lake
The darkest evening of the year.

He gives his harness bells a shake
To ask if there is some mistake.   10
The only other sound's the sweep
Of easy wind and downy flake.

The woods are lovely, dark and deep,
But I have promises to keep,
And miles to go before I sleep,   15
And miles to go before I sleep.

1923

NEW HAMPSHIRE

I met a lady from the South who said
(You won't believe she said it, but she said it):
'None of my family ever worked, or had
A thing to sell.' I don't suppose the work
Much matters. You may work for all of me.   5

I've seen the time I've had to work myself.
The having anything to sell is what
Is the disgrace in man or state or nation.

I met a traveler from Arkansas
Who boasted of his state as beautiful   10
For diamonds and apples. 'Diamonds
And apples in commercial quantities?'
I asked him, on my guard. 'Oh, yes,' he answered,
Off his. The time was evening in the Pullman.
'I see the porter's made your bed,' I told him.   15

I met a Californian who would
Talk California—a state so blessed,
He said, in climate, none had ever died there
A natural death, and Vigilance Committees
Had had to organize to stock the graveyards   20
And vindicate the state's humanity.
'Just the way Stefansson runs on,' I murmured,
'About the British Arctic. That's what comes
Of being in the market with a climate.'

I met a poet from another state,   25
A zealot full of fluid inspiration,
Who in the name of fluid inspiration,
But in the best style of bad salesmanship,
Angrily tried to make me write a protest
(In verse I think) against the Volstead Act.   30
He didn't even offer me a drink
Until I asked for one to steady *him*.
This is called having an idea to sell.

It never could have happened in New Hampshire.

The only person really soiled with trade   35
I ever stumbled on in old New Hampshire
Was someone who had just come back ashamed
From selling things in California.
He'd built a noble mansard roof with balls
On turrets like Constantinople, deep   40

In woods some ten miles from a railroad station,
As if to put forever out of mind
The hope of being, as we say, received.
I found him standing at the close of day
Inside the threshold of his open barn,   45
Like a lone actor on a gloomy stage—
And recognized him through the iron gray
In which his face was muffled to the eyes
As an old boyhood friend, and once indeed
A drover with me on the road to Brighton.   50
His farm was 'grounds,' and not a farm at all;
His house among the local sheds and shanties
Rose like a factor's at a trading station.
And he was rich, and I was still a rascal.
I couldn't keep from asking impolitely,   55
Where had he been and what had he been doing?
How did he get so? (Rich was understood.)
In dealing in 'old rags' in San Francisco.
Oh, it was terrible as well could be.
We both of us turned over in our graves.   60
Just specimens is all New Hampshire has,
One each of everything as in a show-case
Which naturally she doesn't care to sell.

She had one President (pronounce him Purse,
And make the most of it for better or worse.   65
He's your one chance to score against the state).
She had one Daniel Webster. He was all
The Daniel Webster ever was or shall be.
She had the Dartmouth needed to produce him.

I call her old. She has one family   70
Whose claim is good to being settled here
Before the era of colonization,
And before that of exploration even.
John Smith remarked them as he coasted by
Dangling their legs and fishing off a wharf   75
At the Isles of Shoals, and satisfied himself
They weren't Red Indians, but veritable
Pre-primitives of the white race, dawn people,

Like those who furnished Adam's sons with wives;
However uninnocent they may have been   80
In being there so early in our history.
They'd been there then a hundred years or more.
Pity he didn't ask what they were up to
At that date with a wharf already built,
And take their name. They've since told me their name— 85
Today an honored one in Nottingham.
As for what they were up to more than fishing—
Suppose they weren't behaving Puritanly,
The hour had not yet struck for being good,
Mankind had not yet gone on the Sabbatical.   90
It became an explorer of the deep
Not to explore too deep in others' business.
Did you but know of him, New Hampshire has
One real reformer who would change the world
So it would be accepted by two classes,   95
Artists the minute they set up as artists,
Before, that is, they are themselves accepted,
And boys the minute they get out of college.
I can't help thinking those are tests to go by.

And she has one I don't know what to call him,   100
Who comes from Philadelphia every year
With a great flock of chickens of rare breeds
He wants to give the educational
Advantages of growing almost wild
Under the watchful eye of hawk and eagle—   105
Dorkings because they're spoken of by Chaucer,
Sussex because they're spoken of by Herrick.

She has a touch of gold. New Hampshire gold—
You may have heard of it. I had a farm
Offered me not long since up Berlin way   110
With a mine on it that was worked for gold;
But not gold in commercial quantities,
Just enough gold to make the engagement rings
And marriage rings of those who owned the farm.
What gold more innocent could one have asked for?   115
One of my children ranging after rocks

Lately brought home from Andover or Canaan
A specimen of beryl with a trace
Of radium. I know with radium
The trace would have to be the merest trace   120
To be below the threshold of commercial;
But trust New Hampshire not to have enough
Of radium or anything to sell.

A specimen of everything, I said.
She has one witch—old style. She lives in Colebrook.   125
(The only other witch I ever met
Was lately at a cut-glass dinner in Boston.
There were four candles and four people present.
The witch was young, and beautiful (new style),
And open-minded. She was free to question   130
Her gift for reading letters locked in boxes.
Why was it so much greater when the boxes
Were metal than it was when they were wooden?
It made the world seem so mysterious.
The S'ciety for Psychical Research   135
Was cognizant. Her husband was worth millions.
I think he owned some shares in Harvard College.)

New Hampshire *used* to have at Salem
A company we called the White Corpuscles,
Whose duty was at any hour of night   140
To rush in sheets and fools' caps where they smelled
A thing the least bit doubtfully perscented
And give someone the Skipper Ireson's Ride.

One each of everything as in a show-case.
More than enough land for a specimen   145
You'll say she has, but there there enters in
Something else to protect her from herself.
There quality makes up for quantity.
Not even New Hampshire farms are much for sale.
The farm I made my home on in the mountains   150
I had to take by force rather than buy.
I caught the owner outdoors by himself
Raking up after winter, and I said,

'I'm going to put you off this farm: I want it!'
'Where are you going to put me? In the road?'   155
'I'm going to put you on the farm next to it.'
'Why won't the farm next to it do for you?'
'I like this better.' It was really better.

Apples? New Hampshire has them, but unsprayed,
With no suspicion in stem-end or blossom-end   160
Of vitriol or arsenate of lead,
And so not good for anything but cider.
Her unpruned grapes are flung like lariats
Far up the birches out of reach of man.

A state producing precious metals, stones,   165
And—writing; none of these except perhaps
The precious literature in quantity
Or quality to worry the producer
About disposing of it. Do you know,
Considering the market, there are more   170
Poems produced than any other thing?
No wonder poets sometimes have to *seem*
So much more business-like than business men.
Their wares are so much harder to get rid of.

She's one of the two best states in the Union.   175
Vermont's the other. And the two have been
Yoke-fellows in the sap-yoke from of old
In many Marches. And they lie like wedges,
Thick end to thin end and thin end to thick end,
And are a figure of the way the strong   180
Of mind and strong of arm should fit together,
One thick where one is thin and vice versa.
New Hampshire raises the Connecticut
In a trout hatchery near Canada,
But soon divides the river with Vermont.   185
Both are delightful states for their absurdly
Small towns—Lost Nation, Bungey, Muddy Boo,
Poplin, Still Corners (so called not because
The place is silent all day long, nor yet
Because it boasts a whisky still—because   190

It set out once to be a city and still
Is only corners, cross-roads in a wood).
And I remember one whose name appeared
Between the pictures on a movie screen
Election night once in Franconia,   195
When everything had gone Republican
And Democrats were sore in need of comfort:
Easton goes Democratic, Wilson 4
Hughes 2. And everybody to the saddest
Laughed the loud laugh, the big laugh at the little.   200
New York (five million) laughs at Manchester,
Manchester (sixty or seventy thousand) laughs
At Littleton (four thousand), Littleton
Laughs at Franconia (seven hundred), and
Franconia laughs, I fear,—did laugh that night—   205
At Easton. What has Easton left to laugh at,
And like the actress exclaim, 'Oh, my God' at?
There's Bungey; and for Bungey there are towns,
Whole townships named but without population.

Anything I can say about New Hampshire   210
Will serve almost as well about Vermont,
Excepting that they differ in their mountains.
The Vermont mountains stretch extended straight;
New Hampshire mountains curl up in a coil.

I had been coming to New Hampshire mountains.   215
And here I am and what am I to say?
Here first my theme becomes embarrassing.
Emerson said, 'The God who made New Hampshire
Taunted the lofty land with little men.'
Another Massachusetts poet said,   220
'I go no more to summer in New Hampshire.
I've given up my summer place in Dublin.'
But when I asked to know what ailed New Hampshire,
She said she couldn't stand the people in it,
The little men (it's Massachusetts speaking)   225
And when I asked to know what ailed the people,
She said, 'Go read your own books and find out.'
I may as well confess myself the author

Of several books against the world in general.
To take them as against a special state   230
Or even nation's to restrict my meaning.
I'm what is called a sensibilitist,
Or otherwise an environmentalist.
I refuse to adapt myself a mite
To any change from hot to cold, from wet   235
To dry, from poor to rich, or back again.
I make a virtue of my suffering
From nearly everything that goes on round me.
In other words, I know wherever I am,
Being the creature of literature I am,   240
I shall not lack for pain to keep me awake.
Kit Marlowe taught me how to say my prayers:
'Why, this is Hell, nor am I out of it.'
Samoa, Russia, Ireland, I complain of,
No less than England, France, and Italy.   245
Because I wrote my novels in New Hampshire
Is no proof that I aimed them at New Hampshire.

When I left Massachusetts years ago
Between two days, the reason why I sought
New Hampshire, not Connecticut,   250
Rhode Island, New York, or Vermont was this:
Where I was living then, New Hampshire offered
The nearest boundary to escape across.
I hadn't an illusion in my hand-bag
About the people being better there   255
Than those I left behind. I thought they weren't.
I thought they couldn't be. And yet they were.
I'd sure had no such friends in Massachusetts
As Hall of Windham, Gay of Atkinson,
Bartlett of Raymond (now of Colorado),   260
Harris of Derry, and Lynch of Bethlehem.

The glorious bards of Massachusetts seem
To want to make New Hampshire people over.
They taunt the lofty land with little men.
I don't know what to say about the people.   265
For art's sake one could almost wish them worse

Rather than better. How are we to write
The Russian novel in America
As long as life goes so unterribly?
There is the pinch from which our only outcry   270
In literature to date is heard to come.
We get what little misery we can
Out of not having cause for misery.
It makes the guild of novel writers sick
To be expected to be Dostoievskis   275
On nothing worse than too much luck and comfort.
This is not sorrow, though; it's just the vapors,
And recognized as such in Russia itself
Under the new régime, and so forbidden.
If well it is with Russia, then feel free   280
To say so or be stood against the wall
And shot. It's Pollyanna now or death.
This, then, is the new freedom we hear tell of;
And very sensible. No state can build
A literature that shall at once be sound   285
And sad on a foundation of well-being.

To show the level of intelligence
Among us: it was just a Warren farmer
Whose horse had pulled him short up in the road
By me, a stranger. This is what he said,   290
From nothing but embarrassment and want
Of anything more sociable to say:
'You hear those hound-dogs sing on Moosilauke?
Well they remind me of the hue and cry
We've heard against the Mid-Victorians   295
And never rightly understood till Bryan
Retired from politics and joined the chorus.
The matter with the Mid-Victorians
Seems to have been a man named John L. Darwin.'
'Go 'long,' I said to him, he to his horse.   300

I knew a man who failing as a farmer
Burned down his farmhouse for the fire insurance,
And spent the proceeds on a telescope
To satisfy a life-long curiosity

About our place among the infinities.   305
And how was that for other-worldliness?

If I must choose which I would elevate—
The people or the already lofty mountains,
I'd elevate the already lofty mountains.
The only fault I find with old New Hampshire   310
Is that her mountains aren't quite high enough.
I was not always so; I've come to be so.
How, to my sorrow, how have I attained
A height from which to look down critical
On mountains? What has given me assurance   315
To say what height becomes New Hampshire mountains,
Or any mountains? Can it be some strength
I feel as of an earthquake in my back
To heave them higher to the morning star?
Can it be foreign travel in the Alps?   320
Or having seen and credited a moment
The solid molding of vast peaks of cloud
Behind the pitiful reality
Of Lincoln, Lafayette, and Liberty?
Or some such sense as says how high shall jet   325
The fountain in proportion to the basin?
No, none of these has raised me to my throne
Of intellectual dissatisfaction,
But the sad accident of having seen
Our actual mountains given in a map   330
Of early times as twice the height they are—
Ten thousand feet instead of only five—
Which shows how sad an accident may be.
Five thousand is no longer high enough.
Whereas I never had a good idea   335
About improving people in the world,
Here I am over-fertile in suggestion,
And cannot rest from planning day or night
How high I'd thrust the peaks in summer snow
To tap the upper sky and draw a flow   340
Of frosty night air on the vale below
Down from the stars to freeze the dew as starry.

The more sensibilitist I am
The more I seem to want my mountains wild;
The way the wiry gang-boss liked the log-jam.   345
After he'd picked the lock and got it started,
He dodged a log that lifted like an arm
Against the sky to break his back for him,
Then came in dancing, skipping, with his life
Across the roar and chaos, and the words   350
We saw him say along the zigzag journey
Were doubtless as the words we heard him say
On coming nearer: 'Wasn't she an *i*-deal
Son-of-a-bitch? You bet she was an *i*-deal.'

For all her mountains fall a little short,   355
Her people not quite short enough for Art,
She's still New Hampshire, a most restful state.

Lately in converse with a New York alec
About the new school of the pseudo-phallic,
I found myself in a close corner where   360
I had to make an almost funny choice.
'Choose you which you will be—a prude, or puke,
Mewling and puking in the public arms.'
'Me for the hills where I don't have to choose.'
'But if you had to choose, which would you be?'   365
I wouldn't be a prude afraid of nature.
I know a man who took a double ax
And went alone against a grove of trees;
But his heart failing him, he dropped the ax
And ran for shelter quoting Matthew Arnold: 370
'Nature is cruel, man is sick of blood;
There's been enough shed without shedding mine.
Remember Birnam Wood! The wood's in flux!'
He had a special terror of the flux
That showed itself in dendrophobia.   375
The only decent tree had been to mill
And educated into boards, he said.
He knew too well for any earthly use
The line where man leaves off and nature starts,
And never over-stepped it save in dreams.   380

He stood on the safe side of the line talking;
Which is sheer Matthew Arnoldism,
The cult of one who owned himself 'a foiled,
Circuitous wanderer,' and 'took dejectedly
His seat upon the intellectual throne.'   385
Agreed in frowning on these improvised
Altars the woods are full of nowadays,
Again as in the days when Ahaz sinned
By worship under green trees in the open.
Scarcely a mile but that I come on one,   390
A black-cheeked stone and stick of rain-washed charcoal
Even to say the groves were God's first temples
Comes too near to Ahaz' sin for safety.
Nothing not built with hands of course is sacred.
But here is not a question of what's sacred;   395
Rather of what to face or run away from.
I'd hate to be a runaway from nature.
And neither would I choose to be a puke
Who cares not what he does in company,
And, when he can't do anything, falls back   400
On words, and tries his worst to make words speak
Louder than actions, and sometimes achieves it.
It seems a narrow choice the age insists on.
How about being a good Greek, for instance?
That course, they tell me, isn't offered this year.   405
'Come, but this isn't choosing—puke or prude?'
Well, if I have to choose one or the other,
I choose to be a plain New Hampshire farmer
With an income in cash of say a thousand
(From say a publisher in New York City).   410
It's restful to arrive at a decision,
And restful just to think about New Hampshire.
At present I am living in Vermont.

                                                        1923

ACQUAINTED WITH THE NIGHT

I have been one acquainted with the night.
I have walked out in rain—and back in rain.
I have outwalked the furthest city light.

I have looked down the saddest city lane.
I have passed by the watchman on his beat   5
And dropped my eyes, unwilling to explain.

I have stood still and stopped the sound of feet
When far away an interrupted cry
Came over houses from another street,

But not to call me back or say good-by;   10
And further still at an unearthly height,
One luminary clock against the sky

Proclaimed the time was neither wrong nor right.
I have been one acquainted with the night.
                                                    1928

DUST IN THE EYES

If, as they say, some dust thrown in my eyes
Will keep my talk from getting overwise,
I'm not the one for putting off the proof.
Let it be overwhelming, off a roof
And round a corner, blizzard snow for dust,   5
And blind me to a standstill if it must.
                                                    1928

THE LOVELY SHALL BE CHOOSERS

The Voice said, 'Hurl her down!'

The Voices, 'How far down?'

'Seven levels of the world.'

'How much time have we?'

'Take twenty years.   5
She *would* refuse love safe with wealth and honor!
The lovely shall be choosers, shall they?
Then let them choose!'

'Then we shall let her choose?'

'Yes, let her choose.   10
Take up the task beyond her choosing.'

Invisible hands crowded on her shoulder
In readiness to weigh upon her.
But she stood straight still,
In broad round ear-rings, gold and jet with pearls   15
And broad round suchlike brooch,
Her cheeks high colored,
Proud and the pride of friends.

The Voice asked, 'You can let her choose?'
'Yes, we can let her and still triumph.'   20

'Do it by joys, and leave her always blameless.
Be her first joy her wedding,
That though a wedding,
Is yet—well something they know, he and she.
And after that her next joy   25
That though she grieves, her grief is secret:
Those friends know nothing of her grief to make
    it shameful.
Her third joy that though now they cannot help
    but know,
They move in pleasure too far off
To think much or much care.   30
Give her a child at either knee for fourth joy
To tell once and once only, for them never to forget,
How once she walked in brightness,
And make them see it in the winter firelight.
But give her friends for then she dare not tell   35
For their foregone incredulousness.
And be her next joy this:
Her never having deigned to tell them.
Make her among the humblest even
Seem to them less than they are.   40
Hopeless of being known for what she has been,
Failing of being loved for what she is,

Give her the comfort for her sixth of knowing
She fails from strangeness to a way of life
She came to from too high too late to learn.   45
Then send some *one* with eyes to see
And wonder at her where she is,
And words to wonder in her hearing how she came
    there,
But without time to linger for her story.
Be her last joy her heart's going out to this one   50
So that she almost speaks.
You know them—seven in all.'

'Trust us,' the Voices said.

                                                      1929

MOON COMPASSES

I stole forth dimly in the dripping pause
Between two downpours to see what there was.
And a masked moon had spread down compass rays
To a cone mountain in the midnight haze,
As if the final estimate were hers,   5
And as it measured in her calipers,
The mountain stood exalted in its place.
So love will take between the hands a face. . . .

                                                      1934

TWO TRAMPS IN MUD TIME

Out of the mud two strangers came
And caught me splitting wood in the yard.
And one of them put me off my aim
By hailing cheerily 'Hit them hard!'
I knew pretty well why he dropped behind   5
And let the other go on a way.
I knew pretty well what he had in mind:
He wanted to take my job for pay.

Good blocks of oak it was I split,
As large around as the chopping block;   10
And every piece I squarely hit
Fell splinterless as a cloven rock.
The blows that a life of self-control
Spares to strike for the common good
That day, giving a loose to my soul,   15
I spent on the unimportant wood.

The sun was warm but the wind was chill.
You know how it is with an April day
When the sun is out and the wind is still,
You're one month on in the middle of May.   20
But if you so much as dare to speak,
A cloud comes over the sunlit arch,
A wind comes off a frozen peak,
And you're two months back in the middle of March.

A bluebird comes tenderly up to alight   25
And turns to the wind to unruffle a plume
His song so pitched as not to excite
A single flower as yet to bloom.
It is snowing a flake: and he half knew
Winter was only playing possum.   30
Except in color he isn't blue,
But he wouldn't advise a thing to blossom.

The water for which we may have to look
In summertime with a witching-wand,
In every wheelrut's now a brook,   35
In every print of a hoof a pond.
Be glad of water, but don't forget
The lurking frost in the earth beneath
That will steal forth after the sun is set
And show on the water its crystal teeth.   40

The time when most I loved my task
These two must make me love it more
By coming with what they came to ask.
You'd think I never had felt before

The weight of an ax-head poised aloft,   45
The grip on earth of outspread feet.
The life of muscles rocking soft
And smooth and moist in vernal heat.

Out of the woods two hulking tramps
(From sleeping God knows where last night,   50
But not long since in the lumber camps).
They thought all chopping was theirs of right.
Men of the woods and lumberjacks,
They judged me by their appropriate tool.
Except as a fellow handled an ax,   55
They had no way of knowing a fool.

Nothing on either side was said.
They knew they had but to stay their stay
And all their logic would fill my head:
As that I had no right to play   60
With what was another man's work for gain.
My right might be love but theirs was need.
And where the two exist in twain
Theirs was the better right—agreed.

But yield who will to their separation,   65
My object in living is to unite
My avocation and my vocation
As my two eyes make one in sight.
Only where love and need are one,
And the work is play for mortal stakes,   70
Is the deed ever really done
For Heaven and the future's sakes.

                                          1934

NOT QUITE SOCIAL

Some of you will be glad I did what I did,
And the rest won't want to punish me too severely
For finding a thing to do that though not forbid
Yet wasn't enjoined and wasn't expected clearly.

To punish me overcruelly wouldn't be right   5
For merely giving you once more gentle proof
That the city's hold on a man is no more tight
Than when its walls rose higher than any roof.

You may taunt me with not being able to flee the earth.
You have me there, but loosely as I would be held.   10
The way of understanding is partly mirth.
I would not be taken as ever having rebelled.

And anyone is free to condemn me to death—
If he leaves it to nature to carry out the sentence.
I shall will to the common stock of air my breath   15
And pay a death-tax of fairly polite repentance.

                                                        1935

THE WHITE-TAILED HORNET

The white-tailed hornet lives in a balloon
That floats against the ceiling of the woodshed.
The exit he comes out at like a bullet
Is like the pupil of a pointed gun.
And having power to change his aim in flight,   5
He comes out more unerring than a bullet.
Verse could be written on the certainty
With which he penetrates my best defense
Of whirling hands and arms about the head
To stab me in the sneeze-nerve of a nostril.   10
Such is the instinct of it I allow.
Yet how about the insect certainty
That in the neighborhood of home and children
Is such an execrable judge of motives
As not to recognize in me the exception   15
I like to think I am in everything—
One who would never hang above a bookcase
His Japanese crepe-paper globe for trophy?
He stung me first and stung me afterward.
He rolled me off the field head over heels,   20
And would not listen to my explanations.

That's when I went as visitor to his house.
As visitor at my house he is better.
Hawking for flies about the kitchen door,
In at one door perhaps and out another,   25
Trust him then not to put you in the wrong,
He won't misunderstand your freest movements.
Let him light on your skin unless you mind
So many prickly grappling feet at once.
He's after the domesticated fly   30
To feed his thumping grubs as big as he is.
Here he is at his best, but even here—
I watched him where he swooped, he pounced, he
     struck;
But what he found he had was just a nailhead.
He struck a second time. Another nailhead.   35
'Those are just nailheads. Those are fastened down.'
Then disconcerted and not unannoyed,
He stooped and struck a little huckleberry
The way a player curls around a football.
'Wrong shape, wrong color, and wrong scent,' I
     said.   40
The huckleberry rolled him on his head.
At last it was a fly. He shot and missed;
And the fly circled round him in derision.
But for the fly he might have made me think
He had been at his poetry, comparing   45
Nailhead with fly and fly with huckleberry:
How like a fly, how very like a fly.
But the real fly he missed would never do;
The missed fly made me dangerously skeptic.

Won't this whole instinct matter bear revision?   50
Won't almost any theory bear revision?
To err is human, not to, animal.
Or so we pay the compliment to instinct,
Only too liberal of our compliment
That really takes away instead of gives.   55
Our worship, humor, conscientiousness
Went long since to the dogs under the table.
And serves us right for having instituted

Downward comparisons. As long on earth
As our comparisons were stoutly upward   60
With gods and angels, we were men at least,
But little lower than the gods and angels.
But once comparisons were yielded downward,
Once we began to see our images
Reflected in the mud and even dust,   65
'Twas disillusion upon disillusion.
We were lost piecemeal to the animals,
Like people thrown out to delay the wolves.
Nothing but fallibility was left us,
And this day's work made even that seem doubtful.   70

1936

THE SILKEN TENT

She is as in a field a silken tent
At midday when a sunny summer breeze
Has dried the dew and all its ropes relent,
So that in guys it gently sways at ease,
And its supporting central cedar pole,   5
That is its pinnacle to heavenward
And signifies the sureness of the soul,
Seems to owe naught to any single cord,
But strictly held by none, is loosely bound
By countless silken ties of love and thought   10
To everything on earth the compass round, .
And only by one's going slightly taut
In the capriciousness of summer air
Is of the slightest bondage made aware.

1939

THE MOST OF IT

He thought he kept the universe alone;
For all the voice in answer he could wake
Was but the mocking echo of his own

From some tree-hidden cliff across the lake.
Some morning from the boulder-broken beach   5
He would cry out on life, that what it wants
Is not its own love back in copy speech,
But counter-love, original response.
And nothing ever came of what he cried
Unless it was the embodiment that crashed   10
In the cliff's talus on the other side,
And then in the far distant water splashed,
But after a time allowed for it to swim,
Instead of proving human when it neared
And someone else additional to him,   15
As a great buck it powerfully appeared,
Pushing the crumpled water up ahead,
And landed pouring like a waterfall,
And stumbled through the rocks with horny tread,
And forced the underbrush—and that was all.   20

                                              1942

THE SUBVERTED FLOWER

She drew back; he was calm:
'It is this that had the power.'
And he lashed his open palm
With the tender-headed flower.
He smiled for her to smile,   5
But she was either blind
Or willfully unkind.
He eyed her for a while
For a woman and a puzzle.
He flicked and flung the flower,   10
And another sort of smile
Caught up like finger tips
The corners of his lips
And cracked his ragged muzzle.
She was standing to the waist   15
In goldenrod and brake,
Her shining hair displaced.
He stretched her either arm

As if she made it ache
To clasp her—not to harm; 20
As if he could not spare
To touch her neck and hair.
'If this has come to us
And not to me alone—'
So she thought she heard him say; 25
Though with every word he spoke
His lips were sucked and blown
And the effort made him choke
Like a tiger at a bone.
She had to lean away. 30
She dared not stir a foot,
Lest movement should provoke
The demon of pursuit
That slumbers in a brute.
It was then her mother's call 35
From inside the garden wall
Made her steal a look of fear
To see if he could hear
And would pounce to end it all
Before her mother came. 40
She looked and saw the shame:
A hand hung like a paw,
An arm worked like a saw
As if to be persuasive,
An ingratiating laugh 45
That cut the snout in half,
An eye become evasive.
A girl could only see
That a flower had marred a man,
But what she could not see 50
Was that the flower might be
Other than base and fetid:
That the flower had done but part,
And what the flower began
Her own too meager heart 55
Had terribly completed.
She looked and saw the worst.
And the dog or what it was,

Obeying bestial laws,
A coward save at night,   60
Turned from the place and ran.
She heard him stumble first
And use his hands in flight.
She heard him bark outright.
And oh, for one so young   65
The bitter words she spit
Like some tenacious bit
That will not leave the tongue.
She plucked her lips for it,
And still the horror clung.   70
Her mother wiped the foam
From her chin, picked up her comb
And drew her backward home.

                                                 1942

IN A POEM

The sentencing goes blithely on its way,
And takes the playfully objected rhyme
As surely as it keeps the stroke and time
In having its undeviable say.

                                                 1942

ETHEREALIZING

A theory if you hold it hard enough
And long enough gets rated as a creed:
Such as that flesh is something we can slough
So that the mind can be entirely freed.
Then when the arms and legs have atrophied,   5
And brain is all that's left of mortal stuff,
We can lie on the beach with the seaweed
And take our daily tide baths smooth and rough.
There once we lay as blobs of jellyfish
At evolution's opposite extreme.   10
But now as blobs of brain we'll lie and dream,

With only one vestigial creature wish:
Oh, may the tide be soon enough at high
To keep our abstract verse from being dry.

1947

ANY SIZE WE PLEASE

No one was looking at his lonely case,
So like a half-mad outpost sentinel,
Indulging an absurd dramatic spell,
Albeit not without some shame of face,
He stretched his arms out to the dark of space   5
And held them absolutely parallel
In infinite appeal. Then saying, 'Hell'
He drew them in for warmth of self-embrace.
He thought if he could have his space all curved
Wrapped in around itself and self-befriended,   10
His science needn't get him so unnerved.
He had been too all out, too much extended.
He slapped his breast to verify his purse
And hugged himself for all his universe.

1947

THE BROKEN DROUGHT

The prophet of disaster ceased to shout.
Something was going right outside the hall.
A rain though stingy had begun to fall
That rather hurt his theory of the drought
And all the great convention was about.   5
A cheer went up that shook the mottoed wall.
He did as Shakespeare says, you may recall,
Good orators *will* do when they are out.
Yet in his heart he was unshaken sure
The drought was one no spit of rain could cure.   10
It was the drought of deserts. Earth would soon
Be uninhabitable as the moon.
What for that matter had it ever been?
Who advised man to come and live therein?

1947

CARL SANDBURG

Carl [August] Sandburg (1878-   ) was born in Galesburg, Illinois, the son of Swedish immigrants, and was largely educated among the intermittent employments available to a young man in the Middle West before the turn of the century. He has been house painter, infantryman (in the Spanish-American War), political organizer, and journalist. Harriet Monroe's magazine, *Poetry*, had already begun to publish the newer poets, when, in 1914, Sandburg's first poems appeared there, but the loose, colloquial rhythms of his work added a new dimension to the poetic impulse coming from Chicago.

Sandburg writes of and from the Midwest, of the lives of city and farm people caught by the pressures of economic and social change. Not quite in the tradition of Whitman, for he has more humor and more anger, he nevertheless speaks of what seems often to be the modern derivative of Whitman's Americana, and his long labor over his biography of Lincoln (*The Prairie Years*, 1926, and *The War Years*, 1939) marks a deep emotional response to that image of the democratic ideal.

Always reluctant to define his craft or limit his material, Sandburg—again much in Whitman's manner—has himself become an image of the national bardic poet, often accompanying himself on his guitar. He has said that he favors "simple poems . . . which continue to have an appeal for simple people. I have written by different methods and in a wide miscellany of moods and have seldom been afraid to travel in lands and seas where I met fresh scenes and new songs. All my life I have been trying to learn to read, to see and hear, and to write."

He has published some six volumes of poetry, and three times won the Pulitzer Prize. The text of the poems in this anthology is taken from *Collected Poems* (1950).

CHICAGO

Hog Butcher for the World,
Tool Maker, Stacker of Wheat,
Player with Railroads and the Nation's Freight Handler;
Stormy, husky, brawling,
City of the Big Shoulders: 5

They tell me you are wicked and I believe them, for I have seen
your painted women under the gas lamps luring the farm
boys.
And they tell me you are crooked and I answer: Yes, it is true I
have seen the gunman kill and go free to kill again.
And they tell me you are brutal and my reply is: On the faces
of women and children I have seen the marks of wanton
hunger.
And having answered so I turn once more to those who sneer at
this my city, and I give them back the sneer and say to them:
Come and show me another city with lifted head singing so
proud to be alive and coarse and strong and cunning. 10
Flinging magnetic curses amid the toil of piling job on job,
here is a tall bold slugger set vivid against the little soft cities;
Fierce as a dog with tongue lapping for action, cunning as a
savage pitted against the wilderness,
 Bareheaded,
 Shoveling,
 Wrecking, 15
 Planning,
 Building, breaking, rebuilding,
Under the smoke, dust all over his mouth, laughing with white
teeth,
Under the terrible burden of destiny laughing as a young man
laughs,
Laughing even as an ignorant fighter laughs who has never
lost a battle, 20
Bragging and laughing that under his wrist is the pulse, and
under his ribs the heart of the people,
 Laughing!

Laughing the stormy, husky, brawling laughter of Youth, half-
naked, sweating, proud to be Hog Butcher, Tool Maker,
Stacker of Wheat, Player with Railroads and Freight
Handler to the Nation.

1916

TO A CONTEMPORARY BUNKSHOOTER

You come along . . . tearing your shirt . . . yelling about Jesus.
  Where do you get that stuff?
  What do you know about Jesus?
Jesus had a way of talking soft and outside of a few bankers
  and higher-ups among the con men of Jerusalem everybody
  liked to have this Jesus around because he never made any
  fake passes and everything he said went and he helped the
  sick and gave the people hope.

You come along squirting words at us, shaking your fist and
  calling us all dam fools so fierce the froth slobbers over your
  lips . . . always blabbing we're all going to hell straight off
  and you know all about it.

5

I've read Jesus' words. I know what he said. You don't throw
  any scare into me. I've got your number. I know how much
  you know about Jesus.
He never came near clean people or dirty people but they felt
  cleaner because he came along. It was your crowd of bankers
  and business men and lawyers hired the sluggers and mur-
  derers who put Jesus out of the running.

I say the same bunch backing you nailed the nails into the
  hands of this Jesus of Nazareth. He had lined up against him
  the same crooks and strong-arm men now lined up with you
  paying your way.

This Jesus was good to look at, smelled good, listened good. He
  threw out something fresh and beautiful from the skin of his
  body and the touch of his hands wherever he passed along.

You slimy bunkshooter, you put a smut on every human
blossom in reach of your rotten breath belching about hell-
fire and hiccupping about this Man who lived a clean life in
Galilee.   10

When are you going to quit making the carpenters build
emergency hospitals for women and girls driven crazy with
wrecked nerves from your gibberish about Jesus—I put it to
you again: Where do you get that stuff; what do you know
about Jesus?

Go ahead and bust all the chairs you want to. Smash a whole
wagon load of furniture at every performance. Turn sixty
somersaults and stand on your nutty head. If it wasn't for
the way you scare the women and kids I'd feel sorry for you
and pass the hat.
I like to watch a good four-flusher work, but not when he
starts people puking and calling for the doctors.
I like a man that's got nerve and can pull off a great original
performance, but you—you're only a bug-house peddler of
second-hand gospel—you're only shoving out a phoney imita-
tion of the goods this Jesus wanted free as air and sunlight.

You tell people living in shanties Jesus is going to fix it up all
right with them by giving them mansions in the skies after
they're dead and the worms have eaten 'em.   15
You tell $6 a week department store girls all they need is Jesus;
you take a steel trust wop, dead without having lived, gray
and shrunken at forty years of age, and you tell him to look
at Jesus on the cross and he'll be all right.
You tell poor people they don't need any more money on pay-
day and even if it's fierce to be out of a job, Jesus'll fix that
up all right, all right—all they gotta do is take Jesus the way
you say.
I'm telling you Jesus wouldn't stand for the stuff you're hand-
ing out. Jesus played it different. The bankers and lawyers
of Jerusalem got their sluggers and murderers to go after
Jesus just because Jesus wouldn't play their game. He didn't
sit in with the big thieves.

I don't want a lot of gab from a bunkshooter in my religion.
I won't take my religion from any man who never works ex-
    cept with his mouth and never cherishes any memory except
    the face of the woman on the American silver dollar.   20
I ask you to come through and show me where you're pouring
    out the blood of your life.
I've been to this suburb of Jerusalem they call Golgotha,
    where they nailed Him, and I know if the story is straight it
    was real blood ran from His hands and the nail-holes, and
    it was real blood spurted in red drops where the spear of the
    Roman soldier rammed in between the ribs of this Jesus of
    Nazareth.
                                                                   1916

I AM THE PEOPLE, THE MOB

I am the people—the mob—the crowd—the mass.
Do you know that all the great work of the world is done
    through me?
I am the workingman, the inventor, the maker of the world's
    food and clothes.
I am the audience that witnesses history. The Napoleons come
    from me and the Lincolns. They die. And then I send forth
    more Napoleons and Lincolns.
I am the seed ground. I am a prairie that will stand for much
    plowing. Terrible storms pass over me. I forget. The best of
    me is sucked out and wasted. I forget. Everything but Death
    comes to me and makes me work and give up what I have.
    And I forget.   5
Sometimes I growl, shake myself and spatter a few red drops for
    history to remember. Then—I forget.
When I, the People, learn to remember, when I, the People,
    use the lessons of yesterday and no longer forget who robbed
    me last year, who played me for a fool—then there will be no
    speaker in all the world say the name: "The People," with
    any fleck of a sneer in his voice or any far-off smile of
    derision.
The mob—the crowd—the mass—will arrive then.
                                                                   1916

LANGUAGES

There are no handles upon a language
Whereby men take hold of it
And mark it with signs for its remembrance.
It is a river, this language,
Once in a thousand years   5
Breaking a new course
Changing its way to the ocean.
It is mountain effluvia
Moving to valleys
And from nation to nation   10
Crossing borders and mixing.
Languages die like rivers.
Words wrapped round your tongue today
And broken to shape of thought
Between your teeth and lips speaking   15
Now and today
Shall be faded hieroglyphics
Ten thousand years from now.
Sing—and singing—remember
Your song dies and changes   20
And is not here tomorrow
Any more than the wind
Blowing ten thousand years ago.

1916

OLD TIMERS

I am an ancient reluctant conscript.

On the soup wagons of Xerxes I was a cleaner of pans.

On the march of Miltiades' phalanx I had a haft and head;
I had a bristling gleaming spear-handle.

Red-headed Caesar picked me for a teamster.   5
He said, "Go to work, you Tuscan bastard,
Rome calls for a man who can drive horses."

The units of conquest led by Charles the Twelfth,
The whirling whimsical Napoleonic columns:
They saw me one of the horseshoers.   10

I trimmed the feet of a white horse Bonaparte swept the
    night stars with.

Lincoln said, "Get into the game; your nation takes you."
And I drove a wagon and team and I had my arm shot off
At Spotsylvania Court House.

I am an ancient reluctant conscript.   15

                                                            1917

JOLIET

On the one hand the steel works.
On the other hand the penitentiary.
Santa Fé trains and Alton trains
Between smokestacks on the west
And gray walls on the east.   5
And Lockport down the river.

Part of the valley is God's.
And part is man's.
The river course laid out
A thousand years ago.   10
The canals ten years back.

The sun on two canals and one river
Makes three stripes of silver
Or copper and gold
Or shattered sunflower leaves.   15
    Talons of an iceberg
    Scraped out this valley.
    Claws of an avalanche loosed here.

                                                            1918

THEY ALL WANT TO PLAY HAMLET

They all want to play Hamlet.
They have not exactly seen their fathers killed
Nor their mothers in a frame-up to kill,
Nor an Ophelia dying with a dust gagging the heart,
Not exactly the spinning circles of singing golden spiders,   5
Not exactly this have they got at nor the meaning of flowers—
    O flowers, flowers slung by a dancing girl—in the saddest
    play the inkfish, Shakespeare, ever wrote;
Yet they all want to play Hamlet because it is sad like all actors
    are sad and to stand by an open grave with a joker's skull in
    the hand and then to say over slow and say over slow wise,
    keen, beautiful words masking a heart that's breaking,
    breaking,
This is something that calls and calls to their blood.
They are acting when they talk about it and they know it is
    acting to be particular about it and yet: They all want to
    play Hamlet.

                                1920

THE SINS OF KALAMAZOO

The sins of Kalamazoo are neither scarlet nor crimson.
The sins of Kalamazoo are a convict gray, a dishwater drab.
And the people who sin the sins of Kalamazoo are neither
    scarlet nor crimson.
They run to drabs and grays—and some of them sing they shall
    be washed whiter than snow—and some: We should worry.

Yes, Kalamazoo is a spot on the map   5
And the passenger trains stop there
And the factory smokestacks smoke
And the grocery stores are open Saturday nights
And the streets are free for citizens who vote
And inhabitants counted in the census.   10
Saturday night is the big night.

Listen with your ears on a Saturday night in Kalamazoo
And say to yourself: I hear America, I hear, *what* do I hear?

Main street there runs through the middle of the town
And there is a dirty post office   15
And a dirty city hall
And a dirty railroad station
And the United States flag cries, cries the Stars and Stripes to
   the four winds on Lincoln's birthday and the Fourth of July.

Kalamazoo kisses a hand to something far off.
Kalamazoo calls to a long horizon, to a shivering silver angel,
   to a creeping mystic what-is-it.   20
"We're here because we're here," is the song of Kalamazoo.
"We don't know where we're going but we're on our way," are
   the words.
There are hound dogs of bronze on the public square, hound
   dogs looking far beyond the public square.

Sweethearts there in Kalamazoo
Go to the general delivery window of the post office   25
And speak their names and ask for letters
And ask again, "Are you sure there is nothing for me?
I wish you'd look again—there must be a letter for me."

And sweethearts go to the city hall
And tell their names and say, "We want a license."   30
And they go to an installment house and buy a bed on time and
   a clock
And the children grow up asking each other, "What can we do
   to kill time?"
They grow up and go to the railroad station and buy tickets for
   Texas, Pennsylvania, Alaska.
"Kalamazoo is all right," they say. "But I want to see the
   world."
And when they have looked the world over they come back say-
   ing it is all like Kalamazoo.   35

The trains come in from the east and hoot for the crossings,
And buzz away to the peach country and Chicago to the west

Or they come from the west and shoot on to the Battle Creek
 breakfast bazaars
And the speedbug heavens of Detroit.

"I hear America, I hear, *what* do I hear?"   40
Said a loafer lagging along on the sidewalks of Kalamazoo,
Lagging along and asking questions, reading signs.

Oh yes, there is a town named Kalamazoo,
A spot on the map where the trains hesitate.
I saw the sign of a five and ten cent store there   45
And the Standard Oil Company and the International Har-
 vester
And a graveyard and a ball grounds
And a short order counter where a man can get a stack of
 wheats
And a pool hall where a rounder leered confidential like and
 said:
"Lookin' for a quiet game?"   50

The loafer lagged along and asked,
"Do you make guitars here?
Do you make boxes the singing wood winds ask to sleep in?
Do you rig up strings the singing wood winds sift over and sing
 low?"
The answer: "We manufacture musical instruments here."   55

Here I saw churches with steeples like hatpins,
Undertaking rooms with sample coffins in the show window
And signs everywhere satisfaction is guaranteed,
Shooting galleries where men kill imitation pigeons,
And there were doctors for the sick,   60
And lawyers for people waiting in jail,
And a dog catcher and a superintendent of streets,
And telephones, water-works, trolley cars,
And newspapers with a splatter of telegrams from sister cities
 of Kalamazoo the round world over.

And the loafer lagging along said: 65
Kalamazoo, you ain't in a class by yourself;

I seen you before in a lot of places.
If you are nuts America is nuts.
     And lagging along he said bitterly:
     Before I came to Kalamazoo I was silent.   70
     Now I am gabby, God help me, I am gabby.

Kalamazoo, both of us will do a fadeaway.
I will be carried out feet first
And time and the rain will chew you to dust
And the winds blow you away.   75
And an old, old mother will lay a green moss cover on my bones
And a green moss cover on the stones of your post office and city
     hall.
     Best of all
I have loved your kiddies playing run-sheep-run
And cutting their initials on the ball ground fence.   80
They knew every time I fooled them who was fooled and how.

     Best of all
I have loved the red gold smoke of your sunsets;
I have loved a moon with a ring around it
Floating over your public square;   85
I have loved the white dawn frost of early winter silver
And purple over your railroad tracks and lumber yards.

     The wishing heart of you I loved, Kalamazoo.
     I sang bye-lo, bye-lo to your dreams.
I sang bye-lo to your hopes and songs.   90
I wished to God there were hound dogs of bronze on your pub-
     lic square,
Hound dogs with bronze paws looking to a long horizon with
     a shivering silver angel,
     a creeping mystic what-is-it.
                                                   1920

SLABS OF THE SUNBURNT WEST

1

Into the night, into the blanket of night,
Into the night rain gods, the night luck gods,
Overland goes the overland passenger train.

Stand up, sandstone slabs of red,
Tell the overland passengers who burnt you.   5

Tell 'em how the jacks and screws loosened you.
Tell 'em who shook you by the heels and stood you on your
    heads,
Who put the slow pink of sunset mist on your faces.

Panels of the cold gray open night,
Gates of the Great American Desert,   10
    Skies keeping the prayers of the wagon men,
    The riders with picks, shovels and guns,
On the old trail, the Santa Fé trail, the Raton pass
Panels, skies, gates, listen tonight while we send up our prayers
    on the Santa Fé trail.

    (A colossal bastard frog   15
    squats in stone.
    Once he squawked.
    Then he was frozen and
    shut up forever.)

Into the night the overland passenger train,
Slabs of sandstone red sink to the sunset red,
Blankets of night cover 'em up.   20
Night rain gods, night luck gods, are looking on.

March on, processions.
Tie your hat to the saddle and ride, O Rider.
Let your ponies drag their navels in the sand.
Go hungry; leave your bones in the desert sand.   25

When the desert takes you the wind is clean.
The winds say so on a noisy night.
    The fingerbone of a man
    lay next to the handle of a frying pan
    and the footbone of a horse.
"Clean, we are clean," the winds whimper on a noisy night.

Into the night the overland passenger train,   30
And the engineer with an eye for signal lights,
And the porters making up berths for passengers,
And the boys in the diner locking the icebox—
And six men with cigars in the buffet car mention "civiliza-
    tion," "history," "God."

Into the blanket of night goes the overland train,   35
Into the black of the night the processions march,
    The ghost of a pony goes by,
    A hat tied to the saddle,
    The wagon tongue of a prairie schooner
    And the handle of a Forty-niner's pickax   40
    Do a shiver dance in the desert dust,
    In the coyote gray of the alkali dust.
And—six men with cigars in the buffet car mention "civiliza-
    tion," "history," "God."

Sleep, O wonderful hungry people.
Take a shut-eye, take a long old snooze,
    and be good to yourselves;   45
Into the night the overland passenger train
And the sleepers cleared for a morning sun
    and the Grand Canyon of Arizona.

2

    A bluejay blue
    and a gray mouse gray
    ran up the canyon walls.

A rider came to the rim
Of a slash and a gap of desert dirt—   50
A long-legged long-headed rider

On a blunt and a blurry jackass—
Riding and asking, "How come? How come?"
And the long-legged long-headed rider said:
"Between two ears of a blurry jackass   55
I see ten miles of auburn, gold and purple—
I see doors open over doorsills
And always another door and a doorsill.
Cheat my eyes, fill me with the float
Of your dream, you auburn, gold, and purple.   60
Cheat me, blow me off my pins onto footless floors.
Let me put footsteps in an airpath.
Cheat me with footprints on auburn, gold, purple
Out to the last violet shimmer of the float
Of the dream—and I will come straddling a jackass,   65
Singing a song and letting out hallelujahs
To the doorsill of the last footprint."

And the man took a stub lead pencil
And made a long memo in shorthand
On the two blurry jackass ears:—   70

"God sits with long whiskers in the sky."
I said it when I was a boy.
I said it because long-whiskered men
Put it in my head to say it.
        They lied . . . about you . . . God . . .   75
        They lied. . . .

The other side of the five doors
and doorsills put in my house—
how many hinges, panels, doorknobs,
how many locks and lintels,
put on the doors and doorsills
winding and wild between
the first and the last doorsill of all?

"Out of the footprints on ten miles
of auburn, gold and purple—an old song comes:
These bones shall rise again,
Yes, children, these bones shall rise.   80

"Yonder past my five doors
are fifty million doors, maybe,
stars with knobs and locks and lintels,
stars with riders of rockets,
stars with swimmers of fire.

"Cheat my eyes—and I come again—
straddling a jackass—singing a song—
letting out hallelujahs.

"If God is a proud and a cunning Bricklayer,
Or if God is a King in a white gold Heaven,
Or if God is a Boss and a Watchman always watching,   85
I come riding the old ride of the humiliation,
Straddling a jackass, singing a song,
Letting out hallelujahs.

"Before a ten mile float
of auburn, gold, and purple,
footprints on a sunset airpath haze,
     I ask:
How can I taste with my tongue a tongueless God?   90
How can I touch with my fingers a fingerless God?
How can I hear with my ears an earless God?
Or smell of a God gone noseless long ago?
Or look on a God who never needs eyes for looking?

"My head is under your foot, God.   95
My head is a pan of alkali dust
your foot kicked loose—your foot of air
with its steps on the sunset airpath haze.

          (A bluejay blue
          and a gray mouse gray
          ran up the canyon walls.)

"Sitting at the rim of the big gap
at the high lash of the frozen storm line,
I ask why I go on five crutches,
tongues, ears, nostrils—all cripples—
eyes and nose—both cripples—

I ask why these five cripples
limp and squint and gag with me,
why they say with the oldest frozen faces:
    Man is a poor stick and a sad squirt;
    if he is poor he can't dress up;
    if he dresses up he don't know any place to go.

"Away and away on some green moon
a blind blue horse eats white grass   100
    And the blind blue horse knows more than I do
    because he saw more than I have seen
    and remembered it after he went blind.

"And away and away on some other green moon
is a sea-kept child who lacks a nose I got
and fingers like mine and all I have.
And yet the sea-kept child knows more than
I do and sings secrets alien to me as light
to a nosing mole underground.
I understand this child as a yellow-belly
catfish in China understands peach pickers
at sunrise in September in a Michigan orchard.

    "The power and lift of the sea
    and the flame of the old earth fires under,
I sift their meanings of sand in my fingers.   105
I send out five sleepwalkers to find out who I am,
    my name and number, where I came from,
    and where I am going.
They go out, look, listen, wonder, and shoot a fire-white rocket
    across the night sky; the shot and the flare of the rocket
    dies to a whisper; and the night is the same as it always was.
They come back, my five sleepwalkers; they have an answer for
    me, they say; they tell me: *Wait*—the password all of them
    heard when the fire-white rocket shot across the sky and
    died to a whisper, the password is: *Wait*.

"I sit with five binoculars, amplifiers, spectroscopes
I sit looking through five windows, listening, tasting, smelling,
    touching.   110

I sit counting five million smoke fogs.
Repeaters, repeaters, come back to my window-sills.
Some are pigeons coming to coo and coo and clean their tail
     feathers and look wise at me.
Some are pigeons coming with broken wings to die with pain
     in their eyes on my window-sills.

"I walk the high lash of the frozen storm line;   115
I sit down with my feet in a ten-mile gravel pit.
Here I ask why I am a bag of sea-water fastened
to a frame of bones put walking on land—here I
look at crawlers, crimson, spiders, spotted with
purple spots on their heads, flinging silver nets,
two, four, six, against the sun.
Here I look two miles down to the ditch of the sea
and pick a winding ribbon, a river eater, a water
grinder; it is a runner sent to run by a stop-watch,
it is a wrecker on a rush job."

          (A bluejay blue
          and a gray mouse gray
          ran up the canyon walls.)

Battering rams, blind mules, mounted policemen,
trucks hauling caverns of granite, elephants
grappling gorillas in a death strangle, cathedrals,
arenas, platforms, somersaults of telescoped rail-
road train wrecks, exhausted egg heads, piles of
skulls, mountains of empty sockets, mummies of kings
and mobs, memories of work gangs and wrecking crews,
sobs of wind and water storms, all frozen and held
on paths leading on to spirals of new zigzags—   120

An arm-chair for a one-eyed giant;
two pine trees grow in the left arm of the chair;
a bluejay comes, sits, goes, comes again;
a bluejay shoots and twitters . . . out and across . . .
tumbled skyscrapers and wrecked battleships,
walls of crucifixions and wedding breakfasts;
ruin, ruin—a brute gnashed, dug, kept on—

kept on and quit: and this is It.
Falling away, the brute is working.
Sheets of white veils cross a woman's face.
An eye socket glooms and wonders.
The brute hangs his head and drags on to the job.   125
The mother of mist and light and air murmurs: Wait.

The weavers of light weave best in red,
     better in blue.
The weavers of shadows weave at sunset;
          the young black-eyed women run, run, run
          to the night star homes; the old women
          sit weaving for the night rain gods,
          the night luck gods.

Eighteen old giants throw a red gold shadow ball;
they pass it along; hands go up and stop it; they
bat up flies and practice; they begin the game, they
knock it for home runs and two-baggers; the pitcher
put it across in an out- and an in-shoot drop; the
Devil is the Umpire; God is the Umpire; the game
is called on account of darkness.

          A bluejay blue
          and a gray mouse gray
          ran up the canyon walls.   130

                              3

Good night; it is scribbled on the panels
of the cold gray open desert.
Good night; on the big sky blanket over the
Santa Fé trail it is woven in the oldest
Indian blanket songs.

Buffers of land, breakers of sea, say it and
say it, over and over, good night, good night.

          Tie your hat to the saddle
          and ride, ride, ride, O Rider.
          Lay your rails and wires

and ride, ride, ride, O Rider.   135
The worn tired star˗ say
you shall die early and die dirty.
The clean cold stars say
you shall die late and die clean.

The runaway stars say
you shall never die at all,
never at all.

1922

THE PEOPLE, YES

1

From the four corners of the earth,
from corners lashed in wind
and bitten with rain and fire,
from places where the winds begin
and fogs are born with mist children,
tall men from tall rocky slopes came
and sleepy men from sleepy valleys,
their women tall, their women sleepy,
with bundles and belongings,
with little ones babbling, "Where to now?
    what next?"

The people of the earth, the family of man,
wanted to put up something proud to look at,
a tower from the flat land of earth
on up through the ceiling into the top of the sky.

And the big job got going,
the caissons and pilings sunk,
floors, walls and winding staircases
aimed at the stars high over,
aimed to go beyond the ladders of the moon.

And God Almighty could have struck them dead
or smitten them deaf and dumb.

And God was a whimsical fixer.   5
God was an understanding Boss
    with another plan in mind,
And suddenly shuffled all the languages,
    changed the tongues of men
    so they all talked different
And the masons couldn't get what the hodcarriers said,
The helpers handed the carpenters the wrong tools,
Five hundred ways to say, ''W h o a r e y o u ?''   10
Changed ways of asking, "Where do we go from here?"
Or of saying, "Being born is only the beginning,"
Or, "Would you just as soon sing as make that noise?"
Or, "What you don't know won't hurt you."
And the material-and-supply men started disputes   15
With the hauling gangs and the building trades
And the architects tore their hair over the blueprints
And the brickmakers and the mule skinners talked back
To the straw bosses who talked back to the superintendents
And the signals got mixed; the men who shovelled the bucket   20
Hooted the hoisting men—and the job was wrecked.

Some called it the Tower of Babel job
And the people gave it many other names.
The wreck of it stood as a skull and a ghost,
    a memorandum hardly begun,
swaying and sagging in tall hostile winds,
held up by slow friendly winds.

2

From Illinois and Indiana came a later myth
Of all the people in the world at Howdeehow
For the first time standing together:
From six continents, seven seas, and several archipelagoes,
From points of land moved by wind and water   5
Out of where they used to be to where they are,
The people of the earth marched and travelled
To gather on a great plain.

At a given signal they would join in a shout,
    So it was planned,   10

One grand hosannah, something worth listening to.
    And they all listened.
    The signal was given.
    And they all listened.
    And the silence was beyond words.   15
They had come to listen, not to make a noise.
    They wanted to hear.
So they all stood still and listened,
Everybody except a little old woman from Kalamazoo
Who gave out a long slow wail over what she was missing
    because she was stone deaf.   20

This is the tale of the Howdeehow powpow,
One of a thousand drolls the people tell of themselves,
Of tall corn, of wide rivers, of big snakes,
Of giants and dwarfs, heroes and clowns,
Grown in the soil of the mass of the people.   25

24

    Who shall speak for the people?
    who has the answers?
    where is the sure interpreter?
    who knows what to say?
Who can write the music jazz-classical
    smokestacks-geraniums hyacinths-biscuits
    now whispering easy
    now boom doom crashing angular
    now tough monotonous tom tom
Who has enough split-seconds and slow sea-tides?

The ships of the sea and the mists of
    night and the sheen of old battle-
    fields and the moon on the city
    rubbish dumps belong to the people.
The crops this year, last and next year,
    and the winds and frosts in many
    orchards and tomato gardens, are
    listed in the people's acquaintance.   5
Horses and wagons, trucks and tractors,
    from the shouting cities to the sleep-

ing prairies, from worn pavements
to mountain mule paths, the people
have strange possessions.
The plow and the hammer, the knife and
the shovel, the planting hoe and the
reaping sickle, everywhere these are
the people's possessions by right of
use.
Their handles are smoothed to the grain
of the wood by the enclosing
thumbs and fingers of familiar
hands,
Maintenance-of-way men in a Tennessee
gang singing, "If I die a railroad
man put a pick and shovel at my
head and my feet and a nine-pound
hammer in my hand,"
Larry, the Kansas section boss, on his
dying bed asking for one last look at
the old hand-car,
His men saying in the coffin on his chest
he should by rights have the spike
maul, the gauge and the old claw-bar.

The early morning in the fields, the
brown thrush warbling and the imi-
tations of the catbird, the neverend-
ing combat with pest and destroyer,
the chores of feeding and watching,
seedtime and harvest,
The clocking of the months toward a
birthing day, the newly dropped
calves and the finished steers loaded
in stock-cars for market, the gamble
on what we'll get tomorrow for
what we put in today—
These are belongings of the people, dusty
with the dust of earth, merciless as
sudden hog cholera, hopeful as a
rainwashed hill of moonlit pines.

10

32

What the people learn out of lifting and hauling and wait-
     ing and losing and laughing
Goes into a scroll, an almanac, a record folding and unfolding,
     and the music goes down and around:
The story goes on and on, happens, forgets to happen, goes out
     and meets itself coming in, puts on disguises and drops
     them.
"Yes yes, go on, go on, I'm listening." You hear that in one
     doorway.
And in the next, "Aw shut up, close your trap, button your
     tongue, you talk too much."   5
          The people, yes, the people,
To the museum, the aquarium, the planetarium, the zoo, they
     go by thousands, coming away to talk about mummies,
     camels, fish and stars,
The police and constables holding every one of them either a
     lawbreaker or lawabiding.
The fingerprint expert swears no two of them ever has finger
     lines and circlings the same.
The handwriting expert swears no one of them ever writes his
     name twice the same way.   10
To the grocer and the banker they are customers, depositors,
     investors.
The politician counts them as voters, the newspaper editor as
     readers, the gambler as suckers.
The priest holds each one an immortal soul in the care of Al-
     mighty God.
          bright accidents from the chromosome
          spill   from the color bowl of the
          chromosomes   some go under in early
          bubbles   some learn from desert blos-
          soms   how to lay up and use thin
          hoardings of night mist

     In an old French town
     the mayor ordered the people
     to hang lanterns in front of their houses

which the people did
but the lanterns gave no light
so the mayor ordered they must
put candles in the lanterns
which the people did
but the candles in the lanterns gave no light
whereupon the mayor ordered
they must light the candles in the lanterns
which the people did
and thereupon there was light.

The cauliflower is a cabbage with a college education.   15
All she needs for housekeeping is a can opener.
        They'll fly high if you give them wings.
Put all your eggs in one basket and watch that basket.
Everybody talks about the weather and nobody does anything
        about it.
The auk flies backward so as to see where it's been.   20
        Handle with care women and glass.
        Women and linen look best by candlelight.
One hair of a woman draws more than a team of horses.
Blessed are they who expect nothing for they shall not be
        disappointed.
You can send a boy to college but you can't make him think. 25
The time to sell is when you have a customer.
Sell the buffalo hide after you have killed the buffalo.
The more you fill a barrel the more it weighs unless you fill it
        with holes.
A pound of iron or a pound of feathers weighs the same.
Those in fear they may cast pearls before swine are often lack-
        ing in pearls.   30
May you live to eat the hen that scratches over your grave.
He seems to think he's the frog's tonsils but he looks to me like
        a plugged nickel.
If you don't like the coat bring back the vest and I'll give you a
        pair of pants.
The coat and the pants do the work but the vest gets the gravy.
"You are singing an invitation to summer," said the teacher,
        "you are not defying it to come."   35

"Sergeant, if a private calls you
a dam fool, what of it?"
"I'd throw him in the guard house."
"And if he just thinks you're a dam
fool and don't say it, then what?"
"Nothing."
"Well, let it go at that."   40

    The white man drew a small circle in the sand
and told the red man, "This is what the Indian
knows," and drawing a big circle around the
small one, "This is what the white man knows."
The Indian took the stick and swept an immense
ring around both circles: "This is where the
white man and the red man know nothing."

On the long dirt road from Nagadoches to Austin
The pioneer driving a yoke of oxen and a cart
met a heavy man in a buggy driving a team
of glossy black horses.
    "I am Sam Houston, Governor of the State of
Texas, and I order you to turn out of the road
for me."   45
    "I am an American citizen and a taxpayer of
Texas and I have as much right to the road as
you."
    "That is an intelligent answer and I salute you
and I will turn out of the road for you."

What did they mean with that Iowa epitaph:
    "She averaged well for this vicinity"?
And why should the old Des Moines editor
    say they could write on his gravestone:
    "He et what was sot before him"?

"I never borrowed your umbrella," said a
    borrower, "and if I did I brought it back."   50
He was quiet as a wooden-legged man on a tin
    roof and busy as a one-armed paper-hanger
    with the hives.

When a couple of fried eggs were offered the
new hired man he said, "I don't dirty my
plate for less than six."

Why did the top sergeant tell the rookie, "Put
on your hat, here comes a woodpecker"?
"Whiskey," taunted the Irish orator, "whiskey
it is that makes you shoot at the landlords
—and miss 'em!"

"Unless you learn," said the father to the son,
"how to tell a horse chestnut from a chest-
nut horse you may have to live on soup made
from the shadow of a starved pigeon."   55
Said Oscar neither laughing nor crying: "We fed
the rats to the cats and the cats to the rats
and was just getting into the big money when
the whole thing went blooey on account of the
overproduction of rats and cats."

Where you been so long?
What good wind blew you in?
Snow again, kid, I didn't get your drift.
Everything now is either swell or lousy.   60
"It won't be long now," was answered,
"The worst is yet to come."
Of the dead merchant prince whose holdings
were colossal the ditch-digger queried,
"How much did he leave? All of it."

"What do you want to be?"
T. R. asked.
Bruere answered, "Just an
earthworm turning over a
little of the soil near me."
"Great men never feel great,"
say the Chinese.   65
"Small men never feel small."

76

The record is a scroll of many indecipherable scrawls,
telling the pay of the people for commencing action
toward redress of wrongs too heavy
to be longer borne.
              "No strike is ever lost": an old cry
heard before the strike begins and heard long after, and
"No strike is ever lost": either a thought or an instinct
equivalent to "Give me liberty or give me death."
              On the horizon a cloud no larger than
a man's hand rolls larger and darker when masses of people
begin saying, "Any kind of death is better than this kind
of life."

          The machine world of the insects
          individual spiders engineering exploits
          interwoven colonies of bees and ants
          clouds of grasshopper destroyers
          —they carry lessons and warnings
              they do what they must
              they are beyond argument.

The flowing of the stream clears it of pollution.   5
The refuse of humanity, the offscourings, the encum-
      berings,
They are who?
They are those who have forgotten work and the price
At which life goes on.
They live in shambles overly foul and in mansions overly   10
Swept and garnished.
The flowing of the stream clears it of pollution.

                          107
              The people will live on.
    The learning and blundering people will live on.
       They will be tricked and sold and again sold
    And go back to the nourishing earth for rootholds,
          The people so peculiar in renewal and comeback,   5
          You can't laugh off their capacity to take it.
    The mammoth rests between his cyclonic dramas.

The people so often sleepy, weary, enigmatic,
is a vast huddle with many units saying:
  "I earn my living.
  I make enough to get by
  and it takes all my time.   10
  If I had more time
  I could do more for myself
  and maybe for others.
  I could read and study
  and talk things over
  and find out about things.
  It takes time.
  I wish I had the time."   15

The people is a tragic and comic two-face:
hero and hoodlum: phantom and gorilla twist-
ing to moan with a gargoyle mouth: "They
buy me and sell me . . . it's a game . . .
sometime I'll break loose . . ."

  Once having marched
Over the margins of animal necessity,
Over the grim line of sheer subsistence
  Then man came   20
To the deeper rituals of his bones,
To the lights lighter than any bones,
To the time for thinking things over,
To the dance, the song, the story,
Or the hours given over to dreaming,   25
  Once having so marched.

Between the finite limitations of the five senses
and the endless yearnings of man for the beyond
the people hold to the humdrum bidding of work and food
while reaching out when it comes their way
for lights beyond the prism of the five senses,
for keepsakes lasting beyond any hunger or death.
  This reaching is alive.
The panderers and liars have violated and smutted it.
  Yet this reaching is alive yet
  for lights and keepsakes.   30

The people know the salt of the sea
and the strength of the winds
lashing the corners of the earth.
The people take the earth
as a tomb of rest and a cradle of hope.
Who else speaks for the Family of Man?
They are in tune and step
with constellations of universal law.

The people is a polychrome,
a spectrum and a prism
held in a moving monolith,
a console organ of changing themes,
a clavilux of color poems
wherein the sea offers fog
and the fog moves off in rain
and the labrador sunset shortens
to a nocturne of clear stars
serene over the shot spray
of northern lights.   35

The steel mill sky is alive.
The fire breaks white and zigzag
shot on a gun-metal gloaming.
Man is a long time coming.
Man will yet win.
Brother may yet line up with brother: 40

This old anvil laughs at many broken hammers.
There are men who can't be bought.
The fireborn are at home in fire.
The stars make no noise.
You can't hinder the wind from blowing.   45
Time is a great teacher.
Who can live without hope?

In the darkness with a great bundle of grief
   the people march.
In the night, and overhead a shovel of stars for
   keeps, the people march:
                              "Where to? what next?"
                                                              1936

WALLACE STEVENS

Wallace Stevens (1879-1955) was born in Reading, Pennsylvania, later settled in Connecticut, and lived what he called "an exceedingly regular and disciplined life." He attended Harvard College, where he was a member of the Literary Board and then president of the Harvard Advocate, to which he contributed editorial essays and short stories. Stevens later received a degree from New York Law School (1904) and took a job on the New York *Tribune*. At about this time also he began writing poems. He first published four brief poems in *Poetry* (November, 1914), after which his work began to circulate in little magazines—notably *Poetry, Others,* and *Broom*—and in anthologies of new verse. By the time he assembled his first volume of poems, *Harmonium* (1923), at the age of forty-four, he had already built a considerable reputation among writers and readers of avant-garde publications. Meanwhile, he had left his law practice for insurance and joined the staff of the Hartford Accident Indemnity Company (1916) as head of the Surety Claims Department. He remained with this firm for the rest of his life, becoming an expert in surety bonds and a vice-president of the Hartford Livestock Insurance Company. During his forty years as an insurance man he continued to write poems. "Poetry and surety claims," he once said, "are not as unlikely a combination as they might seem. There is nothing perfunctory about them, for each case is different."

Stevens published eleven volumes of poems—not counting reissues—from 1923 until his *Collected Poems* (1954) appeared on the occasion of his seventy-fifth birthday. He has been much honored, receiving the Bollingen Prize in Poetry (1949), two National Book Awards (1950, 1954), the Poetry Society's Gold Medal (1951), and the Pulitzer Prize (1955), as well as several honorary degrees. His younger colleagues have called him the poet's poet, more awarded than read. This could not have surprised Stevens, who once patiently wrote:

> The poem must resist the intelligence
> Almost successfully.

Stevens' understanding—and consequently ours—of his poetry is bound up in his concepts of the imagination and of the function of the poet. The poet's job, he thought, is certainly not to comfort people or to lead them out of their confusion; and yet it is his function to help people live their lives. He must do it by making his imagination theirs. Stevens explained this conviction with a metaphor about pressure. Acutal events, he said, exert an awesome pressure on our lives, which a possible poet must be capable of resisting or evading. It is not a matter of escape but of resistance to the exterior realities with an equal pressure from within oneself. (After all, he said, "a poet's words are the things that do not exist without words.") This resisting pressure of the imagination "seems, in the last analysis, to have something to do with our self-preservation; and that, no doubt, is why the expression of it, the sound of its words, helps us to live our lives." Stevens was articulate about poetry, and some of his essays on the subject were collected in the *Necessary Angel* (1951).

The text of these selections is *The Collected Poems of Wallace Stevens* (New York, 1954).

SUNDAY MORNING

I

Complacencies of the peignoir, and late
Coffee and oranges in a sunny chair,
And the green freedom of a cockatoo
Upon a rug mingle to dissipate
The holy hush of ancient sacrifice.   5
She dreams a little, and she feels the dark
Encroachment of that old catastrophe,
As a calm darkens among water-lights.
The pungent oranges and bright, green wings
Seem things in some procession of the dead,   10
Winding across wide water, without sound.
The day is like wide water, without sound,
Stilled for the passing of her dreaming feet
Over the seas, to silent Palestine,
Dominion of the blood and sepulchre.   15

II

Why should she give her bounty to the dead?
What is divinity if it can come
Only in silent shadows and in dreams?
Shall she not find in comforts of the sun,
In pungent fruit and bright, green wings, or else   20
In any balm or beauty of the earth,
Things to be cherished like the thought of heaven?
Divinity must live within herself:
Passions of rain, or moods in falling snow;
Grievings in loneliness, or unsubdued   25
Elations when the forest blooms; gusty
Emotions on wet roads on autumn nights;
All pleasures and all pains, remembering
The bough of summer and the winter branch.
These are the measures destined for her soul.   30

III

Jove in the clouds had his inhuman birth.
No mother suckled him, no sweet land gave
Large-mannered motions to his mythy mind.
He moved among us, as a muttering king,
Magnificent, would move among his hinds,   35
Until our blood, commingling, virginal,
With heaven; brought such requital to desire
The very hinds discerned it, in a star.
Shall our blood fail? Or shall it come to be
The blood of paradise? And shall the earth   40
Seem all of paradise that we shall know?
The sky will be much friendlier then than now,
A part of labor and a part of pain,
And next in glory to enduring love,
Not this dividing and indifferent blue.   45

IV

She says, "I am content when wakened birds,
Before they fly, test the reality

Of misty fields, by their sweet questionings;
But when the birds are gone, and their warm **fields**
Return no more, where, then, is paradise?"   50
There is not any haunt of prophecy,
Nor any old chimera of the grave,
Neither the golden underground, nor isle
Melodious, where spirits gat them home,
Nor visionary south, nor cloudy palm   55
Remote on heaven's hill, that has endured
As April's green endures; or will endure
Like her remembrance of awakened birds,
Or her desire for June and evening, tipped
By the consummation of the swallow's wings.   60

V

She says, "But in contentment I still feel
The need of some imperishable bliss."
Death is the mother of beauty; hence from her,
Alone, shall come fulfilment to our dreams
And our desires. Although she strews the leaves   65
Of sure obliteration on our paths,
The path sick sorrow took, the many paths
Where triumph rang its brassy phrase, or love
Whispered a little out of tenderness,
She makes the willow shiver in the sun   70
For maidens who were wont to sit and gaze
Upon the grass, relinquished to their feet.
She causes boys to pile new plums and pears
On disregarded plate. The maidens taste
And stray impassioned in the littering leaves.   75

VI

Is there no change of death in paradise?
Does ripe fruit never fall? Or do the boughs
Hang always heavy in that perfect sky,
Unchanging, yet so like our perishing earth,
With rivers like our own that seek for seas   80
They never find, the same receding shores

That never touch with inarticulate pang?
Why set the pear upon those river-banks
Or spice the shores with odors of the plum?
Alas, that they should wear our colors there, 85
The silken weavings of our afternoons,
And pick the strings of our insipid lutes!
Death is the mother of beauty, mystical,
Within whose burning bosom we devise
Our earthly mothers waiting, sleeplessly. 90

VII

Supple and turbulent, a ring of men
Shall chant in orgy on a summer morn
Their boisterous devotion to the sun,
Not as a god, but as a god might be,
Naked among them, like a savage source. 95
Their chant shall be a chant of paradise,
Out of their blood, returning to the sky;
And in their chant shall enter, voice by voice,
The windy lake wherein their lord delights,
The trees, like serafin, and echoing hills, 100
That choir among themselves long afterward.
They shall know well the heavenly fellowship
Of men that perish and of summer morn.
And whence they came and whither they shall go
The dew upon their feet shall manifest. 105

VIII

She hears, upon that water without sound,
A voice that cries, "The tomb in Palestine
Is not the porch of spirits lingering.
It is the grave of Jesus, where he lay."
We live in an old chaos of the sun, 110
Or old dependency of day and night,
Or island solitude, unsponsored, free,
Of that wide water, inescapable.
Deer walk upon our mountains, and the quail
Whistle about us their spontaneous cries; 115

Sweet berries ripen in the wilderness;
And, in the isolation of the sky,
At evening, casual flocks of pigeons make
Ambiguous undulations as they sink,
Downward to darkness, on extended wings.   120

                                              1915

PETER QUINCE AT THE CLAVIER

I

Just as my fingers on these keys
Make music, so the selfsame sounds
On my spirit make a music, too.

Music is feeling, then, not sound;
And thus it is that what I feel,   5
Here in this room, desiring you,

Thinking of your blue-shadowed silk,
Is music. It is like the strain
Waked in the elders by Susanna.

Of a green evening, clear and warm,   10
She bathed in her still garden, while
The red-eyed elders watching, felt

The basses of their beings throb
In witching chords, and their thin blood
Pulse pizzicati of Hosanna.   15

II

In the green water, clear and warm,
Susanna lay.
She searched
The touch of springs,
And found   20

Concealed imaginings.
She sighed,
For so much melody.

Upon the bank, she stood
In the cool   25
Of spent emotions.
She felt, among the leaves,
The dew
Of old devotions.

She walked upon the grass,   30
Still quavering.
The winds were like her maids,
On timid feet,
Fetching her woven scarves,
Yet wavering.   35

A breath upon her hand
Muted the night.
She turned—
A cymbal crashed,
And roaring horns.   40

III

Soon, with a noise like tambourines,
Came her attendant Byzantines.

They wondered why Susanna cried
Against the elders by her side;

And as they whispered, the refrain   45
Was like a willow swept by rain.

Anon, their lamps' uplifted flame
Revealed Susanna and her shame.

And then, the simpering Byzantines
Fled, with a noise like tambourines.   50

IV

Beauty is momentary in the mind—
The fitful tracing of a portal;
But in the flesh it is immortal.
The body dies; the body's beauty lives.
So evenings die, in their green going,   55
A wave, interminably flowing.
So gardens die, their meek breath scenting
The cowl of winter, done repenting.
So maidens die, to the auroral
Celebration of a maiden's choral.   60
Susanna's music touched the bawdy strings
Of those white elders; but, escaping,
Left only Death's ironic scraping.
Now, in its immortality it plays
On the clear viol of her memory,   65
And makes a constant sacrament of praise.

                                            1915

SIX SIGNIFICANT LANDSCAPES

I

An old man sits
In the shadow of a pine tree
In China.
He sees larkspur,
Blue and white,   5
At the edge of the shadow,
Move in the wind.
His beard moves in the wind.
The pine tree moves in the wind.
Thus water flows   10
Over weeds.

II

The night is of the color
Of a woman's arm:
Night, the female

Obscure,   15
Fragrant and supple,
Conceals herself.
A pool shines,
Like a bracelet
Shaken in a dance.   20

III

I measure myself
Against a tall tree.
I find that I am much taller,
For I reach right up to the sun,
With my eye;   25
And I reach to the shore of the sea
With my ear.
Nevertheless, I dislike
The way the ants crawl
In and out of my shadow.   30

IV

When my dream was near the moon,
The white folds of its gown
Filled with yellow light.
The soles of its feet
Grew red.   35
Its hair filled
With certain blue crystallizations
From stars,
Not far off.

V

Not all the knives of the lamp-posts,   40
Nor the chisels of the long streets,
Nor the mallets of the domes
And high towers,
Can carve
What one star can carve,   45
Shining through the grape-leaves.

VI

Rationalists, wearing square hats,
Think, in square rooms,
Looking at the floor,
Looking at the ceiling.   50
They confine themselves
To right-angled triangles.
If they tried rhomboids,
Cones, waving lines, ellipses—
As, for example, the ellipse of the half-moon—   55
Rationalists would wear sombreros.

                                                  1916

THEORY

I am what is around me.

Women understand this.
One is not duchess
A hundred yards from a carriage.

These, then are portraits: 5
A black vestibule;
A high bed sheltered by curtains.

These are merely instances.

                                                  1917

THIRTEEN WAYS OF LOOKING AT A BLACKBIRD

I

Among twenty snowy mountains,
The only moving thing
Was the eye of the blackbird.

II

I was of three minds,
Like a tree   5
In which there are three blackbirds.

III

The blackbird whirled in the autumn winds.
It was a small part of the pantomime.

IV

A man and a woman
Are one.   10
A man and a woman and a blackbird
Are one.

V

I do not know which to prefer,
The beauty of inflections
Or the beauty of innuendoes,   15
The blackbird whistling
Or just after.

VI

Icicles filled the long window
With barbaric glass.
The shadow of the blackbird   20
Crossed it, to and fro.
The mood
Traced in the shadow
An indecipherable cause.

VII

O thin men of Haddam,   25
Why do you imagine golden birds?
Do you not see how the blackbird
Walks around the feet
Of the women about you?

VIII

I know noble accents   30
And lucid, inescapable rhythms;
But I know, too,
That the blackbird is involved
In what I know.

IX

When the blackbird flew out of sight,   35
It marked the edge
Of one of many circles.

X

At the sight of blackbirds
Flying in a green light,
Even the bawds of euphony   40
Would cry out sharply.

XI

He rode over Connecticut
In a glass coach.
Once, a fear pierced him,
In that he mistook   45
The shadow of his equipage
For blackbirds.

XII

The river is moving.
The blackbird must be flying.

XIII

It was evening all afternoon.   50
It was snowing
And it was going to snow.
The blackbird sat
In the cedar-limbs.

                                                   1917

ANECDOTE OF THE JAR

I placed a jar in Tennessee,
And round it was, upon a hill.
It made the slovenly wilderness
Surround that hill.

The wilderness rose up to it,   5
And sprawled around, no longer wild,
The jar was round upon the ground
And tall and of a port in air.

It took dominion everywhere.
The jar was gray and bare.   10
It did not give of bird or bush,
Like nothing else in Tennessee.

1919

THE SNOW MAN

One must have a mind of winter
To regard the frost and the boughs
Of the pine-trees crusted with snow;

And have been cold a long time
To behold the junipers shagged with ice,   5
The spruces rough in the distant glitter

Of the January sun; and not to think
Of any misery in the sound of the wind,
In the sound of a few leaves,

Which is the sound of the land   10
Full of the same wind
That is blowing in the same bare place

For the listener, who listens in the snow,
And, nothing himself, beholds
Nothing that is not there and the nothing that is.   15

                                                              1921

THE BIRD WITH THE COPPERY, KEEN CLAWS

Above the forest of the parakeets,
A parakeet of parakeets prevails,
A pip of life amid a mort of tails.

(The rudiments of tropics are around,
Aloe of ivory, pear of rusty rind.)   5
His lids are white because his eyes are blind.

He is not paradise of parakeets,
Of his gold ether, golden alguazil,
Except because he broods there and is still.

Panache upon panache, his tails deploy   10
Upward and outward, in green-vented forms,
His tip a drop of water full of storms.

But though the turbulent tinges undulate
As his pure intellect applies its laws,
He moves not on his coppery, keen claws.   15

He munches a dry shell while he exerts
His will, yet never ceases, perfect cock,
To flare, in the sun-pallor of his rock.

                                                              1921

A HIGH-TONED OLD CHRISTIAN WOMAN

Poetry is the supreme fiction, madame.
Take the moral law and make a nave of it
And from the nave build haunted heaven. Thus,
The conscience is converted into palms,

Like windy citherns hankering for hymns.   5
We agree in principle. That's clear. But take
The opposing law and make a peristyle,
And from the peristyle project a masque
Beyond the planets. Thus, our bawdiness,
Unpurged by epitaph, indulged at last,   10
Is equally converted into palms,
Squiggling like saxophones. And palm for palm,
Madame, we are where we began. Allow,
Therefore, that in the planetary scene
Your disaffected flagellants, well-stuffed,   15
Smacking their muzzy bellies in parade,
Proud of such novelties of the sublime,
Such tink and tank and tunk-a-tunk-tunk,
May, merely may, madame, whip from themselves
A jovial hullabaloo among the spheres.   20
This will make widows wince. But fictive things
Wink as they will. Wink most when widows wince.

                                        1922

THE EMPEROR OF ICE-CREAM

Call the roller of big cigars,
The muscular one, and bid him whip
In kitchen cups concupiscent curds.
Let the wenches dawdle in such dress
As they are used to wear, and let the boys   5
Bring flowers in last month's newspapers.
Let be be finale of seem.
The only emperor is the emperor of ice-cream.

Take from the dresser of deal,
Lacking the three glass knobs, that sheet   10
On which she embroidered fantails once
And spread it so as to cover her face.
If her horny feet protrude, they come
To show how cold she is, and dumb.
Let the lamp affix its beam.   15
The only emperor is the emperor of ice-cream.

                                        1922

TO THE ONE OF FICTIVE MUSIC

Sister and mother and diviner love,
And of the sisterhood of the living dead
Most near, most clear, and of the clearest bloom,
And of the fragrant mothers the most dear
And queen, and of diviner love the day   5
And flame and summer and sweet fire, no thread
Of cloudy silver sprinkles in your gown
Its venom of renown, and on your head
No crown is simpler than the simple hair.

Now, of the music summoned by the birth   10
That separates us from the wind and sea,
Yet leaves us in them, until earth becomes,
By being so much of the things we are,
Gross effigy and simulacrum, none
Gives motion to perfection more serene   15
Than yours, out of our imperfections wrought,
Most rare, or ever of more kindred air
In the laborious weaving that you wear.

For so retentive of themselves are men
That music is intensest which proclaims   20
The near, the clear, and vaunts the clearest bloom,
And of all vigils musing the obscure,
That apprehends the most which sees and names,
As in your name, an image that is sure,
Among the arrant spices of the sun,   25
O bough and bush and scented vine, in whom
We give ourselves our likest issuance.

Yet not too like, yet not so like to be
Too near, too clear, saving a little to endow
Our feigning with the strange unlike, whence springs   30
The difference that heavenly pity brings.
For this, musician, in your girdle fixed
Bear other perfumes. On your pale head wear

A band entwining, set with fatal stones.
Unreal, give back to us what once you gave: 5
The imagination that we spurned and crave.

1922

TWO FIGURES IN DENSE VIOLET NIGHT

I had as lief be embraced by the porter at the hotel
As to get no more from the moonlight
Than your moist hand.

Be the voice of night and Florida in my ear.
Use dusky words and dusky images.   5
Darken your speech.

Speak, even, as if I did not hear you speaking,
But spoke for you perfectly in my thoughts,
Conceiving words,

As the night conceives the sea-sounds in silence,   10
And out of their droning sibilants makes
A serenade.

Say, puerile, that the buzzards crouch on the ridge-pole
And sleep with one eye watching the stars fall
Below Key West.   15

Say that the palms are clear in a total blue,
Are clear and are obscure; that it is night;
That the moon shines.

1923

POETRY IS A DESTRUCTIVE FORCE

That's what misery is,
Nothing to have at heart.
It is to have or nothing.

It is a thing to have,
A lion, an ox in his breast,   5
To feel it breathing there.

Corazon, stout dog,
Young ox, bow-legged bear,
He tastes its blood, not spit.

He is like a man   10
In the body of a violent beast.
Its muscles are his own . . .

The lion sleeps in the sun.
Its nose is on its paws.
It can kill a man.   15

                                              1938

THE POEMS OF OUR CLIMATE

I

Clear water in a brilliant bowl,
Pink and white carnations. The light
In the room more like a snowy air,
Reflecting snow. A newly-fallen snow
At the end of winter when afternoons return.   5
Pink and white carnations—one desires
So much more than that. The day itself
Is simplified: a bowl of white,
Cold, a cold porcelain, low and round,
With nothing more than the carnations there.   10

II

Say even that this complete simplicity
Stripped one of all one's torments, concealed
The evilly compounded, vital I
And made it fresh in a world of white,
A world of clear water, brilliant-edged,   15

Still one would want more, one would need more,
More than a world of white and snowy scents.

III

There would still remain the never-resting mind,
So that one would want to escape, come back
To what had been so long composed.   20
The imperfect is our paradise.
Note that, in this bitterness, delight,
Since the imperfect is so hot in us,
Lies in flawed words and stubborn sounds.

                                                      1938

PRELUDE TO OBJECTS

I

If he will be heaven after death,
If, while he lives, he hears himself
Sounded in music, if the sun,
Stormer, is the color of a self
As certainly as night is the color   5
Of a self, if, without sentiment,
He is what he hears and sees and if,
Without pathos, he feels what he hears
And sees, being nothing otherwise,
Having nothing otherwise, he has not   10
To go to the Louvre to behold himself.
Granted each picture is a glass,
That the walls are mirrors multiplied,
That the marbles are gluey pastiches, the stairs
The sweep of an impossible elegance,   15
And the notorious views from the windows
Wax wasted, monarchies beyond
The S. S. *Normandie*, granted
One is always seeing and feeling oneself,
That's not by chance. It comes to this: 20
That the guerilla I should be booked

And bound. Its nigger mystics should change
Foolscap for wigs. Academies
As of a tragic science should rise.

II

Poet, patting more nonsense foamed   25
From the sea, conceive for the courts
Of these academies, the diviner health
Disclosed in common forms. Set up
The rugged black, the image. Design
The touch. Fix quiet. Take the place   30
Of parents, lewdest of ancestors.
We are conceived in your conceits.

                                                      1938

OF MODERN POETRY

The poem of the mind in the act of finding
What will suffice. It has not always had
To find: the scene was set; it repeated what
Was in the script.
                    Then the theatre was changed   5
To something else. Its past was a souvenir.
It has to be living, to learn the speech of the place.
It has to face the men of the time and to meet
The women of the time. It has to think about war
And it has to find what will suffice. It has   10
To construct a new stage. It has to be on that stage
And, like an insatiable actor, slowly and
With meditation, speak words that in the ear,
In the delicatest ear of the mind, repeat,
Exactly, that which it wants to hear, at the sound   15
Of which, an invisible audience listens,
Not to the play, but to itself, expressed
In an emotion as of two people, as of two
Emotions becoming one. The actor is
A metaphysician in the dark, twanging   20

An instrument, twanging a wiry string that gives
Sounds passing through sudden rightnesses, wholly
Containing the mind, below which it cannot descend,
Beyond which it has no will to rise.

               It must   25
Be the finding of a satisfaction, and may
Be of a man skating, a woman dancing, a woman
Combing. The poem of the act of the mind.

                         1940

ASIDES ON THE OBOE

The prologues are over. It is a question, now,
Of final belief. So, say that final belief
Must be in a fiction. It is time to choose.

I

That obsolete fiction of the wide river in
An empty land; the gods that Boucher killed;   5
And the metal heroes that time granulates—
The philosophers' man alone still walks in dew,
Still by the sea-side mutters milky lines
Concerning an immaculate imagery.
If you say on the hautboy man is not enough,   10
Can never stand as god, is ever wrong
In the end, however naked, tall, there is still
The impossible possible philosophers' man,
The man who has had the time to think enough,
The central man, the human globe, responsive   15
As a mirror with a voice, the man of glass,
Who in a million diamonds sums us up.

II

He is the transparence of the place in which
He is and in his poems we find peace.
He sets this peddler's pie and cries in summer,   20
The glass man, cold and numbered, dewily cries,

"Thou art not August unless I make thee so."
Clandestine steps upon imagined stairs
Climb through the night, because his cuckoos call.

III

One year, death and war prevented the jasmine scent   25
And the jasmine islands were bloody martyrdoms.
How was it then with the central man? Did we
Find peace? We found the sum of men. We found,
If we found the central evil, the central good.
We buried the fallen without jasmine crowns.   30
There was nothing he did not suffer, no; nor we.

It was not as if the jasmine ever returned.
But we and the diamond globe at last were one.
We had always been partly one. It was as we came
To see him, that we were wholly one, as we heard   35
Him chanting for those buried in their blood,
In the jasmine haunted forests, that we knew
The glass man, without external reference.

                                                    1940

THE WOMAN IN SUNSHINE

It is only that this warmth and movement are like
The warmth and movement of a woman.

It is not that there is any image in the air
Nor the beginning nor end of a form:

It is empty. But a woman in threadless gold   5
Burns us with brushings of her dress

And a dissociated abundance of being,
More definite for what she is—

Because she is disembodied,
Bearing the odors of the summer fields,   10

Confessing the taciturn and yet indifferent,
Invisibly clear, the only love.

1950

WORLD WITHOUT PECULIARITY

The day is great and strong—
But his father was strong, that lies now
In the poverty of dirt.

Nothing could be more hushed than the way
The moon moves toward the night,   5
But what his mother was returns and cries on his
    breast.

The red ripeness of round leaves is thick
With the spices of red summer,
But she that he loved turns cold at his light touch.

What good is it that the earth is justified,   10
That it is complete, that it is an end,
That in itself it is enough?

It is the earth itself that is humanity. . .
He is the inhuman son and she,
She is the fateful mother, whom he does not know.   15

She is the day, the walk of the moon
Among the breathless spices and, sometimes,
He, too, is human and difference disappears

And the poverty of dirt, the thing upon his breast,
The hating woman, the meaningless place,   20
Become a single being, sure and true.

1950

THE PLAIN SENSE OF THINGS

After the leaves have fallen, we return
To a plain sense of things. It is as if
We had come to an end of the imagination,
Inanimate in an inert savoir.

It is difficult even to choose the adjective   5
For this blank cold, this sadness without cause.
The great structure has become a minor house.
No turban walks across the lessened floors.

The greenhouse never so badly needed paint.
The chimney is fifty years old and slants to one side.   10
A fantastic effort has failed, a repetition
In a repetitiousness of men and flies.

Yet the absence of the imagination had
Itself to be imagined. The great pond,
The plain sense of it, without reflections, leaves,   15
Mud, water like dirty glass, expressing silence

Of a sort, silence of a rat come out to see,
The great pond and its waste of the lilies, all this
Had to be imagined as an inevitable knowledge,
Required, as a necessity requires.   20

                                                    1952

EZRA POUND

Ezra Weston Loomis Pound (1885-   ) was born in Hailey, Idaho, and spent his early years in Pennsylvania. He attended the University of Pennsylvania for two years as a special student, was graduated from Hamilton College (1905), and received an A.M. (1906) from the University of Pennsylvania, where he returned to study Romance linguistics. After a year's travel in Europe, he taught for four months at Wabash College, Indiana, until he was dismissed from the faculty. He returned to Italy, where his first book of poems, *A Lume Spento* (1908), was published, then lived in London for twelve years, in Paris for four years, and in Italy until the close of World War II. During his European residence, Pound's opinions about politics and economics led him to Fascism, and he broadcast propaganda for Mussolini's government. Under indictment for treason immediately following the war, he was returned to the United States and committed to a mental hospital in Washington, D. C. He has since been released from custody and has returned to Italy. His notoriety grew in 1949, in the course of a widely publicized dispute, when the Fellows of the Library of Congress, with a grant from the Bollingen Foundation, awarded Pound a cash prize for the best book of poems in the previous year by an American citizen. The book was *The Pisan Cantos* (1948), also included in *The Cantos of Ezra Pound* (1948).

These Cantos and an earlier volume, *Personae* (1926), account for most of Pound's poetry. *Personae* is a selection from a dozen previous titles, published from 1908 to 1921; it was reissued in 1949, containing all the verse, exclusive of the Cantos, that Pound wished to preserve. The Cantos have been published piecemeal since 1917; the 1948 volume collects eighty-four of the one hundred poems which Pound intended to complete the series. These are described by Elizabeth Drew and John L. Sweeney, in *Directions in Modern Poetry* (1940), as "a mosaic of translation, historical anecdote, quotation, economic discussion, and lyrical description, dealing mainly with the Greek and Latin classics, medieval France, Renaissance Italy and modern England and America. . . . Pound uses a structure of factual instances and

343

statistics. .... His characters are a mixed company of classical gods, heroes and poets, Chinese sages, Italian princes, pontiffs and art patrons, armament makers, bankers and politicians." His theme involves the debased values of civilization, past and present, seen "in the ascendancy of financial jobbery."

Pound's influence on contemporary English and American poetry is enormous. There is scarcely a poet of note who does not owe him some debt. As a literary critic and an editor of *Poetry* and *The Little Review*, he secured a hearing for dozens of colleagues. Even more significant are his technical discoveries, made in the process of experimenting with verse forms and language. Pound has been more responsible than any other writer for the contemporary revolution in poetics. He has naturalized, to modern English, the properties of a dozen languages: old and modern French, German, and Italian; Chinese, Japanese, Spanish, Provençal, Anglo-Saxon, Greek, classical and medieval Latin. With his early translation of the tenth-century "The Seafarer," Pound adapted to modern English the alliterative stressed line of Anglo-Saxon poetry. The range of his experimentation is suggested in the first of his Cantos, an adaptation of a medieval Latin translation of an episode in Homer's *Odyssey* which retains the structure and measurement of the Anglo-Saxon line.

His translations of Chinese verse reflect Pound's insistence on the precision of a word, an image, or a concept, and his conviction about the responsibility of the artist in this respect. He once wrote: "When words cease to cling close to things, kingdoms fall, empires wane and diminish. Rome went because it was no longer the fashion to hit the nail on the head." His poetry reflects the social criticism and literary scholarship which he has exercised and recorded in nine volumes of essays. Notable among these are the long essay, "How to Read," in *Polite Essays* (1937), and a collection of essays in *Make It New* (1934). His writings also include treatises on economics and politics; an experiment in autobiography, *Indiscretions* (1923); and *The Letters of Ezra Pound, 1907-1941* (1950).

The texts of these selections are *Personae* (1926) and *The Cantos of Ezra Pound* (1948).

BALLAD OF THE GOODLY FERE

Simon Zelotes speaketh it somewhile after the Crucifixion
Fere=Mate, Companion

Ha' we lost the goodliest fere o' all
For the priests and the gallows tree?
Aye lover he was of brawny men,
O' ships and the open sea.

When they came wi' a host to take Our Man   5
His smile was good to see,
"First let these go!" quo' our Goodly Fere,
"Or I'll see ye damned," says he.

Aye he sent us out through the crossed high spears
And the scorn of his laugh rang free,   10
"Why took ye not me when I walked about
Alone in the town?" says he.

Oh we drunk his "Hale" in the good red wine
When we last made company,
No capon priest was the Goodly Fere   15
But a man o' men was he.

I ha' seen him drive a hundred men
Wi' a bundle o' cords swung free,
That they took the high and holy house
For their pawn and treasury.   20

They'll no' get him a' in a book I think
Though they write it cunningly;
No mouse of the scrolls was the Goodly Fere
But aye loved the open sea.

If they think they ha' snared our Goodly Fere   25
They are fools to the last degree.

"I'll go to the feast," quo' our Goodly Fere,
"Though I go to the gallows tree."

"Ye ha' seen me heal the lame and blind,
And wake the dead," says he,   30
"Ye shall see one thing to master all:
'Tis how a brave man dies on the tree."

A son of God was the Goodly Fere
That bade us his brothers be.
I ha' seen him cow a thousand men.   35
I have seen him upon the tree.

He cried no cry when they drave the nails
And the blood gushed hot and free,
The hounds of the crimson sky gave tongue
But never a cry cried he.   40

I ha' seen him cow a thousand men
On the hills o' Galilee,
They whined as he walked out calm between,
Wi' his eyes like the grey o' the sea,

Like the sea that brooks no voyaging   45
With the winds unleashed and free,
Like the sea that he cowed at Genseret
Wi' twey words spoke' suddently.

A master of men was the Goodly Fere,
A mate of the wind and sea,   50
If they think they ha' slain our Goodly Fere
They are fools eternally.

I ha' seen him eat o' the honey-comb
Sin' they nailed him to the tree.

                                              1909

ERAT HORA

"Thank you, whatever comes." And then she turned
And, as the ray of sun on hanging flowers
Fades when the wind hath lifted them aside,
Went swiftly from me. Nay, whatever comes
One hour was sunlit and the most high gods   5
May not make boast of any better thing
Than to have watched that hour as it passed.

1911

TENZONE

Will people accept them?
  (i.e. these songs).
As a timorous wench from a centaur
  (or a centurion),
Already they flee, howling in terror.   5

Will they be touched with the verisimilitudes?
  Their virgin stupidity is untemptable.
I beg you, my friendly critics,
Do not set about to procure me an audience.

I mate with my free kind upon the crags;
  the hidden recesses   10
Have heard the echo of my heels,
  in the cool light,
  in the darkness.

1913

DANCE FIGURE

For the Marriage in Cana of Galilee

Dark eyed,
O woman of my dreams,
Ivory sandaled,

There is none like thee among the dancers,
None with swift feet.   5

I have not found thee in the tents,
In the broken darkness.
I have not found thee at the well-head
Among the women with pitchers.

Thine arms are as a young sapling under the bark;   10
Thy face as a river with lights.

White as an almond are thy shoulders;
As new almonds stripped from the husk.
They guard thee not with eunuchs;
Not with bars of copper.   15

Gilt turquoise and silver are in the place of thy rest.
A brown robe, with threads of gold woven in patterns,
     hast thou gathered about thee,
O Nathat-Ikanaie, "Tree-at-the-river."

As a rillet among the sedge are thy hands upon me;
Thy fingers a frosted stream.   20

Thy maidens are white like pebbles;
Their music about thee!

There is none like thee among the dancers;
None with swift feet.

                                                        1913

A PACT

I make a pact with you, Walt Whitman—
I have detested you long enough.
I come to you as a grown child
Who has had a pig-headed father;
I am old enough now to make friends.   5
It was you that broke the new wood,

Now is a time for carving.
We have one sap and one root—
Let there be commerce between us.

1913

IN A STATION OF THE METRO

The apparition of these faces in the crowd;
Petals on a wet, black bough.

1913

THE GARDEN
En robe de parade.

Samain

Like a skein of loose silk blown against a wall
She walks by the railing of a path in Kensington
    Gardens,
And she is dying piece-meal
    of a sort of emotional anaemia.

And round about there is a rabble   5
Of the filthy, sturdy, unkillable infants of the very poor.
They shall inherit the earth.

In her is the end of breeding.
Her boredom is exquisite and excessive.
She would like some one to speak to her,   10
And is almost afraid that
    I will commit that indiscretion.

1913

FURTHER INSTRUCTIONS

Come, my songs, let us express our baser passions,
Let us express our envy of the man with a steady job
    and no worry about the future.

You are very idle, my songs.
I fear you will come to a bad end.
You stand about in the streets,   5
You loiter at the corners and bus-stops,
You do next to nothing at all.

You do not even express our inner nobilities,
You will come to a very bad end.

And I?   10
I have gone half cracked,
I have talked to you so much that I almost see you
        about me,
Insolent little beasts, shameless, devoid of clothing!

But you, newest song of the lot,
You are not old enough to have done much mischief,   15
I will get you a green coat out of China
With dragons worked upon it,
I will get you the scarlet silk trousers
From the statue of the infant Christ in Santa Maria
        Novella,
Lest they say we are lacking in taste,   20
Or that there is no caste in this family.

                                                          1913

LES MILLWIN

The little Millwins attend the Russian Ballet.
The mauve and greenish souls of the little Millwins
Were seen lying along the upper seats
Like so many unused boas.

The turbulent and undisciplined host of art students—   5
The rigorous deputation from "Slade"—
Was before them.

With arms exalted, with fore-arms
Crossed in great futuristic X's, the art students
Exulted, they beheld the splendours of *Cleopatra*.   10

And the little Millwins beheld these things;
With their large and anaemic eyes they looked out
        upon this configuration.

Let us therefore mention the fact,
For it seems to us worthy of record.

1913

ANCIENT MUSIC

Winter is icummen in,
Lhude sing Goddamm,
Raineth drop and staineth slop,
And how the wind doth ramm!
        Sing: Goddamm.   5
Skiddeth bus and sloppeth us,
An ague hath my ham.
Freezeth river, turneth liver,
        Damn you, sing: Goddamm.
Goddamm, Goddamm, 'tis why I am, Goddamm,   10
        So 'gainst the winter's balm.
Sing goddamm, damm, sing Goddamm,
Sing goddamm, sing goddamm, DAMN.

1915

CANTO I

And then went down to the ship,
Set keel to breakers, forth on the godly sea, and
We set up mast and sail on that swart ship,
Bore sheep aboard her, and our bodies also
Heavy with weeping, and winds from sternward   5
Bore us out onward with bellying canvas
Circe's this craft, the trim-coifed goddess.
Then sat we amidships, wind jamming the tiller,
Thus with stretched sail, we went over sea till day's end.
Sun to his slumber, shadows o'er all the ocean,   10
Came we then to the bounds of deepest water,

To the Kimmerian lands, and peopled cities
Covered with close-webbed mist, unpierced ever
With glitter of sun-rays
Nor with stars stretched, nor looking back from heaven   15
Swartest night stretched over wretched men there.
The ocean flowing backward, came we then to the place
Aforesaid by Circe.
Here did they rites, Perimedes and Eurylochus,
And drawing sword from my hip   20
I dug the ell-square pitkin;
Poured we libations unto each the dead,
First mead and then sweet wine, water mixed with
    white flour.
Then prayed I many a prayer to the sickly death's-heads;
As set in Ithaca, sterile bulls of the best   25
For sacrifice, heaping the pyre with goods,
A sheep to Tiresias only, black and a bell-sheep.
Dark blood flowed in the fosse,
Souls out of Erebus, cadaverous dead, of brides
Of youths and of the old who had borne much;   30
Souls stained with recent tears, girls tender,
Men many, mauled with bronze lance heads,
Battle spoil, bearing yet dreory arms,
These many crowded about me; with shouting,
Pallor upon me, cried to my men for more beasts;   35
Slaughtered the herds, sheep slain of bronze;
Poured ointment, cried to the gods,
To Pluto the strong, and praised Proserpine;
Unsheathed the narrow sword,
I sat to keep off the impetuous impotent dead,   40
Till I should hear Tiresias.
But first Elpenor came, our friend Elpenor,
Unburied, cast on the wide earth,
Limbs that we left in the house of Circe,
Unwept, unwrapped in sepulchre, since toils urged
    other.   45
Pitiful spirit. And I cried in hurried speech;
"Elpenor, how art thou come to this dark coast?
"Cam'st thou afoot, outstripping seamen?"
    And he in heavy speech:

"Ill fate and abundant wine. I slept in Circe's ingle. 50
"Going down the long ladder unguarded,
"I fell against the buttress,
"Shattered the nape-nerve, the soul sought Avernus.
"But thou, O King, I bid remember me, unwept, un-
    buried,
"Heap up mine arms, be tomb by sea-bord, and in-
    scribed: 55
"*A man of no fortune, and with a name to come.*
"And set my oar up, that I swung mid fellows."

And Anticlea came, whom I beat off, and then Tiresias
    Theban,
Holding his golden wand, knew me, and spoke first:
"A second time? why? man of ill star, 60
"Facing the sunless dead and this joyless region?
"Stand from the fosse, leave me my bloody bever
"For soothsay."
        And I stepped back,
And he strong with the blood, said then: "Odysseus
"Shalt return through spiteful Neptune, over dark seas, 65
"Lose all companions." And then Anticlea came.
Lie quiet Divus. I mean, that is Andreas Divus,
In officina Wecheli, 1538, out of Homer.
And he sailed, by Sirens and thence outward and away
And unto Circe.
        Venerandam, 70
In the Cretan's phrase, with the golden crown,
    Aphrodite,
Cypri munimenta sortita est, mirthful, oricalchi, with
    golden
Girdles and breast bands, thou with dark eyelids
Bearing the golden bough of Argicida. So that:
                                1917

PHANOPOEIA

I

ROSE WHITE, YELLOW, SILVER

The swirl of light follows me through the square,
The smoke of incense
Mounts from the four horns of my bed-posts,
The water-jet of gold light bears us up through the
    ceilings;
Lapped in the gold-coloured flame I descend through
    the aether.   5
The silver ball forms in my hand,
It falls and rolls to your feet.

1918

HUGH SELWYN MAUBERLEY

(Life and Contacts)

"Vocat aestus in umbram."
    Nemesianus, Ec. IV.

I

E. P. ODE POUR L'ELECTION DE SON SEPULCHRE

For three years, out of key with his time,
He strove to resuscitate the dead art
Of poetry; to maintain "the sublime"
In the old sense. Wrong from the start—

No, hardly, but seeing he had been born   5
In a half savage country, out of date;
Bent resolutely on wringing lilies from the acorn;
Capaneus; trout for factitious bait;

Ἴδμεν γάρ τοι πάνθ, ὄσ' ἐνὶ Τροίῃ [1]
Caught in the unstopped ear;   10
Giving the rocks small lee-way
The chopped seas held him, therefore, that year.

His true Penelope was Flaubert,
He fished by obstinate isles;
Observed the elegance of Circe's hair   15
Rather than the mottoes on sun-dials.

Unaffected by "the march of events,"
He passed from men's memory in *l'an trentiesme*
De son eage; the case presents
No adjunct to the Muses' diadem.   20

II

The age demanded an image
Of its accelerated grimace,
Something for the modern stage,
Not, at any rate, an Attic grace;

Not, not certainly, the obscure reveries   5
Of the inward gaze;
Better mendacities
Than the classics in paraphrase!

The "age demanded" chiefly a mould in plaster,
Made with no loss of time,   10
A prose kinema, not, not assuredly, alabaster
Or the "sculpture" of rhyme.

III

The tea-rose tea-gown, etc.
Supplants the mousseline of Cos,
The pianola "replaces"
Sappho's barbitos.

1 "For surely we know all about Troy"

Christ follows Dionysus,   5
Phallic and ambrosial
Made way for macerations;
Caliban casts out Ariel.

All things are a flowing,
Sage Heracleitus says;   10
But a tawdry cheapness
Shall outlast our days.

Even the Christian beauty
Defects—after Samothrace;
We see τὸ καλὸν [1]   15
Decreed in the market place.

Faun's flesh is not to us,
Nor the saint's vision.
We have the press for wafer;
Franchise for circumcision.   20

All men, in law, are equals.
Free of Pisistratus,
We choose a knave or an eunuch
To rule over us.

O bright Apollo,   25
τίν' ἄνδρα, τίν' ἥρωα, τίνα θεόν, [2]
What god, man, or hero
Shall I place a tin wreath upon!

IV

These fought in any case,
and some believing,
        pro domo, in any case. . .

Some quick to arm,
some for adventure,   5

[1] the beautiful
[2] Translated in line 27.

some from fear of weakness,
some from fear of censure,
some for love of slaughter, in imagination,
learning later. . .
some in fear, learning love of slaughter;   10

Died some, pro patria,
        non "dulce" non "et decor". . .
walked eye-deep in hell
believing in old men's lies, then unbelieving
came home, home to a lie,   15
home to many deceits,
home to old lies and new infamy;
usury age-old and age-thick
and liars in public places.

Daring as never before, wastage as never before.   20
Young blood and high blood,
fair cheeks, and fine bodies;

fortitude as never before

frankness as never before,
disillusions as never told in the old days,   25
hysterias, trench confessions,
laughter out of dead bellies.

                          V

There died a myriad,
And of the best, among them,
For an old bitch gone in the teeth,
For a botched civilization,

Charm, smiling at the good mouth,   5
Quick eyes gone under earth's lid,

For two gross of broken statues,
For a few thousand battered books.

YEUX GLAUQUES

Gladstone was still respected,
When John Ruskin produced
"King's Treasuries"; Swinburne
And Rossetti still abused.

Foetid Buchanan lifted up his voice   5
When that faun's head of hers
Became a pastime for
Painters and adulterers.

The Burne-Jones cartoons
Have preserved her eyes;   10
Still, at the Tate, they teach
Cophetua to rhapsodize;

Thin like brook-water,
With a vacant gaze.
The English Rubaiyat was still-born   15
In those days.

The thin, clear gaze, the same
Still darts out faun-like from the half-ruin'd face,
Questing and passive. . . .
"Ah, poor Jenny's case". . .   20

Bewildered that a world
Shows no surprise
At her last maquero's
Adulteries.

"SIENE MI FE'; DISFECEMI MAREMMA"

Among the pickled foetuses and bottled bones,
Engaged in perfecting the catalogue,
I found the last scion of the
Senatorial families of Strasbourg, Monsieur Verog.

For two hours he talked of Gallifet;   5
Of Dowson; of the Rhymers' Club;
Told me how Johnson (Lionel) died
By falling from a high stool in a pub. . .

But showed no trace of alcohol
At the autopsy, privately performed—   10
Tissue preserved—the pure mind
Arose toward Newman as the whiskey warmed.

Dowson found harlots cheaper than hotels;
Headlam for uplift; Image impartially imbued
With raptures for Bacchus, Terpsichore and the Church.   15
So spoke the author of "The Dorian Mood,"

M. Verog, out of step with the decade,
Detached from his contemporaries,
Neglected by the young,
Because of these reveries.   20

BRENNBAUM

The sky-like limpid eyes,
The circular infant's face,
The stiffness from spats to collar
Never relaxing into grace;

The heavy memories of Horeb, Sinai and the forty
    years,   5
Showed only when the daylight fell
Level across the face
Of Brennbaum "The Impeccable."

MR. NIXON

In the cream gilded cabin of his steam yacht
Mr. Nixon advised me kindly, to advance with fewer
Dangers of delay. "Consider
    "Carefully the reviewer.

"I was as poor as you are;   5
"When I began I got, of course,
"Advance on royalties, fifty at first," said Mr. Nixon,
"Follow me, and take a column
"Even if you have to work free.

"Butter reviewers. From fifty to three hundred   10
"I rose in eighteen months;
"The hardest nut I had to crack
"Was Dr. Dundas.

"I never mentioned a man but with the view
"Of selling my own works.   15
"The tip's a good one, as for literature
"It gives no man a sinecure.

"And no one knows, at sight, a masterpiece.
"And give up verse, my boy,
"There's nothing in it."   20

  .   .   .   .

Likewise a friend of Bloughram's once advised me:
Don't kick against the pricks,
Accept opinion. The "Nineties" tried your game
And died, there's nothing in it.

X

Beneath the sagging roof
The stylist has taken shelter,
Unpaid, uncelebrated,
At last from the world's welter

Nature receives him;   5
With a placid and uneducated mistress
He exercises his talents
And the soil meets his distress.

The haven from sophistications and contentions
Leaks through its thatch;   10
He offers succulent cooking;
The door has a creaking latch.

XI

"Conservatrix of Milésien"
Habits of mind and feeling,
Possibly. But in Ealing
With the most bank-clerkly of Englishmen?

No, "Milésian" is an exaggeration.   5
No instinct has survived in her
Older than those her grandmother
Told her would fit her station.

XII

"Daphne with her thighs in bark
Stretches toward me her leafy hands,"—
Subjectively. In the stuffed-satin drawing-room
I await The Lady Valentine's commands,

Knowing my coat has never been   5
Of precisely the fashion
To stimulate, in her,
A durable passion;

Doubtful, somewhat, of the value
Of well-gowned approbation   10
Of literary effort,
But never of The Lady Valentine's vocation:

Poetry, her border of ideas,
The edge, uncertain, but a means of blending
With other strata   15
Where the lower and higher have ending;

A hook to catch the Lady Jane's attention,
A modulation toward the theatre,
Also, in the case of revolution,
A possible friend and comforter.   20

.   .   .   .

Conduct, on the other hand, the soul
"Which the highest cultures have nourished"

To Fleet St. where
Dr. Johnson flourished;

Beside this thoroughfare
The sale of half-hose has   25
Long since superseded the cultivation
Of Pierian roses.

ENVOI (1919)

Go, dumb-born book,
Tell her that sang me once that song of Lawes;
Hadst thou but song
As thou hast subjects known,
Then were there cause in thee that should condone   5
Even my faults that heavy upon me lie,
And build her glories their longevity.

Tell her that sheds
Such treasure in the air,
Recking naught else but that her graces give   10
Life to the moment,
I would bid them live
As roses might, in magic amber laid,
Red overwrought with orange and all made
One substance and one colour   15
Braving time.

Tell her that goes
With song upon her lips
But sings not out the song, nor knows
The maker of it, some other mouth,   20
May be as fair as hers,
Might, in new ages, gain her worshippers,
When our two dusts with Waller's shall be laid,
Siftings on siftings in oblivion,
Till change hath broken down   25
All things save Beauty alone.

MAUBERLEY

1920

"Vacuos exercet aera morsus."

I

Turned from the "eau-forte
Par Jaquemart"
To the strait head
Of Messalina:

"His true Penelope   5
Was Flaubert,"
And his tool
The engraver's.

Firmness,
Not the full smile,   10
His art, but an art
In profile;

Colourless
Pier Francesca,
Pisanello lacking the skill   15
To forge Achaia.

II

*"Qu'est ce qu'ils savent de l'amour, et qu'est ce qu'ils
peuvent comprendre?*
*S'ils ne comprennent pas la poésie, s'ils ne sentent pas
la musique, qu'est ce qu'ils peuvent comprendre de cette
passion en comparaison avec laquelle la rose est grossière
et le parfum des violettes un tonnerre?"*

                                                    Caid Ali

For three years, diabolus in the scale,
He drank ambrosia,

All passes, ANANGKE prevails,
Came end, at last, to that Arcadia.

He had moved amid her phantasmagoria,   5
Amid her galaxies,
NUKTIS 'AGALMA

.   .   .   .

Drifted . . . drifted precipitate,
Asking time to be rid of. . .
Of his bewilderment; to designate   10
His new found orchid. . . .

To be certain . . . certain . . .
(Amid aerial flowers) . . . time for arrangements—
Drifted on
To the final estrangement;   15

Unable in the supervening blankness
To sift TO AGATHON from the chaff
Until he found his sieve . . .
Ultimately, his seismograph:

—Given that is his "fundamental passion,"   20
This urge to convey the relation
Of eye-lid and cheek-bone
By verbal manifestations;

To present the series
Of curious heads in medallion—   25

He had passed, inconscient, full gaze,
The wide-banded irides
And botticellian sprays implied
In their diastasis;

Which anaethesis, noted a year late,   30
And weighed, revealed his great affect,
(Orchid), mandate
Of Eros, a retrospect

. . .

Mouths biting empty air,
The still stone dogs,   35
Caught in metamorphosis, were
Left him as epilogues.

"THE AGE DEMANDED"

For this agility chance found
Him of all men, unfit
As the red-beaked steeds of
The Cytheraean for a chain bit.

The glow of porcelain   5
Brought no reforming sense
To his perception
Of the social inconsequence.

Thus, if her colour
Came against his gaze,   10
Tempered as if
It were through a perfect glaze

He made no immediate application
Of this to relation of the state
To the individual, the month was more temperate   15
Because this beauty had been.

        The coral isle, the lion-coloured sand
        Burst in upon the porcelain revery:
        Impetuous troubling
        Of his imagery.   20

Mildness, amid the neo-Nietzschean clatter,
His sense of graduations,
Quite out of place amid
Resistance to current exacerbations,

Invitation, mere invitation to perceptivity   25
Gradually led him to the isolation
Which these presents place
Under a more tolerant, perhaps, examination.

By constant elimination
The manifest universe   30
Yielded an armour
Against utter consternation,

A Minoan undulation,
Seen, we admit, amid ambrosial circumstances
Strengthened him against   35
The discouraging doctrine of chances,

And his desire for survival,
Faint in the most strenuous moods,
Became an Olympian *apathein*
In the presence of selected perceptions.   40

A pale gold, in the aforesaid pattern,
The unexpected palms
Destroying, certainly, the artist's urge,
Left him delighted with the imaginary
Audition of the phantasmal sea-surge,   45

Incapable of the least utterance or composition,
Emendation, conservation of the "better tradition,"
Refinement of medium, elimination of superfluities,
August attraction or concentration.

Nothing, in brief, but maudlin confession,   50
Irresponse to human aggression,
Amid the precipitation, down-float
Of insubstantial manna,
Lifting the faint susurrus
Of his subjective hosannah.   55

Ultimate affronts to
Human redundancies;

Non-esteem of self-styled "his betters"
Leading, as he well knew,
To his final   60
Exclusion from the world of letters.

IV

Scattered Moluccas
Not knowing, day to day,
The first day's end, in the next noon;
The placid water
Unbroken by the Simoon;   5

Thick foliage
Placid beneath warm suns,
Tawn fore-shores
Washed in the cobalt of oblivions;

Or through dawn-mist   10
The grey and rose
Of the juridical
Flamingoes;

A consciousness disjunct,
Being but this overblotted   15
Series
Of intermittences;

Coracle of Pacific voyages,
The unforecasted beach;
Then on an oar   20
Read this:

"I was
And I no more exist;
Here drifted
An hedonist."   25

MEDALLION

Luini in porcelain!
The grand piano
Utters a profane
Protest with her clear soprano.

The sleek head emerges   5
From the gold-yellow frock
As Anadyomene in the opening
Pages of Reinach.

Honey-red, closing the face-oval,
A basket-work of braids which seem as if they were   10
Spun in King Minos' hall
From metal, or intractable amber;

The face-oval beneath the glaze,
Bright in its suave bounding-line, as,
Beneath half-watt rays,   15
The eyes turn topaz.

                                                        1920

ROBINSON JEFFERS

John Robinson Jeffers (1887-   ) was born in Pittsburgh, Pennsylvania. He writes: "My parents carried me about Europe a good deal. . . . When I was fifteen I was brought home. Next year my family moved to California and I graduated at eighteen from Occidental College, Los Angeles. After that, desultory years at the University of Southern California, University of Zurich, Medical School in Los Angeles, University of Washington but with faint interest. I wasn't deeply interested in anything, but poetry." He married Una Call Kuster in 1913, and they settled in Carmel, California, on a high slope overlooking Carmel Bay, among the granite rocks.

Jeffers published his first poem in 1903, and, in 1912, with the income from a legacy, subsidized his first volume of poetry, *Flagons and Apples*. After a second volume of poems, *Californians* (1916), and a number of rejections from publishers, he subsidized a volume entitled *Tamar and Other Poems* (1924), the first of his major works and the one which largely established his reputation. This volume was revised and reissued by a publisher the following year, with another title poem added: *Roan Stallion, Tamar, and Other Poems* (1925), the most widely circulated of all his writings. Between this volume and his *Selected Poems* (1938)—excluding separate editions of single poems—Jeffers published ten titles; characteristically, they are made up of clusters of short poems amplifying the theme of a long narrative poem. Most of his narratives are domestications of Greek legends— "The Tower Beyond Tragedy" (1924) and "Solstice" (1935), for instance— or Biblical stories—such as "Tamar" (1924) and "Dear Judas" (1929), located on the landscape near Carmel. The conviction of many of the poems is the need "to uncenter the human mind from itself." Jeffers contends: "All past cultures have died of introversion, at last, and so will this one, but the individual can be free of the net, in his mind." In the preface to *The Double Axe and Other Poems* (1948) he again speaks to the point: the burden of his poems, he says, "is to present a certain philosophical attitude, which might be called Inhumanism, a shifting of emphasis and significance from man to not-man; the rejection of human solipsism and recognition of the transhuman magnificence." As for the legends he naturalizes, and which bear these convictions, he observes: "We turn to the classic stories, I suppose, as to Greek sculpture, for a more ideal and also more normal beauty, because the myths of our own race were never developed, and have been alienated from us."

Since *The Selected Poetry of Robinson Jeffers* (New York, 1938), the poet has published an adaptation of *Medea* (1946), and three volumes of poems. The 1938 volume is the text of all the following poems published by that date. The text of the last two selections is *Hungerfield and Other Poems* (New York, 1954), and of the two preceding those, *Be Angry at the Sun* (New York, 1941).

ROAN STALLION

The dog barked; then the woman stood in the doorway, and
    hearing iron strike stone down the steep road
Covered her head with a black shawl and entered the light rain;
    she stood at the turn of the road.
A nobly formed woman; erect and strong as a new tower; the
    features stolid and dark
But sculptured into a strong grace; straight nose with a high
    bridge, firm and wide eyes, full chin,
Red lips; she was only a fourth part Indian; a Scottish sailor had
    planted her in young native earth,   5
Spanish and Indian, twenty-one years before. He had named her
    California when she was born;
That was her name; and had gone north.
                She heard the hooves
    and wheels come nearer, up the steep road.
The buckskin mare, leaning against the breastpiece, plodded
    into sight round the wet bank.
The pale face of the driver followed; the burnt-out eyes; they
    had fortune in them. He sat twisted
On the seat of the old buggy, leading a second horse by a long
    halter, a roan, a big one,   10

That stepped daintily; by the swell of the neck, a stallion.
"What have you got, Johnny? " "Maskerel's stallion.
Mine now. I won him last night, I had very good luck." He was
quite drunk. "They bring their mares up here now.
I keep this fellow. I got money besides, but I'll not show you."
"Did you buy something, Johnny,
For our Christine? Christmas comes in two days, Johnny." "By
God, forgot," he answered laughing.
"Don't tell Christine it's Christmas; after while I get her some-
thing, maybe." But California: 15
"I shared your luck when you lost: you lost *me* once, Johnny,
remember? Tom Dell had me two nights
Here in the house: other times we've gone hungry: now that
you've won, Christine will have her Christmas.
We share your luck, Johnny. You give me money, I go down
to Monterey to-morrow,
Buy presents for Christine, come back in the evening. Next day
Christmas." "You have wet ride," he answered
Giggling. "Here money. Five dollar; ten; twelve dollar. You
buy two bottles of rye whiskey for Johnny."   20
"All right. I go to-morrow."
                            He was an outcast Hollander; not
old, but shriveled with bad living.
The child Christine inherited from his race blue eyes, from his
life a wizened forehead; she watched
From the house-door her father lurch out of the buggy and lead
with due respect the stallion
To the new corral, the strong one; leaving the wearily breathing
buckskin mare to his wife to unharness.

Storm in the night; the rain on the thin shakes of the roof like
the ocean on rock streamed battering; once thunder   25
Walked down the narrow canyon into Carmel valley and wore
away westward; Christine was wakeful
With fears and wonders; her father lay too deep for storm to
touch him.
                    Dawn comes late in the year's dark,
Later into the crack of a canyon under redwoods; and Cali-
fornia slipped from bed

An hour before it; the buckskin would be tired; there was a little
  barley, and why should Johnny
Feed all the barley to his stallion? That is what he would do.
  She tip-toed out of the room.   30
Leaving her clothes, he'd waken if she waited to put them on,
  and passed from the door of the house
Into the dark of the rain; the big black drops were cold through
  The thin shift, but the wet earth
Pleasant under her naked feet. There was a pleasant smell in the
  stable; and moving softly,
Touching things gently with the supple bend of the unclothed
  body, was pleasant. She found a box,
Filled it with sweet dry barley and took it down to the old
  corral. The little mare sighed deeply   35
At the rail in the wet darkness; and California returning be-
  tween two redwoods up to the house
Heard the happy jaws grinding the grain. Johnny could mind
  the pigs and chickens. Christine called to her
When she entered the house, but slept again under her hand.
  She laid the wet night-dress on a chair-back
And stole into the bedroom to get her clothes. A plank creaked.
  and he wakened. She stood motionless
Hearing him stir in the bed. When he was quiet she stooped
  after her shoes, and he said softly,   40
"What are you doing? Come back to bed." "It's late, I'm going
  to Monterey, I must hitch up."
"You come to bed first. I been away three days. I give you
  money, I take back the money
And what you do in town then?" She sighed sharply and came
  to the bed.
              He reaching his hands from it
Felt the cool curve and firmness of her flank, and half rising
  caught her by the long wet hair.
She endured, and to hasten the act she feigned desire; she had
  not for long, except in dream, felt it.   45
Yesterday's drunkenness made him sluggish and exacting; she
  saw, turning her head sadly,
The windows were bright gray with dawn; he embraced her still,
  stopping to talk about the stallion.

At length she was permitted to put on her clothes. Clear day-
light over the steep hills;
Gray-shining cloud over the tops of the redwoods; the winter
stream sang loud; the wheels of the buggy
Slipped in deep slime, ground on washed stones at the road-
edge. Down the hill the wrinkled river smothered the ford.   50
You must keep to the bed of stones: she knew the way by willow
and alder: the buckskin halted mid-stream,
Shuddering, the water her own color washing up to the traces;
but California, drawing up
Her feet out of the whirl onto the seat of the buggy swung the
whip over the yellow water
And drove to the road.
           All morning the clouds were racing
northward like a river. At noon they thickened.
When California faced the southwind home from Monterey it
was heavy with level rainfall.   55
She looked seaward from the foot of the valley; red rays cried
sunset from a trumpet of streaming
Cloud over Lobos, the southwest occident of the solstice. Twi-
light came soon, but the tired mare
Feared the road more than the whip. Mile after mile of slow
gray twilight.
           Then, quite suddenly, darkness.
"Christine will be asleep. It is Christmas Eve. The ford. That
hour of daylight wasted this morning!"
She could see nothing; she let the reins lie on the dashboard and
knew at length by the cramp of the wheels   60
And the pitch down, they had reached it. Noise of wheels on
stones, plashing of hooves in water; a world
Of sounds; no sight; the gentle thunder of water; the mare
snorting, dipping her head, one knew,
To look for footing, in the blackness, under the stream. The
hushing and creaking of the sea-wind
In the passion of invisible willows.
           The mare stood still; the
woman shouted to her; spared whip,
For a false leap would lose the track of the ford. She stood.
"The baby's things," thought California,   65

"Under the seat: the water will come over the floor"; and rising
in the midst of the water
She tilted the seat; fetched up the doll, the painted wooden
chickens, the woolly bear, the book
Of many pictures, the box of sweets: she brought them all from
under the seat and stored them, trembling,
Under her clothes, about the breasts, under the arms; the cor-
ners of the cardboard boxes
Cut into the soft flesh; but with a piece of rope for a girdle and
wound about the shoulders   70
All was made fast. The mare stood still as if asleep in the midst
of the water. Then California
Reached out a hand over the stream and fingered her rump;
the solid wet convexity of it
Shook like the beat of a great heart. "What are you waiting
for?" But the feel of the animal surface
Had wakened a dream, obscured real danger with a dream of
danger. "What for? For the water-stallion
To break out of the stream, that is what the rump strains for,
him to come up flinging foam sidewise,   75
Fore-hooves in air, crush me and the rig and curl over his
woman." She flung out with the whip then;
The mare plunged forward. The buggy drifted sidelong: was
she off ground? Swimming? No: by the splashes.
The driver, a mere prehensile instinct, clung to the side-irons
of the seat and felt the force
But not the coldness of the water, curling over her knees,
breaking up to the waist
Over her body. They'd turned. The mare had turned up stream
and was wallowing back into shoal water.   80
Then California dropped her forehead to her knees, having
seen nothing, feeling a danger,
And felt the brute weight of a branch of alder, the pendulous
light leaves brush her bent neck
Like a child's fingers. The mare burst out of the water and
stopped on the slope to the ford. The woman climbed down
Between the wheels and went to her head. "Poor Dora," she
called her by her name, "there, Dora. Quietly,"
And led her around, there was room to turn on the margin,
the head to the gentle thunder of the water.   85

She crawled on hands and knees, felt for the ruts, and shifted
the wheels into them. "You can see, Dora.
I can't. But this time you'll go through it." She climbed into the
seat and shouted angrily. The mare
Stopped, her two forefeet in the water. She touched with the
whip. The mare plodded ahead and halted.
Then California thought of prayer: "Dear little Jesus,
Dear baby Jesus born to-night, your head was shining   90
Like silver candles. I've got a baby too, only a girl. You had light
wherever you walked.
Dear baby Jesus give me light." Light streamed: rose, gold, rich
purple, hiding the ford like a curtain.
The gentle thunder of water was a noise of wing-feathers, the
fans of paradise lifting softly.
The child afloat on radiance had a baby face, but the angels had
birds' heads, hawks' heads,
Bending over the baby, weaving a web of wings about him. He
held in the small fat hand   95
A little snake with golden eyes, and California could see clearly
on the under radiance
The mare's pricked ears, a sharp black fork against the shining
light-fall. But it dropped; the light of heaven
Frightened poor Dora. She backed; swung up the water,
And nearly oversetting the buggy turned and scrambled back-
ward; the iron wheel-tires rang on bowlders.

Then California weeping climbed between the wheels. Her wet
clothes and the toys packed under   100
Dragged her down with their weight; she stripped off cloak and
dress and laid the baby's things in the buggy;
Brought Johnny's whiskey out from under the seat; wrapped all
in the dress, bottles and toys, and tied them
Into a bundle that would sling over her back. She unharnessed
the mare, hurting her fingers
Against the swollen straps and the wet buckles. She tied the
pack over her shoulders, the cords
Crossing her breasts, and mounted. She drew up her shift about
her waist and knotted it, naked thighs   105
Clutching the sides of the mare, bare flesh to the wet withers,
and caught the mane with her right hand,

The looped-up bridle-reins in the other. "Dora, the baby gives
you light." The blinding radiance
Hovered the ford. "Sweet baby Jesus give us light." Cataracts of
light and Latin singing
Fell through the willows; the mare snorted and reared: the roar
and thunder of the invisible water;
The night shaking open like a flag, shot with the flashes; the
baby face hovering; the water   110
Beating over her shoes and stockings up to the bare thighs; and
over them, like a beast
Lapping her belly; the wriggle and pitch of the mare swimming;
the drift, the sucking water; the blinding
Light above and behind with not a gleam before, in the throat
of darkness; the shock of the fore-hooves
Striking bottom, the struggle and surging lift of the haunches.
She felt the water streaming off her
From the shoulders down; heard the great strain and sob of the
mare's breathing, heard the horseshoes grind on gravel.   115
When California came home the dog at the door snuffed at her
without barking; Christine and Johnny
Both were asleep; she did not sleep for hours, but kindled fire
and knelt patiently over it,
Shaping and drying the dear-bought gifts for Christmas
morning.

She hated (she thought) the proud-necked stallion.
He'd lean the big twin masses of his breast on the rail, his red-
brown eyes flash the white crescents,
She admired him then, she hated him for his uselessness, serving
nothing   120
But Johnny's vanity. Horses were too cheap to breed. She
thought, if he could range in freedom,
Shaking the red-roan mane for a flag on the bare hills.
                                                          A man
brought up a mare in April;
Then California, though she wanted to watch, stayed with
Christine indoors. When the child fretted
The mother told her once more about the miracle of the ford;
her prayer to the little Jesus

The Christmas Eve when she was bringing the gifts home; the
  appearance, the lights, the Latin singing,   125
The thunder of wing-feathers and water, the shining child, the
  cataracts of splendor down the darkness.
"A little baby," Christine asked, "the God is a baby?" "The
  child of God. That was his birthday.
His mother was named Mary: we pray to her too: God came to
  her. He was not the child of a man
Like you or me. God was his father: she was the stallion's wife—
  what did I say—God's wife,"
She said with a cry, lifting Christine aside, pacing the planks
  of the floor. "She is called more blessed   130
Than any woman. She was so good, she was more loved." "Did
  God live near her house? " "He lives
Up high, over the stars; he ranges on the bare blue hill of the
  sky." In her mind a picture
Flashed, of the red-roan mane shaken out for a flag on the bare
  hills, and she said quickly, "He's more
Like a great man holding the sun in his hand." Her mind giving
  her words the lie, "But no one
Knows, only the shining and the power. The power, the terror,
  the burning fire covered her over . . ."   135
"Was she burnt up, mother? " "She was so good and lovely, she
  was the mother of the little Jesus.
If you are good nothing will hurt you." "What did she think?"
  "She loved, she was not afraid of the hooves—
Hands that had made the hills and sun and moon, and the sea
  and the great redwoods, the terrible strength,
She gave herself without thinking." "You only saw the baby,
  mother?" "Yes, and the angels about him,
The great wild shining over the black river." Three times she
  had walked to the door, three times returned,   140
And now the hand that had thrice hung on the knob, full of
  prevented action, twisted the cloth
Of the child's dress that she had been mending. "Oh, oh, I've
  torn it." She struck at the child and then embraced her
Fiercely, the small blonde sickly body.
                               Johnny came in, his face
  reddened as if he had stood

Near fire, his eyes triumphing. "Finished," he said, and looked
  with malice at Christine. "I go
Down valley with Jim Carrier; owes me five dollar, fifteen I
  charge him, he brought ten in his pocket.   145
Has grapes on the ranch, maybe I take a barrel red wine instead
  of money. Be back to-morrow.
To-morrow night I tell you—Eh, Jim," he laughed over his
  shoulder, "I say to-morrow evening
I show her how the red fellow act, the big fellow. When I come
  home." She answered nothing, but stood
In front of the door, holding the little hand of her daughter, in
  the path of sun between the redwoods,
While Johnny tied the buckskin mare behind Carrier's buggy,
  and bringing saddle and bridle tossed them   150
Under the seat. Jim Carrier's mare, the bay, stood with drooped
  head and started slowly, the men
Laughing and shouting at her; their voices could be heard down
  the steep road, after the noise
Of the iron-hooped wheels died from the stone. Then one might
  hear the hush of the wind in the tall redwoods,
The tinkle of the April brook, deep in its hollow.
                                         Humanity is
  the start of the race; I say
Humanity is the mould to break away from, the crust to break
  through, the coal to break into fire,   155
The atom to be split.
                          Tragedy that breaks man's face and a
  white fire flies out of it; vision that fools him
Out of his limits, desire that fools him out of his limits, un-
  natural crime, inhuman science,
Slit eyes in the mask; wild loves that leap over the walls of
  nature, the wild fence-vaulter science,
Useless intelligence of far stars, dim knowledge of the spinning
  demons that make an atom,
These break, these pierce, these deify, praising their God shrilly
  with their fierce voices: not in a man's shape   160
He approves the praise, he that walks lightning-naked on the
  Pacific, that laces the suns with planets,
The heart of the atom with electrons: what is humanity in this
  cosmos? For him, the last

Least taint of a trace in the dregs of the solution; for itself, the
    mold to break away from, the coal
To break into fire, the atom to be split.
                     After the child slept,
    after the leopard-footed evening
Had glided oceanward, California turned the lamp to its least
    flame and glided from the house.   165
She moved sighing, like a loose fire, backward and forward on
    the smooth ground by the door.
She heard the night-wind that draws down the valley like the
    draught in a flue under clear weather
Whisper and toss in the tall redwoods; she heard the tinkle of
    the April brook deep in its hollow.
Cooled by the night the odors that the horses had left behind
    were in her nostrils; the night
Whitened up the bare hill; a drift of coyotes by the river cried
    bitterly against moonrise;   170
Then California ran to the old corral, the empty one where they
    kept the buckskin mare,
And leaned, and bruised her breasts on the rail, feeling the sky
    whiten. When the moon stood over the hill
She stole to the house. The child breathed quietly. Herself: to
    sleep? She had seen Christ in the night at Christmas.
The hills were shining open to the enormous night of the April
    moon: empty and empty,
The vast round backs of the bare hills? If one should ride up
    high might not the Father himself   175
Be seen brooding His night, cross-legged, chin in hand,
    squatting on the last dome? More likely
Leaping the hills, shaking the red-roan mane for a flag on the
    bare hills. She blew out the lamp.
Every fiber of flesh trembled with faintness when she came to
    the door; strength lacked, to wander
Afoot into the shining of the hill, high enough, high enough . . .
    the hateful face of a man had taken
The strength that might have served her, the corral was empty.
    The dog followed her, she caught him by the collar,   180
Dragged him in fierce silence back to the door of the house,
    latched him inside.
                  It was like daylight

Outdoors, and she hastened without faltering down the foot-
path, through the dark fringe of twisted oak-brush,
To the open place in a bay of the hill. The dark strength of the
stallion had heard her coming; she heard him
Blow the shining air out of his nostrils, she saw him in the white
lake of moonlight
Move like a lion along the timbers of the fence, shaking the
nightfall   185
Of the great mane; his fragrance came to her; she leaned on the
fence;
He drew away from it, the hooves making soft thunder in the
trodden soil,
Wild love had trodden it, his wrestling with the stranger, the
shame of the day
Had stamped it into mire and powder when the heavy fetlocks
Strained the soft flanks. "Oh, if I could bear you!
If I had the strength. O great God that came down to Mary,
gently you came. But I will ride him   190
Up into the hill, if he throws me, if he tramples me, is it not
my desire
To endure death?" She climbed the fence, pressing her body
against the rail, shaking like fever,
And dropped inside to the soft ground. He neither threatened
her with his teeth nor fled from her coming,
And lifting her hand gently to the upflung head she caught
the strap of the headstall,
That hung under the quivering chin. She unlooped the halter
from the high strength of the neck   195
And the arch the storm-cloud mane hung with live darkness. He
stood; she crushed her breasts
On the hard shoulder, an arm over the withers, the other under
the mass of his throat, and murmuring
Like a mountain dove, "If I could bear you." No way, no help,
a gulf in nature. She murmured, "Come,
We will run on the hill. O beautiful, O beautiful," and led him
To the gate and flung the bars on the ground. He threw his
head downward
To snuff at the bars; and while he stood, she catching mane and
withers with all sudden contracture   200

And strength of her lithe body, leaped, clung hard, and was
  mounted. He had been ridden before; he did not
Fight the weight but ran like a stone falling;
Broke down the slope into the moon-glass of the stream, and
  flattened to his neck
She felt the branches of a buckeye tree fly over her, saw the
  wall of the oak-scrub
End her world: but he turned there, the matted branches
Scraped her right knee, the great slant shoulders   205
Laboring the hill-slope, up, up, the clear hill. Desire had died
  in her
At the first rush, the falling like death, but now it revived,
She feeling between her thighs the labor of the great engine, the
  running muscles, the hard swiftness,
She riding the savage and exultant strength of the world.
  Having topped the thicket he turned eastward,
Running less wildly; and now at length he felt the halter when
  she drew on it; she guided him upward;   210
He stopped and grazed on the great arch and pride of the hill,
  the silent calvary. A dwarfish oakwood
Climbed the other slope out of the dark of the unknown canyon
  beyond; the last wind-beaten bush of it
Crawled up to the height, and California slipping from her
  mount tethered him to it. She stood then,
Shaking. Enormous films of moonlight
Trailed down from the height. Space, anxious whiteness, vast-
  ness. Distant beyond conception the shining ocean   215
Lay light like a haze along the ledge and doubtful world's end.
  Little vapors gleaming, and little
Darknesses on the far chart underfoot symbolized wood and
  valley; but the air was the element, the moon—
Saturate arcs and spires of the air.
                                        Here is solitude, here on
  the calvary, nothing conscious
But the possible God and the cropped grass, no witness, no eye
  but that misformed one, the moon's past fullness.
Two figures on the shining hill, woman and stallion, she
  kneeling to him, brokenly adoring.   220
He cropping the grass, shifting his hooves, or lifting the long
  head to gaze over the world,

Tranquil and powerful. She prayed aloud, "O God, I am not
good enough, O fear, O strength, I am draggled.
Johnny and other men have had me, and O clean power! Here
am I," she said falling before him,
And crawled to his hooves. She lay a long while, as if asleep, in
reach of the fore-hooves, weeping. He avoided
Her head and the prone body. He backed at first; but later
plucked the grass that grew by her shoulder.   225
The small dark head under his nostrils: a small round stone,
that smelt human, black hair growing from it:
The skull shut the light in: it was not possible for any eyes
To know what throbbed and shone under the sutures of the
skull, or a shell full of lightning
Had scared the roan strength, and he'd have broken tether,
screaming, and run for the valley.
                                    The atom bounds-breaking,
Nucleus to the sun, electrons to planets, with recognition   230
Not praying, self-equaling, the whole to the whole, the
microcosm
Not entering nor accepting entrance, more equally, more
utterly, more incredibly conjugate
With the other extreme and greatness; passionately perceptive
of identity. . . .
                                    The fire threw up figures
And symbols meanwhile, racial myths formed and dissolved
in it, the phantom rulers of humanity
That without being are yet more real than what they are born
of, and without shape, shape that which makes them: 235
The nerves and the flesh go by shadowlike, the limbs and the
lives shadowlike, these shadows remain, these shadows
To whom temples, to whom churches, to whom labors and wars,
visions and dreams are dedicate:
Out of the fire in the small round stone that black moss covered,
a crucified man writhed up in anguish;
A woman covered by a huge beast in whose mane the stars were
netted, sun and moon were his eyeballs,
Smiled under the unendurable violation, her throat swollen
with the storm and blood-flecks gleaming   240
On the stretched lips; a woman—no, a dark water, split by jets
of lightning, and after a season

What floated up out of the furrowed water, a boat, a fish, a
   fire-globe?
            It had wings, the creature,
And flew against the fountain of lightning, fell burnt out of the
   cloud back to the bottomless water . . .
Figures and symbols, castings of the fire, played in her brain;
   but the white-fire was the essence,
The burning in the small round shell of bone that black hair
   covered, that lay by the hooves on the hilltop.   245

She rose at length, she unknotted the halter; she walked and led
   the stallion; two figures, woman and stallion,
Came down the silent emptiness of the dome of the hill, under
   the cataract of the moonlight.

The next night there was moon through cloud. Johnny had re-
   turned half drunk toward evening, and California
Who had known him for years with neither love nor loathing
   to-night hating him had let the child Christine
Play in the light of the lamp for hours after her bedtime; who
   fell asleep at length on the floor   250
Beside the dog; then Johnny: "Put her to bed." She gathered
   the child against her breasts, she laid her
In the next room, and covered her with a blanket. The window
   was white, the moon had risen. The mother
Lay down by the child, but after a moment Johnny stood in
   the doorway. "Come drink." He had brought home
Two jugs of wine slung from the saddle, part payment for the
   stallion's service; a pitcher of it
Was on the table, and California sadly came and emptied her
   glass. Whiskey, she thought,   255
Would have erased him till to-morrow; the thin red wine. . . .
"We have a good evening," he laughed, pouring it.
"One glass yet then I show you what the red fellow did." She
   moving toward the house-door his eyes
Followed her, the glass filled and the red juice ran over the
   table. When it struck the floor-planks
He heard and looked. "Who stuck the pig?" he muttered
   stupidly, "here's blood, here's blood," and trailed his fingers

In the red lake under the lamplight. While he was looking down
  the door creaked, she had slipped outdoors,   260
And he, his mouth curving like a faun's imagined the chase
  under the solemn redwoods, the panting
And unresistant victim caught in a dark corner. He emptied the
  glass and went outdoors
Into the dappled lanes of moonlight. No sound but the April
  brook's. "Hey Bruno," he called, "find her.
Bruno, go find her." The dog after a little understood and
  quested, the man following.
When California crouching by an oak-bush above the house
  heard them come near she darted   265
To the open slope and ran down hill. The dog barked at her
  heels, pleased with the game, and Johnny
Followed in silence. She ran down to the new corral, she saw
  the stallion
Move like a lion along the timbers of the fence, the dark arched
  neck shaking the nightfall
Of the great mane; she threw herself prone and writhed under
  the bars, his hooves backing away from her
Made muffled thunder in the soft soil. She stood in the midst
  of the corral, panting, but Johnny   270
Paused at the fence. The dog ran under it, and seeing the
  stallion move, the woman standing quiet,
Danced after the beast, with white-tooth feints and dashes.
  When Johnny saw the formidable dark strength
Recoil from the dog, he climbed up over the fence.

The child Christine waked when her mother left her
And lay half dreaming, in the half-waking dream she saw the
  ocean come up out of the west   275
And cover the world, she looked up through clear water at the
  tops of the redwoods. She heard the door creak
And the house empty; her heart shook her body, sitting up on
  the bed, and she heard the dog
And crept toward light, where it gleamed under the crack of
  the door. She opened the door, the room was empty.
The table-top was a red lake under the lamplight. The color of
  it was terrible to her;

She had seen the red juice drip from a coyote's muzzle, her
    father had shot one day in the hills   280
And carried him home over the saddle: she looked at the rifle on
    the wall-rack: it was not moved:
She ran to the door, the dog was barking and the moon was
    shining: she knew wine by the odor
But the color frightened her, the empty house frightened her,
    she followed down hill in the white lane of moonlight
The friendly noise of the dog. She saw in the big horse's corral,
    on the level shoulder of the hill,
Black on white, the dark strength of the beast, the dancing
    fury of the dog, and the two others.   285
One fled, one followed; the big one charged, rearing; one fell
    under his fore-hooves. She heard her mother
Scream: without thought she ran to the house, she dragged a
    chair past the red pool and climbed to the rifle,
Got it down from the wall and lugged it somehow through the
    door and down the hillside, under the hard weight
Sobbing. Her mother stood by the rails of the corral, she gave
    it to her. On the far side
The dog flashed at the plunging stallion; in the midst of the
    space the man, slow-moving, like a hurt worm   290
Crawling, dragged his body by inches toward the fence-line.
    Then California, resting the rifle
On the top rail, without doubting, without hesitance,
Aimed for the leaping body of the dog, and when it stood, fired.
    It snapped, rolled over, lay quiet.
"O mother you've hit Bruno!" "I couldn't see the sights in the
    moonlight," she answered quietly. She stood
And watched, resting the rifle-butt on the ground. The stallion
    wheeled, freed from his torment, the man   295
Lurched up to his knees, wailing a thin and bitter bird's cry,
    and the roan thunder
Struck; hooves left nothing alive but teeth tore up the remnant.
    "O mother, shoot, shoot!" Yet California
Stood carefully watching, till the beast fed all his fury stretched
    neck to utmost, head high,
And wrinkled back the upper lip from the teeth, yawning
    obscene disgust over—not a man—

A smear on the moon-lake earth; then California moved by
  some obscure human fidelity   300
Lifted the rifle. Each separate nerve-cell of her brain flaming
  the stars fell from their places
Crying in her mind: she fired three times before the haunches
  crumpled sidewise, the forelegs stiffening,
And the beautiful strength settled to earth: she turned then on
  her little daughter the mask of a woman
Who has killed God. The night-wind veering, the smell of the
  spilt wine drifted down hill from the house.

                                                              1925

ANTE MORTEM

It is likely enough that lions and scorpions
Guard the end; life never was bonded to be endurable nor the
  act of dying
Unpainful; the brain burning too often
Earns, though it held itself detached from the object, often a
  burnt age.
No matter, I shall not shorten it by hand.   5
Incapable of body or unmoved of brain is no evil, one always
  went envying
The quietness of stones. But if the striped blossom
Insanity spread lewd splendors and lightning terrors at the
  end of the forest;
Or intolerable pain work its known miracle,
Exile the monarch soul, set a sick monkey in the office . . . re-
  member me   10
Entire and balanced when I was younger,
And could lift stones, and comprehend in the praises the
  cruelties of life.

                                                              1927

THE OLD MAN'S DREAM AFTER HE DIED
from "Cawdor"

Gently with delicate mindless fingers
Decomposition began to pick and caress the unstable chemistry
Of the cells of the brain; Oh very gently, as the first weak
    breath of wind in a wood: the storm is still far,
The leaves are stirred faintly to a gentle whispering: the nerve-
    cells, by what would soon destroy them, were stirred
To a gentle whispering. Or one might say the brain began to
    glow, with its light, in the starless   5
Darkness under the dead bone sky; like bits of rotting wood on
    the floor of the night forest
Warm rains have soaked, you see them beside the path shine
    like vague eyes. So gently the dead man's brain
Glowing by itself made and enjoyed its dream.

                                        The nights
    of many years before this time
He had been dreaming the sweetness of death, as a starved man
    dreams bread, but now decomposition   10
Reversed the chemistry; who had adored in sleep under so many
    disguises the dark redeemer
In death across a thousand metaphors of form and action cele-
    brated life. Whatever he had wanted
To do or become was now accomplished, each bud that had
    been nipped and fallen grew out to a branch,
Sparks of desire forty years quenched flamed up fulfilment.
Out of time, undistracted by the nudging pulse-beat, perfectly
    real to itself being insulated   15
From all touch of reality the dream triumphed, building from
    past experience present paradise
More intense as the decay quickened, but ever more primitive
    as it proceeded, until the ecstasy
Soared through a flighty carnival of wines and women to the
    simple delight of eating flesh, and tended
Even higher, to an unconditional delight. But then the inter-
    connections between the groups of the brain

Failing, the dreamer and the dream split into multitude. Soon
the altered cells became unfit to express   20
Any human or at all describable form of consciousness.

                                                          Pain
  and pleasure are not to be thought
Important enough to require balancing: these flashes of post-
  mortal felicity by mindless decay
Played on the breaking harp by no means countervalued the
  excess of previous pain. Such discords
In the passionate terms of human experience are not resolved,
  nor worth it.   25
                                                          1928

                            ANTRIM

No spot of earth where men have so fiercely for ages of time
Fought and survived and cancelled each other,
Pict and Gael and Dane, McQuillan, Clandonnel, O'Neill,
Savages, the Scot, the Norman, the English,
Here in the narrow passage and the pitiless north, perpetual   5
Betrayals, relentless resultless fighting.
A random fury of dirks in the dark: a struggle for survival
Of hungry blind cells of life in the womb.
But now the womb has grown old, her strength has gone forth;
  a few red carts in a fog creak flax to the dubs,
And sheep in the high heather cry hungrily that life is hard; a
  plaintive peace; shepherds and peasants.   10

We have felt the blades meet in the flesh in a hundred
  ambushes
And the groaning blood bubble in the throat;
In a hundred battles the heavy axes bite the deep bone,
The mountain suddenly stagger and be darkened.
Generation on generation we have seen the blood of boys   15
And heard the moaning of women massacred,
The passionate flesh and nerves have flamed like pitch-pine and
  fallen
And lain in the earth softly dissolving.

I have lain and been humbled in all these graves, and mixed
  new flesh with the old and filled the hollow of my mouth
With maggots and rotten dust and ages of repose. I lie here and
  plot the agony of resurrection.   20

                                 1931

THE PLACE FOR NO STORY

  The coast hills at Sovranes Creek:
  No trees, but dark scant pasture drawn thin
  Over rock shaped like flame;
  The old ocean at the land's foot, the vast
  Gray extension beyond the long white violence;   5
  A herd of cows and the bull
  Far distant, hardly apparent up the dark slope;
  And the gray air haunted with hawks:
  This place is the noblest thing I have ever seen.
    No imaginable   10
  Human presence here could do anything
  But dilute the lonely self-watchful passion.

                                 1932

FIRE ON THE HILLS

The deer were bounding like blown leaves
Under the smoke in front of the roaring wave of the brush-fire;
I thought of the smaller lives that were caught.
Beauty is not always lovely; the fire was beautiful, the terror
Of the deer was beautiful; and when I returned   5
Down the black slopes after the fire had gone by, an eagle
Was perched on the jag of a burnt pine,
Insolent and gorged, cloaked in the folded storms of his
    shoulders.
He had come from far off for the good hunting
With fire for his beater to drive the game; the sky was merciless   10
Blue, and the hills merciless black,

The sombre-feathered great bird sleepily merciless between
   them.
I thought, painfully, but the whole mind,
The destruction that brings an eagle from heaven is better
   than mercy.

1932

SECOND-BEST

A Celtic spearman forcing the cromlech-builder's brown
   daughter;
A blond Saxon, a slayer of Britons,
Building his farm outside the village he'd burned; a Norse
Voyager, wielder of oars and a sword,
Thridding the rocks at the fjord sea-end, hungry as a hawk;   5
A hungry Gaelic chiefling in Ulster,
Whose blood with the Norseman's rotted in the rain on a
   heather hill:
These by the world's time were very recent
Forefathers of yours. And you are a maker of verses. The pallid
Pursuit of the world's beauty on paper,   10
Unless a tall angel comes to require it, is a pitiful pastime.
If, burnished new from God's eyes, an angel:
And the ardors of the simple blood showing clearly a little
   ridiculous
In this changed world:—write and be quiet.

1932

THE CRUEL FALCON

Contemplation would make a good life, keep it strict,
   only
The eyes of a desert skull drinking the sun,
Too intense for flesh, lonely
Exultations of white bone;
Pure action would make a good life, let it be sharp—   5
Set between the throat and the knife.
A man who knows death by heart

Is the man for that life.
In pleasant peace and security
How suddenly the soul in a man begins to die.   10
He shall look up above the stalled oxen
Envying the cruel falcon,
And dig under the straw for a stone
To bruise himself on.

1935

REARMAMENT

These grand and fatal movements toward death: the grandeur
     of the mass
Makes pity a fool, the tearing pity
For the atoms of the mass, the persons, the victims, makes it
     seem monstrous
To admire the tragic beauty they build.
It is beautiful as a river flowing or a slowly gathering   5
Glacier on a high mountain rock-face,
Bound to plow down a forest, or as frost in November,
The gold and flaming death-dance for leaves,
Or a girl in the night of her spent maidenhood, bleeding and
     kissing.
I would burn my right hand in a slow fire   10
To change the future . . . I should do foolishly. The beauty of
     modern
Man is not in the persons but in the
Disastrous rhythm, the heavy and mobile masses, the dance of
     the
Dream-led masses down the dark mountain.

1935

FLIGHT OF SWANS

One who sees giant Orion, the torches of winter midnight,
Enormously walking above the ocean in the west of heaven;
And watches the track of this age of time at its peak of flight
Waver like a spent rocket, wavering toward new discoveries,

Mortal examinations of darkness, soundings of depth;   5
And watches the long coast mountain vibrate from bronze to
    green,
Bronze to green, year after year, and all the streams
Dry and flooded, dry and flooded, in the racing seasons;
And knows that exactly this and not another is the world,
The ideal is phantoms for bait, the spirit is a flicker on a
    grave;—   10
May serve, with a certain detachment, the fugitive human race,
Or his own people, or his own household; but hardly himself;
And will not wind himself into hopes nor sicken with despairs.
He has found the peace and adored the God; he handles in
    autumn
The germs of far-future spring.   15
                              Sad sons of the stormy fall,
No escape, you have to inflict and endure; surely it is time for
    you
To learn to touch the diamond within to the diamond outside,
Thinning your humanity a little between the invulnerable
    diamonds,
Knowing that your angry choices and hopes and terrors are in
    vain,
But life and death not in vain; and the world is like a flight
    of swans.   20

                                                    1935

NEW YEAR'S EVE

Staggering homeward between the stream and the trees the
    unhappy drunkard
Babbles a woeful song and babbles
The end of the world, the moon's like fired Troy in a flying
    cloud, the storm
Rises again, the stream's in flood.
The moon's like the sack of Carthage, the Bastile's broken,
    pedlars and empires   5
Still deal in luxury, men sleep in prison.
Old Saturn thinks it was better in his grandsire's time but that's
    from the brittle

Arteries, it neither betters nor worsens.
(Nobody knows my love the falcon.)
It has always bristled with phantoms, always factitious, mildly
    absurd;   10
The organism, with no precipitous
Degeneration, slight imperceptible discounts of sense and
    faculty,
Adapts itself to the culture-medium.
(Nobody crawls to the test-tube rim.
Nobody knows my love the falcon.)   15
The star's on the mountain, the stream snoring in flood; the
    brainlit drunkard
Crosses midnight and stammers to bed.
The inhuman nobility of things, the ecstatic beauty, the in-
    veterate steadfastness
Uphold the four posts of the bed.
(Nobody knows my love the falcon.)   20

                          1937

SELF-CRITICISM IN FEBRUARY

The bay is not blue but sombre yellow
With wrack from the battered valley, it is speckled with violent
    foam-heads
And tiger-striped with long lovely storm-shadows.
You love this better than the other mask; better eyes than yours
Would feel the equal beauty in the blue.   5
It is certain you have loved the beauty of storm dispropor-
    tionately.
But the present time is not pastoral, but founded
On violence, pointed for more massive violence: perhaps it is
    not
Perversity but need that perceives the storm-beauty.
Well, bite on this: your poems are too full of ghosts and
    demons,   10
And people like phantoms—how often life's are—
And passion so strained that the clay mouths go praying for
    destruction—
Alas, it is not unusual in life;

To every soul at some time. *But why insist on it? And now*
For the worst fault: you have never mistaken   15
Demon nor passion nor idealism for the real God.
Then what is most disliked in those verses
Remains most true. *Unfortunately. If only you could sing*
That God is love, or perhaps that social
Justice will soon prevail. I can tell lies in prose.   20

                                              1937

PRESCRIPTION OF PAINFUL ENDS

Lucretius felt the change of the world in his time, the great
     republic riding to the height
Whence every road leads downward; Plato in his time watched
     Athens
Dance the down path. The future is a misted landscape, no
     man sees clearly, but at cyclic turns
There is a change felt in the rhythm of events, as when an ex-
     hausted horse
Falters and recovers, then the rhythm of the running hoofbeats
     is changed: he will run miles yet,   5
But he must fall: we have felt it again in our own life time,
     slip, shift and speed-up
In the gallop of the world; and now perceive that, come peace
     or war, the progress of Europe and America
Becomes a long process of deterioration—starred with famous
     Byzantiums and Alexandrias,
Surely—but downward. One desires at such times
To gather the insights of the age summit against future loss,
     against the narrowing mind and the tyrants,   10
The pedants, the mystagogues, the barbarians: one builds
     poems for treasuries, time-conscious poems: Lucretius
Sings his great theory of natural origins and of wise conduct;
     Plato smiling carves dreams, bright cells
Of incorruptible wax to hive the Greek honey.
                                        Our own
     time, much greater and far less fortunate,
Has acids for honey, and for fine dreams   15

The immense vulgarities of misapplied science and decaying
  Christianity: therefore one christens each poem, in dutiful
Hope of burning off at least the top layer of the time's unclean-
  ness, from the acid-bottles.

1940

THE EXCESSES OF GOD

Is it not by his high superfluousness we know
Our God? For to equal a need
Is natural, animal, mineral: but to fling
Rainbows over the rain
And beauty above the moon, and secret rainbows   5
On the domes of deep sea-shells,
And make the necessary embrace of breeding
Beautiful also as fire,
Not even the weeds to multiply without blossom
Nor the birds without music: 10
There is the great humaneness at the heart of things,
The extravagant kindness, the fountain
Humanity can understand, and would flow likewise
If power and desire were perch-mates.

[written before 1925] 1941

THE BEAUTY OF THINGS

To feel and speak the astonishing beauty of things—earth,
  stone and water,
Beast, man and woman, sun, moon and stars—
The blood-shot beauty of human nature, its thoughts, frenzies
  and passions,
And unhuman nature its towering reality—
For man's half dream; man, you might say, is nature dreaming,
  but rock   5
And water and sky are constant—to feel
Greatly, and understand greatly, and express greatly, the
  natural

Beauty, is the sole business of poetry.
The rest's diversion: those holy or noble sentiments, the
  intricate ideas,
The love, lust, longing: reasons, but not the reason.   10

                                                          1951

OCEAN

The gray whales are going south: I see their fountains
Rise from black sea: great dark bulks of hot blood
Plowing the deep cold sea to their trysting-place
Off Mexican California, where water is warm, and love
Finds massive joy: from the flukes to the blowhole the whole
  giant   5
Flames like a star. In February storm the ocean
Is black and rainbowed; the high spouts of white spray
Rise and fall over in the wind. There is no April in the ocean;
How do these creatures know that spring is at hand? They re-
  member their ancestors
That crawled on earth: the little fellows like otters, who took to
  sea   10
And have grown great. Go out to the ocean, little ones,
You will grow great or die.

                            And here the small trout
Flicker in the streams that tumble from the coast mountain,
Little quick flames of life: but from time to time   15
One of them goes mad, wanting room and freedom; he slips
  between the rock jaws
And takes to sea, where from time immemorial
The long sharks wait. If he lives he becomes a steelhead,
A rainbow trout grown beyond nature in the ocean. Go out to
  the great ocean,
Grow great or die.   20
                         O ambitious children,
It would be wiser no doubt to rest in the brook
And remain little. But if the devil drives
I hope you will scull far out to the wide ocean and find your
  fortune, and beware of teeth.

It is not important. There are deeps you will never reach and
    peaks you will never explore,   25
Where the great squids and kraken lie in the gates, in the awful
    twilight
The whip-armed hungers; and mile under mile below,
Deep under deep, on the deep floor, in the darkness
Under the weight of the world: like lighted galleons the ghost-
    fish,
With phosphorescent portholes along their flanks,   30
Sail over and eat each other: the condition of life,
To eat each other: but in the slime below
Prodigious worms as great and as slow as glaciers burrow in the
    sediment,
Mindless and blind, huge tubes of muddy flesh
Sucking not meat but carrion, drippings and offal   35
From the upper sea. They move a yard in a year,
Where there are no years, no sun, no seasons, darkness and
    slime;
They spend nothing on action, all on gross flesh.
                               O ambitious ones,
Will you grow great, or die? It hardly matters; the words are
    comparative;   40
Greatness is but less little; and death's changed life.
                                      1954

ARCHIBALD MacLEISH

Archibald MacLeish (1892-   ) was born in Glencoe, Illinois. After graduating from Yale (A.B., 1915), he studied law at Harvard (LL.B., 1919), but practiced actively for but a short time. He saw active service during the First World War, and in 1923 returned to France with his wife and children for a five-year stay.

The first stage of his career as a poet culminates with his return to America in 1928, by which time he had published some five volumes of poetry, including *The Hamlet of A. MacLeish,* a blank verse poem in which the poet marks the spiritual drought of the postwar years. The disillusion and subjectivity of the poems of this early period, often showing the influence of Eliot and Pound, are in marked contrast to his more public poetry of the early 1930s, although both stem from his extreme sensitivity to the problems of his own time.

With *Conquistador* (1932) and *Frescoes for Mr. Rockefeller's City* (1933) MacLeish clearly demonstrated his willingness to involve the artist deeply in matters of immediate social or economic concern. Somewhat later he noted that "the public world with us has *become* the private world and the private world has become the public. We see our private individual lives in terms of the public and numerous lives of those who live beside us. . . . The world of private experience has become the world of crowds and streets and towns and armies and mobs." And his direct concern for the democratic experiment has led him to work not only in poetry but also in verse and radio plays, essays, the ballet, and even the newsreel-like combination of photographs and poetry of *Land of the Free* (1938).

Since *Collected Poems 1917-1952* MacLeish has published one volume of poems and several plays, the most recent of which is *J. B.* (1958), a recounting of the trials of Job in a twentieth-century setting. The 1952 *Collected Poems* provides the text of all the poems published here.

THE END OF THE WORLD

Quite unexpectedly as Vasserot
The armless ambidextrian was lighting
A match between his great and second toe
And Ralph the lion was engaged in biting
The neck of Madame Sossman while the drum   5
Pointed, and Teeny was about to cough
In waltz-time swinging Jocko by the thumb—
Quite unexpectedly the top blew off:

And there, there overhead, there, there, hung over
Those thousands of white faces, those dazed eyes,   10
There in the starless dark the poise, the hover,
There with vast wings across the canceled skies,
There in the sudden blackness the black pall
Of nothing, nothing, nothing—nothing at all.

                                        1925

ARS POETICA

A poem should be palpable and mute
As a globed fruit,

Dumb
As old medallions to the thumb,

Silent as the sleeve-worn stone   5
Of casement ledges where the moss has grown—

A poem should be wordless
As the flight of birds.
                    *

A poem should be motionless in time
As the moon climbs,   10

Leaving, as the moon releases
Twig by twig the night-entangled trees,

Leaving, as the moon behind the winter leaves,
Memory by memory the mind—

A poem should be motionless in time   15
As the moon climbs.

*

A poem should be equal to:
Not true.

For all the history of grief
An empty doorway and a maple leaf.   20

For love
The leaning grasses and two lights above the sea—

A poem should not mean
But be.

                                                        1926

YOU, ANDREW MARVELL

And here face down beneath the sun
And here upon earth's noonward height
To feel the always coming on
The always rising of the night:

To feel creep up the curving east   5
The earthy chill of dusk and slow
Upon those under lands the vast
And ever climbing shadow grow

And strange at Ecbatan the trees
Take leaf by leaf the evening strange   10
The flooding dark about their knees
The mountains over Persia change

And now at Kermanshah the gate
Dark empty and the withered grass

And through the twilight now the late   15
Few travelers in the westward pass

And Baghdad darken and the bridge
Across the silent river gone
And through Arabia the edge
Of evening widen and steal on   20

And deepen on Palmyra's street
The wheel rut in the ruined stone
And Lebanon fade out and Crete
High through the clouds and overblown

And over Sicily the air   25
Still flashing with the landward gulls
And loom and slowly disappear
The sails above the shadowy hulls

And Spain go under and the shore
Of Africa the gilded sand   30
And evening vanish and no more
The low pale light across that land

Nor now the long light on the sea:

And here face downward in the sun
To feel how swift how secretly   35
The shadow of the night comes on . . .

                      1929

MEN

(on a phrase of Apollinaire)

Our history is grave noble and tragic.
We trusted the look of the sun on the green leaves.
We built our towns of stone with enduring ornaments.
We worked the hard flint for basins of water.

We believed in the feel of the earth under us.   5
We planted corn grapes apple-trees rhubarb.
Nevertheless we knew others had died.
Everything we have done has been faithful and dangerous.

We believed in the promises made by the brows of women.
We begot children at night in the warm wool.   10
We comforted those who wept in fear on our shoulders.
Those who comforted us had themselves vanished.

We fought at the dikes in the bright sun for the pride of it.
We beat drums and marched with music and laughter.
We were drunk and lay with our fine dreams in the straw.   15
We saw the stars through the hair of lewd women.

Our history is grave noble and tragic.
Many of us have died and are not remembered.
Many cities are gone and their channels broken.
We have lived a long time in this land and with honor.   20
                                                     1929

AMERICAN LETTER

for Gerald Murphy

The wind is east but the hot weather continues,
Blue and no clouds, the sound of the leaves thin,
Dry like the rustling of paper, scored across
With the slate-shrill screech of the locusts.
                                        The tossing of
Pines is the low sound. In the wind's running   5
The wild carrots smell of the burning sun.
Why should I think of the dolphins at Capo di Mele?
Why should I see in my mind the taut sail
And the hill over St.-Tropez and your hand on the tiller?
Why should my heart be troubled with palms still?   10
I am neither a sold boy nor a Chinese official
Sent to sicken in Pa for some Lo-Yang dish.
This is my own land, my sky, my mountain:

This—not the humming pines and the surf and the sound
At the Ferme Blanche, nor Port Cros in the dusk and the har-
    bor   15
Floating the motionless ship and the sea-drowned star.
I am neither Po Chü-i nor another after
Far from home, in a strange land, daft
For the talk of his own sort and the taste of his lettuces.
This land is my native land. And yet   20
I am sick for home for the red roofs and the olives,
And the foreign words and the smell of the sea fall.
How can a wise man have two countries?
How can a man have the earth and the wind and want
A land far off, alien, smelling of palm-trees   25
And the yellow gorse at noon in the long calms?

It is a strange thing—to be an American.
Neither an old house it is with the air
Tasting of hung herbs and the sun returning
Year after year to the same door and the churn   30
Making the same sound in the cool of the kitchen
Mother to son's wife, and the place to sit
Marked in the dusk by the worn stone at the wellhead—
That—nor the eyes like each other's eyes and the skull
Shaped to the same fault and the hands' sameness.   35
Neither a place it is nor a blood name.
America is West and the wind blowing.
America is a great word and the snow,
A way, a white bird, the rain falling,
A shining thing in the mind and the gulls' call.   40
America is neither a land nor a people,
A word's shape it is, a wind's sweep—
America is alone: many together,
Many of one mouth, of one breath,
Dressed as one—and none brothers among them: 45
Only the taught speech and the aped tongue.
America is alone and the gulls calling.

It is a strange thing to be an American.
It is strange to live on the high world in the stare
Of the naked sun and the stars as our bones live.   50

Men in the old lands housed by their rivers.
They built their towns in the vales in the earth's shelter.
We first inhabit the world. We dwell
On the half earth, on the open curve of a continent.
Sea is divided from sea by the day-fall. The dawn   55
Rides the low east with us many hours;
First are the capes, then are the shorelands, now
The blue Appalachians faint at the day rise;
The willows shudder with light on the long Ohio:
The Lakes scatter the low sun: the prairies   60
Slide out of dark: in the eddy of clean air
The smoke goes up from the high plains of Wyoming:
The steep Sierras arise: the struck foam
Flames at the wind's heel on the far Pacific.
Already the noon leans to the eastern cliff: 65
The elms darken the door and the dust-heavy lilacs.

It is strange to sleep in the bare stars and to die
On an open land where few bury before us:
(From the new earth the dead return no more.)
It is strange to be born of no race and no people.   70
In the old lands they are many together They keep
The wise past and the words spoken in common.
They remember the dead with their hands, their mouths dumb.
They answer each other with two words in their meeting.
They live together in small things. They eat   75
The same dish, their drink is the same and their proverbs.
Their youth is like. They are like in their ways of love.
They are many men. There are always others beside them.
Here it is one man and another and wide
On the darkening hills the faint smoke of the houses.   80
Here it is one man and the wind in the boughs.

Therefore our hearts are sick for the south water.
The smell of the gorse comes back to our night thought.
We are sick at heart for the red roofs and the olives;
We are sick at heart for the voice and the foot fall . . .   85

Therefore we will not go though the sea call us.

This, this is our land, this is our people,
This that is neither a land nor a race. We must reap
The wind here in the grass for our soul's harvest:
Here we must eat our salt or our bones starve.   90
Here we must live or live only as shadows.
This is our race, we that have none, that have had
Neither the old walls nor the voices around us,
This is our land, this is our ancient ground—
The raw earth, the mixed bloods and the strangers,   95
The different eyes, the wind, and the heart's change.
These we will not leave though the old call us.
This our country-earth, our blood, our kind.
Here we will live our years till the earth blind us—

The wind blows from the east. The leaves fall.   100
Far off in the pines a jay rises.
The wind smells of haze and the wild ripe apples.

I think of the masts at Cette and the sweet rain.

                                                        1929

"NOT MARBLE NOR THE GILDED
MONUMENTS"

for Adele

The praisers of women in their proud and beautiful poems,
Naming the grave mouth and the hair and the eyes,
Boasted those they loved should be forever remembered:
These were lies.

The words sound but the face in the Istrian sun is forgotten.   5
The poet speaks but to her dead ears no more.
The sleek throat is gone—and the breast that was troubled to
    listen:
Shadow from door.

Therefore I will not praise your knees nor your fine walking
Telling you men shall remember your name as long   10

As lips move or breath is spent or the iron of English
Rings from a tongue.

I shall say you were young, and your arms straight, and your
     mouth scarlet:
I shall say you will die and none will remember you:
Your arms change, and none remember the swish of your
     garments,   15
Nor the click of your shoe.

Not with my hand's strength, not with difficult labor
Springing the obstinate words to the bones of your breast
And the stubborn line to your young stride and the breath to
     your breathing
And the beat to your haste   20
Shall I prevail on the hearts of unborn men to remember.

(What is a dead girl but a shadowy ghost
Or a dead man's voice but a distant and vain affirmation
Like dream words most)

Therefore I will not speak of the undying glory of women.   25
I will say you were young and straight and your skin fair
And you stood in the door and the sun was a shadow of leaves
     on your shoulders
And a leaf on your hair—

I will not speak of the famous beauty of dead women:
I will say the shape of a leaf lay once on your hair.   30
Till the world ends and the eyes are out and the mouths
     broken
Look! It is there!

                                  1930

INVOCATION TO THE SOCIAL MUSE

Señora, it is true the Greeks are dead.

It is true also that we here are Americans:
That we use the machines: that a sight of the god is unusual:
That more people have more thoughts: that there are

Progress and science and tractors and revolutions and 5
Marx and the wars more antiseptic and murderous
And music in every home: there is also Hoover.

Does the lady suggest we should write it out in The Word?
Does Madame recall our responsibilities? We are
Whores, Fräulein: poets, Fräulein, are persons of 10

Known vocation following troops: they must sleep with
Stragglers from either prince and of both views.
The rules permit them to further the business of neither.

It is also strictly forbidden to mix in maneuvers.
Those that infringe are inflated with praise on the plazas— 15
Their bones are resultantly afterwards found under news-
    papers.

Preferring life with the sons to death with the fathers,
We also doubt on the record whether the sons
Will still be shouting around with the same huzzas—

For we hope Lady to live to lie with the youngest. 20
There are only a handful of things a man likes,
Generation to generation, hungry or

Well fed: the earth's one: life's
One: Mister Morgan is not one.

There is nothing worse for our trade than to be in style. 25

He that goes naked goes further at last than another.
Wrap the bard in a flag or a school and they'll jimmy his
Door down and be thick in his bed—for a month:

(Who recalls the address now of the Imagists?)
But the naked man has always his own nakedness.   30
People remember forever his live limbs.

They may drive him out of the camps but one will take him.
They may stop his tongue on his teeth with a rope's argu-
   ment—
He will lie in a house and be warm when they are shaking.

Besides, Tovarishch, how to embrace an army?   35
How to take to one's chamber a million souls?
How to conceive in the name of a column of marchers?

The things of the poet are done to a man alone
As the things of love are done—or of death when he hears the
Step withdraw on the stair and the clock tick only.   40

Neither his class nor his kind nor his trade may come near him
There where he lies on his left arm and will die,
Nor his class nor his kind nor his trade when the blood is
   jeering

And his knee's in the soft of the bed where his love lies.

I remind you, Barinya, the life of the poet is hard—   45
A hardy life with a boot as quick as a fiver:

Is it just to demand of us also to bear arms?

           1932

SEAFARER

  And learn O voyager to walk
  The roll of earth, the pitch and fall
  That swings across these trees those stars:
  That swings the sunlight up the wall.

And learn upon these narrow beds   5
To sleep in spite of sea, in spite
Of sound the rushing planet makes:
And learn to sleep against this ground.

1933

GEOGRAPHY OF THIS TIME

What is required of us is the recognition of the frontiers be-
tween the centuries. And to take heart: to cross over.

Those who are killed in the place between out of ignorance,
those who wander like cattle and are shot, those who are shot
and are left in the stone fields between the histories—these men   5
may be pitied as the victims of accidents are pitied but their
deaths do not signify. They are neither buried nor otherwise re-
membered but lie in the dead grass in the dry thorn in the worn
light. Their years have no monuments.

There are many such in the sand here—many who did not   10
perceive, who thought the time went on, the years went for-
ward, the history was continuous—who thought tomorrow was
of the same nation as today. There are many who came to the
frontiers between the times and did not know them—who
looked for the sentry-box at the stone bridge, for the barricade   15
in the pines and the declaration in two languages—the warn-
ing and the opportunity to turn. They are dead there in the
down light, in the sheep's barren.

What is required of us is the recognition

⌐with no sign, with no word, with the roads raveled out into   20
ruts and the ruts into dust and the dust stirred by the wind—
the roads from behind us ending in the dust.

What is required of us is the recognition of the frontiers
where the roads end.

We are very far. We are past the place where the light lifts   25
and farther on than the relinquishment of leaves—farther even

than the persistence in the east of the green color. Beyond are
the confused tracks, the guns, the watchers.

What is required of us, Companions, is the recognition of
the frontiers across this history, and to take heart: to cross
over.   30

—to persist and to cross over and survive

But to survive

To cross over.

1942

VOYAGE WEST

There was a time for discoveries—
For the headlands looming above in the
First light and the surf and the
Crying of gulls: for the curve of the
Coast north into secrecy.   5

That time is past.
The last lands have been peopled.
The oceans are known now.

Señora: once the maps have all been made
A man were better dead than find new continents.   10

A man would better never have been born
Than find upon the open ocean flowers
Drifted from islands where there are no islands,

Or midnight, out of sight of any land,
Smell on the altering air the odor of rosemary.   15

No fortune passes that misfortune—

To lift along the evening of the sky,
Certain as sun and sea, a new-found land
Steep from an ocean where no landfall can be.

1948

THE OLD MAN TO THE LIZARD

Lizard, lover of heat, of high
Noon, of the hot stone, the golden
Sun in your unblinking eye—
And they say you are old, lizard, older than

Rocks you run on with those delicate   5
Fishbone fingers, skittering over
Ovens even cricket in his shell
Could never sing in—tell me, lover of

Sun, lover of noon, lizard,
Is it because the sun is gold with   10
Flame you love it so? Or is
Your love because your blood is cold?

1952

THE SHEEP IN THE RUINS

for Learned and Augustus Hand

You, my friends, and you strangers, all of you,
Stand with me a little by the walls
Or where the walls once were.
The bridge was here, the city further:
Now there is neither bridge nor town—   5
A doorway where the roof is down
Opens on a foot-worn stair
That climbs by three steps into empty air.
(What foot went there?)
Nothing in this town that had a thousand steeples   10

Lives now but these flocks of sheep
Grazing the yellow grasses where the bricks lie dead beneath:
Dogs drive them with their brutal teeth.

Can none but sheep live where the walls go under?
Is man's day over and the sheep's begun?   15
And shall we sit here like the mourners on a dunghill
Shrilling with melodious tongue—
Disfiguring our faces with the nails of our despair?
(What dust is this we sift upon our hair?)
Because a world is taken from us as the camels from the man
          of Uz   20
Shall we sit weeping for the world that was
And curse God and so perish?
Shall monuments be grass and sheep inherit them?
Shall dogs rule in the rubble of the arches?

Consider, Oh consider what we are!   25
Consider what it is to be a man—
He who makes his journey by the glimmer of a candle;
Who discovers in his mouth, between his teeth, a word;
Whose heart can bear the silence of the stars—that burden;
Who comes upon his meaning in the blindness of a stone—   30
A girl's shoulder, perfectly harmonious!

Even the talk of it would take us days together.
Marvels men have made, Oh marvels!—and our breath
Brief as it is: our death waiting—
Marvels upon marvels! Works of state—   35
The imagination of the shape of order!
Works of beauty—the cedar door
Perfectly fitted to the sill of basalt!
Works of grace—
The ceremony at the entering of houses,   40
At the entering of lives: the bride among the torches in the
          shrill carouse!

Works of soul—
Pilgrimages through the desert to the sacred boulder:

Through the mid night to the stroke of one!
Works of grace! Works of wonder!   45
All this have we done and more—
And seen—what have we not seen?—

A man beneath the sunlight in his meaning:
A man, one man, a man alone.

In the sinks of the earth that wanderer has gone down.   50
The shadow of his mind is on the mountains.
The word he has said is kept in the place beyond
As the seed is kept and the earth ponders it.
Stones—even the stones remember him:
Even the leaves—his image is in them.   55
And now because the city is a ruin in the waste of air

We sit here and despair!
Because the sheep graze in the dying grove
Our day is over!
We must end   60
Because the talk around the table in the dusk has ended,
Because the fingers of the goddesses are found
Like marble pebbles in the gravelly ground
And nothing answers but the jackal in the desert,—
Because the cloud proposes, the wind says!   65

Because the sheep are pastured where the staring statues lie
We sit upon the sand in silence
Watching the sun go and the shadows change!

Listen, my friends, and you, all of you, strangers,
Listen, the work of man, the work of splendor   70
Never has been ended or will end.
Even where the sheep defile the ruined stair
And dogs are masters—even there
One man's finger in the dust shall trace the circle.

Even among the ruins shall begin the work,   75
Large in the level morning of the light

And beautiful with cisterns where the water whitens,
Rippling upon the lip of stone, and spills
By cedar sluices into pools, and the young builders
String their plumb lines, and the well-laid course　　　　　　80
Blanches its mortar in the sun, and all the morning
Smells of wood-smoke, rope-tar, horse-sweat, pitch-pine,
Men and the trampled mint leaves in the ditch.

One man in the sun alone
Walks between the silence and the stone:　　　　　　　　85
The city rises from his flesh, his bone.

　　　　　　　　　　　　　　　　　　　　　　1952

HYPOCRITE AUTEUR

mon semblable, mon frère

(1)

Our epoch takes a voluptuous satisfaction
In that perspective of the action
Which pictures us inhabiting the end
Of everything with death for only friend.
Not that we love death,　　　　　　　　　　　　5
Not truly, not the fluttering breath,
The obscene shudder of the finished act—
What the doe feels when the ultimate fact
Tears at her bowels with its jaws.

Our taste is for the opulent pause　　　　　　　　10
Before the end comes. If the end is certain
All of us are players at the final curtain:
All of us, silence for a time deferred,
Find time before us for one sad last word.
Victim, rebel, convert, stoic—　　　　　　　　15
Every role but the heroic—
We turn our tragic faces to the stalls
To wince our moment till the curtain falls.

(2)

A world ends when its metaphor has died.

An age becomes an age, all else beside,   20
When sensuous poets in their pride invent
Emblems for the soul's consent
That speak the meanings men will never know
But man-imagined images can show:
It perishes when those images, though seen,   25
No longer mean.

(3)

A world was ended when the womb
Where girl held God became the tomb
Where God lies buried in a man:
Botticelli's image neither speaks nor can   30
To our kind. His star-guided stranger
Teaches no longer, by the child, the manger,
The meaning of the beckoning skies.

Sophocles, when his reverent actors rise
To play the king with bleeding eyes,   35
No longer shows us on the stage advance
God's purpose in the terrible fatality of chance.

No woman living, when the girl and swan
Embrace in verses, feels upon
Her breast the awful thunder of that breast   40
Where God, made beast, is by the blood confessed.

Empty as conch shell by the waters cast
The metaphor still sounds but cannot tell,
And we, like parasite crabs, put on the shell
And drag it at the sea's edge up and down.   45

This is the destiny we say we own.

(4)

But are we sure
The age that dies upon its metaphor
Among these Roman heads, these mediaeval towers,
Is ours?—   50
Or ours the ending of that story?

The meanings in a man that quarry
Images from blinded eyes
And white birds and the turning skies
To make a world of were not spent with these   55
Abandoned presences.

The journey of our history has not ceased:
Earth turns us still toward the rising east,
The metaphor still struggles in the stone,
The allegory of the flesh and bone   60
Still stares into the summer grass
That is its glass,
The ignorant blood
Still knocks at silence to be understood.

Poets, deserted by the world before,   65
Turn round into the actual air:
Invent the age! Invent the metaphor!

                                                                    1952

HART CRANE

Harold Hart Crane (1899-1932) was born in Garrettsville, Ohio, an only child, of parents who were separated when he was seventeen. In 1916 he lived temporarily with his mother on his grandfather's sugar plantation in Cuba, before traveling to New York City where he earned a living in the advertising business and wrote poetry. During 1917 he returned to his father in Cleveland, working first as a laborer and then at menial jobs in his father's candy business, looking for some sort of livelihood which would allow him time to write poetry. But in 1920, no longer able to tolerate his father's hostility to his plans, Crane left home, returned to the advertising business in New York, and rented rooms across the East River from Manhattan, within sight of the Brooklyn Bridge—in a house, as it turned out, from which Washington Roebling had supervised the construction of the Bridge. A year before he published his first volume of poems, *White Buildings* (1926), he conceived of the plan for *The Bridge;* and with the help of Otto Kahn—his father would pay nothing—Crane went to the Isle of Pines and then to Paris to complete his poem. After its publication in 1930, he returned to the United States; then, with a Guggenheim Fellowship and plans for a long poem about Montezuma, he traveled to Mexico. On the return voyage he leaped to his death in the sea.

Crane's despair was partly the consequence of his family (or lack of it) situation, of his father's hostility, of loneliness and self-indulgences to overcome it. But it had more profound causes. Although he had deep and personal religious convictions, he could not successfully find within himself any principle of order to negate the chaos he acutely sensed in the world around him. For nearly twenty years he attempted through his poetry to find or establish some presiding principle, but, except for *The Bridge,* he failed. During the year he completed that poem he published an essay, "Modern Poetry," in Oliver Saylor's anthology, *Revolt in the Arts* (1929), which acknowledged both his own and the typical problems of the contemporary poet. "The poet's concern must be, as always, self-discipline toward a formal integration of experience," he wrote. Poetry is based on "the articulation of contemporary human consciousness *sub specie aeternitatis.* ... The function of poetry in a Machine Age is identical to its function in any other age. . . ." Poets must absorb the machine, "i.e., acclimatize it," like all the human associations of the past. "It demands, however, along with the traditional qualifications of the poet, an extraordinary capacity for surrender, at least temporarily, to the sensations of urban life."

After ten poems had appeared separately from 1927 to 1930, all fifteen poems, grouped into eight parts, of *The Bridge* were published in three separate editions in 1930: first in Paris, then in London, and, after minor revisions, in New York. The text here used is Waldo Frank (ed.), *The Collected Poems of Hart Crane* (1933, 1946, 1948), which reprints the American edition of *The Bridge.*

THE BRIDGE

From going to and fro in the earth,
and from walking up and down in it.
THE BOOK OF JOB

PROEM: TO BROOKLYN BRIDGE

How many dawns, chill from his rippling rest
The seagull's wings shall dip and pivot him,
Shedding white rings of tumult, building high
Over the chained bay waters Liberty—

Then, with inviolate curve, forsake our eyes   5
As apparitional as sails that cross
Some page of figures to be filed away;
—Till elevators drop us from our day . . .

I think of cinemas, panoramic sleights
With multitudes bent toward some flashing scene   10
Never disclosed, but hastened to again,
Foretold to other eyes on the same screen;

And Thee, across the harbor, silver-paced
As though the sun took step of thee, yet left
Some motion ever unspent in thy stride,—   15
Implicitly thy freedom staying thee!

Out of some subway scuttle, cell or loft
A bedlamite speeds to thy parapets,
Tilting there momently, shrill shirt ballooning,
A jest falls from the speechless caravan.   20

Down Wall, from girder into street noon leaks,
A rip-tooth of the sky's acetylene;
All afternoon the cloud-flown derricks turn . . .
Thy cables breathe the North Atlantic still.

And obscure as that heaven of the Jews,   25
Thy guerdon . . . Accolade thou dost bestow
Of anonymity time cannot raise:
Vibrant reprieve and pardon thou dost show.

O harp and altar, of the fury fused,
(How could mere toil align thy choiring strings!)   30
Terrific threshold of the prophet's pledge,
Prayer of pariah, and the lover's cry,—

Again the traffic lights that skim thy swift
Unfractioned idiom, immaculate sigh of stars,
Beading thy path—condense eternity: 35
And we have seen night lifted in thine arms.

Under thy shadow by the piers I waited;
Only in darkness is thy shadow clear.
The City's fiery parcels all undone,
Already snow submerges an iron year . . .   40

O Sleepless as the river under thee,
Vaulting the sea, the prairies' dreaming sod,
Unto us lowliest sometime sweep, descend
And of the curveship lend a myth to God.

1930

I

AVE MARIA

Venient annis, sæcula seris,
Quibus Oceanus vincula rerum
Laxet et ingens pateat tellus
Tiphysque novos detegat orbes
Nec sit terris ultima Thule.

—SENECA

Be with me, Luis de San Angel, now—
imbus,   Witness before the tides can wrest away
e, gazing   The word I bring, O you who reined my suit
ird Spain, Into the Queen's great heart that doubtful day;
kes the
ence of   For I have seen now what no perjured breath   5
faithful
isans of   Of clown nor sage can riddle or gainsay;—
|uest . . . To you, too, Juan Perez, whose counsel fear
And greed adjourned,—I bring you back Cathay!

Here waves climb into dusk on gleaming mail;
Invisible valves of the sea,—locks, tendons   10
Crested and creeping, troughing corridors
That fall back yawning to another plunge.
Slowly the sun's red caravel drops light
Once more behind us. . . . It is morning there—
O where our Indian emperies lie revealed,   15
Yet lost, all, let this keel one instant yield!

I thought of Genoa; and this truth, now proved,
That made me exile in her streets, stood me
More absolute than ever—biding the moon
Till dawn should clear that dim frontier, first seen   20
—The Chan's great continent. . . . Then faith, not fear
Nigh surged me witless. . . . Hearing the surf near—
I, wonder-breathing, kept the watch,—saw
The first palm chevron the first lighted hill.

And lowered. And they came out to us crying,   25
"The Great White Birds!" (O Madre Maria, still
One ship of these thou grantest safe returning;

Assure us through thy mantle's ageless blue!)
And record of more, floating in a casque,
Was tumbled from us under bare poles scudding;   30
And later hurricanes may claim more pawn. . . .
For here between two worlds, another, harsh,

This third, of water, tests the word; lo, here
Bewilderment and mutiny heap whelming
Laughter, and shadow cuts sleep from the heart   35
Almost as though the Moor's flung scimitar
Found more than flesh to fathom in its fall.
Yet under tempest-lash and surfeitings
Some inmost sob, half-heard, dissuades the abyss,
Merges the wind in measure to the waves,   40

Series on series, infinite,—till eyes
Starved wide on blackened tides, accrete—enclose
This turning rondure whole, this crescent ring
Sun-cusped and zoned with modulated fire
Like pearls that whisper through the Doge's hands   45
—Yet no delirium of jewels! O Fernando,
Take of that eastern shore, this western sea,
Yet yield thy God's, thy Virgin's charity!

—Rush down the plenitude, and you shall see
Isaiah counting famine on this lee!   50

*

An herb, a stray branch among salty teeth,
The jellied weeds that drag the shore,—perhaps
Tomorrow's moon will grant us Saltes Bar—
Palos again,—a land cleared of long war.
Some Angelus environs the cordage tree;   55
Dark waters onward shake the dark prow free.

*

O Thou who sleepest on Thyself, apart
Like ocean athwart lanes of death and birth,
And all the eddying breath between dost search
Cruelly with love thy parable of man,—   60

Inquisitor! incognizable Word
Of Eden and the enchained Sepulchre,
Into thy steep savannahs, burning blue,
Utter to loneliness the sail is true.

Who grindest oar, and arguing the mast   65
Subscribest holocaust of ships, O Thou
Within whose primal scan consummately
The glistening seignories of Ganges swim;—
Who sendest greeting by the corposant,
And Teneriffe's garnet—flamed it in a cloud,   70
Urging through night our passage to the Chan;—
Te Deum laudamus, for thy teeming span!

Of all that amplitude that time explores,
A needle in the sight, suspended north,—
Yielding by inference and discard, faith   75
And true appointment from the hidden shoal:
This disposition that thy night relates
From Moon to Saturn in one sapphire wheel:
The orbic wake of thy once whirling feet,
Elohim, still I hear thy sounding heel!   80

White toil of heaven's cordons, mustering
In holy rings all sails charged to the far
Hushed gleaming fields and pendant seething wheat
Of knowledge,—round thy brows unhooded now
—The kindled Crown! acceded of the poles   85
And biassed by full sails, meridians reel
Thy purpose—still one shore beyond desire!
The sea's green crying towers a-sway, Beyond

And kingdoms
                    naked in the
                                        trembling heart—
         Te Deum laudamus
                              O Thou Hand of Fire   90
                                                   1927

II

POWHATAN'S DAUGHTER

> "—*Pocahuntus, a well-featured but wan-*
> *ton yong girle . . . of the age of eleven or*
> *twelve years, get the boyes forth with her*
> *into the market place, and make them*
> *wheele, falling on their hands, turning their*
> *heels upwards, whom she would followe,*
> *and wheele so herself, naked as she was,*
> *all the fort over."*

THE HARBOR DAWN

Insistently through sleep—a tide of voices—
They meet you listening midway in your dream,
The long, tired sounds, fog-insulated noises:
Gongs in white surplices, beshrouded wails,
Far strum of fog horns . . . signals dispersed in veils.

400 years and more . . . or is it from the soundless shore of sleep that time

5

And then a truck will lumber past the wharves
As winch engines begin throbbing on some deck;
Or a drunken stevedore's howl and thud below
Comes echoing alley-upward through dim snow.

And if they take your sleep away sometimes
They give it back again. Soft sleeves of sound
Attend the darkling harbor, the pillowed bay;
Somewhere out there in blankness steam

10

Spills into steam, and wanders, washed away
—Flurried by keen fifings, eddied
Among distant chiming buoys—adrift. The sky,
Cool feathery fold, suspends, distills
This wavering slumber. . . . Slowly—
Immemorially the window, the half-covered chair,
Ask nothing but this sheath of pallid air.

15

20

recalls you   And you beside me, blessèd now while sirens
to your love,
there in a   Sing to us, stealthily weave us into day—
waking   Serenely now, before day claims our eyes
dream to
merge your   Your cool arms murmurously about me lay.
seed

While myriad snowy hands are clustering at the panes—   25

your hands within my hands are deeds;
my tongue upon your throat—singing
arms close; eyes wide, undoubtful
                    dark
                         drink the dawn—
a forest shudders in your hair!   30

—with   The window goes blond slowly. Frostily clears.
whom?   From Cyclopean towers across Manhattan waters
          —Two—three bright window-eyes aglitter, disk
          The sun, released—aloft with cold gulls hither.

Who is the   The fog leans one last moment on the sill.   35
woman with
us in the   Under the mistletoe of dreams, a star—
dawn?...   As though to join us at some distant hill—
whose is the
flesh our feet   Turns in the waking west and goes to sleep.
have moved
upon?   1927

THE RIVER

Stick your patent name on a signboard
... and past   brother—all over—going west—young man
the din and   Tintex—Japalac—Certain-teed Overalls ads
slogans of
the year—   and lands sakes! under the new playbill ripped
          in the guaranteed corner—see Bert Williams what?   5
          Minstrels when you steal a chicken just
          save me the wing for if it isn't
          Erie it ain't for miles around a
          Mazda—and the telegraphic night coming on Thomas

          a Ediford—and whistling down the tracks   10
          a headlight rushing with the sound—can you

imagine—while an EXPRESS makes time like
SCIENCE—COMMERCE and the HOLYGHOST
RADIO ROARS IN EVERY HOME WE HAVE THE NORTHPOLE
WALLSTREET AND VIRGINBIRTH WITHOUT STONES OR   15
WIRES OR EVEN RUNning brooks connecting ears
and no more sermons windows flashing roar
Breathtaking—as you like it . . . eh?

                        So the 20th Century—so
whizzed the Limited—roared by and left   20
three men, still hungry on the tracks, ploddingly
watching the tail lights wizen and converge, slip-
ping gimleted and neatly out of sight.

                        ★

The last bear, shot drinking in the Dakotas
Loped under wires that span the mountain stream.   25
Keen instruments, strung to a vast precision
Bind town to town and dream to ticking dream.   to those
But some men take their liquor slow—and count   whose
—Though they'll confess no rosary nor clue—   addresses are
                                                   never near
The river's minute by the far brook's year.   30
Under a world of whistles, wires and steam
Caboose-like they go ruminating through
Ohio, Indiana—blind baggage—
To Cheyenne tagging . . . Maybe Kalamazoo.

Time's rendings, time's blendings they construe   35
As final reckonings of fire and snow;
Strange bird-wit, like the elemental gist
Of unwalled winds they offer, singing low
My Old Kentucky Home and *Casey Jones,*
Some Sunny Day. I heard a road-gang chanting so.   40
And afterwards, who had a colt's eyes—one said,
"Jesus! Oh I remember watermelon days!" And sped
High in a cloud of merriment, recalled
"—And when my Aunt Sally Simpson smiled," he
        drawled—
"It was almost Louisiana, long ago."   45

"There's no place like Booneville though, Buddy,"
One said, excising a last burr from his vest,
"—For early trouting." Then peering in the can,
"—But I kept on the tracks." Possessed, resigned,
He trod the fire down pensively and grinned,   50
Spreading dry shingles of a beard. . . .

                                                         Behind
My father's cannery works I used to see
Rail-squatters ranged in nomad raillery,
The ancient men—wifeless or runaway
Hobo-trekkers that forever search   55
An empire wilderness of freight and rails.
Each seemed a child, like me, on a loose perch,
Holding to childhood like some termless play.
John, Jake or Charley, hopping the slow freight
—Memphis to Tallahassee—riding the rods,   60
Blind fists of nothing, humpty-dumpty clods.

Yet they touch something like a key perhaps.
From pole to pole across the hills, the states
but who have   —They know a body under the wide rain;
touched her,   Youngsters with eyes like fjords, old reprobates   65
knowing her
without name   With racetrack jargon,—dotting immensity
They lurk across her, knowing her yonder breast
Snow-silvered, sumac-stained or smoky blue—
Is past the valley-sleepers, south or west.
—As I have trod the rumorous midnights, too,   70

And past the circuit of the lamp's thin flame
(O Nights that brought me to her body bare!)
Have dreamed beyond the print that bound her name.
Trains sounding the long blizzards out—I heard
Wail into distances I knew were hers.   75
Papooses crying on the wind's long mane
Screamed redskin dynasties that fled the brain,
—Dead echoes! But I knew her body there,
Time like a serpent down her shoulder, dark,
And space, an eaglet's wing, laid on her hair.   80

Under the Ozarks, domed by Iron Mountain,
The old gods of the rain lie wrapped in pools
Where eyeless fish curvet a sunken fountain
And re-descend with corn from querulous crows.
Such pilferings make up their timeless eatage, 85
Propitiate them for their timber torn
By iron, iron—always the iron dealt cleavage!
They doze now, below axe and powder horn.

nor the
myths of her
fathers . . .

And Pullman breakfasters glide glistening steel
From tunnel into field—iron strides the dew— 90
Straddles the hill, a dance of wheel on wheel.
You have a half-hour's wait at Siskiyou,
Or stay the night and take the next train through.
Southward, near Cairo passing, you can see
The Ohio merging,—borne down Tennessee; 95
And if it's summer and the sun's in dusk
Maybe the breeze will lift the River's musk
—As though the waters breathed that you might know
Memphis Johnny, Steamboat Bill, Missouri Joe.
Oh, lean from the window, if the train slows down, 100
As though you touched hands with some ancient clown,
—A little while gaze absently below
And hum *Deep River* with them while they go.

Yes, turn again and sniff once more—look see,
O Sheriff, Brakeman and Authority— 105
Hitch up your pants and crunch another quid,
For you, too, feed the River timelessly.
And few evade full measure of their fate;
Always they smile out eerily what they seem.
I could believe he joked at heaven's gate— 110
Dan Midland—jolted from the cold brake-beam.

Down, down—born pioneers in time's despite,
Grimed tributaries to an ancient flow—
They win no frontier by their wayward plight,
But drift in stillness, as from Jordan's brow. 115

You will not hear it as the sea; even stone
Is not more hushed by gravity . . . But slow,
As loth to take more tribute—sliding prone
Like one whose eyes were buried long ago

The River, spreading, flows—and spends your dream.   120
What are you, lost within this tideless spell?
You are your father's father, and the stream—
A liquid theme that floating niggers swell.

Damp tonnage and alluvial march of days—
Nights turbid, vascular with silted shale   125
And roots surrendered down of moraine clays:
The Mississippi drinks the farthest dale.

O quarrying passion, undertowed sunlight!
The basalt surface drags a jungle grace
Ochreous and lynx-barred in lengthening might;   130
Patience! and you shall reach the biding place!

Over De Soto's bones the freighted floors
Throb past the City storied of three thrones.
Down two more turns the Mississippi pours
(Anon tall ironsides up from salt lagoons)   135

And flows within itself, heaps itself free.
All fades but one thin skyline 'round . . . Ahead
No embrace opens but the stinging sea;
The River lifts itself from its long bed,

Poised wholly on its dream, a mustard glow   140
Tortured with history, its one will—flow!
—The Passion spreads in wide tongues, choked and slow,
Meeting the Gulf, hosannas silently below.

                                              1928

IV

CAPE HATTERAS

> *The seas all crossed,*
> *weathered the capes, the voyage done . . .*
> —WALT WHITMAN

Imponderable the dinosaur
         sinks slow,
                the mammoth saurian
                      ghoul, the eastern
                            Cape. . .   5
While rises in the west the coastwise range,
                  slowly the hushed land—
Combustion at the astral core—the dorsal change
Of energy—convulsive shift of sand. . .
But we, who round the capes, the promontories
Where strange tongues vary messages of surf   10
Below grey citadels, repeating to the stars
The ancient names—return home to our own
Hearths, there to eat an apple and recall
The songs that gypsies dealt us at Marseille
Or how the priests walked—slowly through Bombay—   15
Or to read you, Walt,—knowing us in thrall

To that deep wonderment, our native clay
Whose depth of red, eternal flesh of Pocahontus—
Those continental folded æons, surcharged
With sweetness below derricks, chimneys, tunnels—   20
Is veined by all that time has really pledged us. . .
And from above, thin squeaks of radio static,
The captured fume of space foams in our ears—
What whisperings of far watches on the main
Relapsing into silence, while time clears   25
Our lenses, lifts a focus, resurrects
A periscope to glimpse what joys or pain
Our eyes can share or answer—then deflects
Us, shunting to a labyrinth submersed
Where each sees only his dim past reversed. . .   30

But that star-glistered salver of infinity,
The circle, blind crucible of endless space,
Is sluiced by motion,—subjugated never.
Adam and Adam's answer in the forest
Left Hesperus mirrored in the lucid pool.   35
Now the eagle dominates our days, is jurist
Of the ambiguous cloud. We know the strident rule
Of wings imperious. . . Space, instantaneous,
Flickers a moment, consumes us in its smile:
A flash over the horizon—shifting gears—   40
And we have laughter, or more sudden tears.
Dream cancels dream in this new realm of fact
From which we wake into the dream of act;
Seeing himself an atom in a shroud—
Man hears himself an engine in a cloud!   45

"—Recorders ages hence"—ah, syllables of faith!
Walt, tell me, Walt Whitman, if infinity
Be still the same as when you walked the beach
Near Paumanok—your lone patrol—and heard the
        wraith
Through surf, its bird note there a long time falling. . .   50
For you, the panoramas and this breed of towers,
Of you—the theme that's statured in the cliff.
O Saunterer on free ways still ahead!
Not this our empire yet, but labyrinth
Wherein your eyes, like the Great Navigator's without ship, 55
Gleam from the great stones of each prison crypt
Of canyoned traffic . . . Confronting the Exchange,
Surviving in a world of stocks,—they also range
Across the hills where second timber strays
Back over Connecticut farms, abandoned pastures,—   60
Sea eyes and tidal, undenying, bright with myth!

The nasal whine of power whips a new universe. . .
Where spouting pillars spoor the evening sky,
Under the looming stacks of the gigantic power house
Stars prick the eyes with sharp ammoniac proverbs,   65
New verities, new inklings in the velvet hummed
Of dynamos, where hearing's leash is strummed. . .

Power's script,—wound, bobbin-bound, refined—
Is stropped to the slap of belts on booming spools, spurred
Into the bulging bouillon, harnessed jelly of the stars.   70
Towards what? The forked crash of split thunder parts
Our hearing momentwise; but fast in whirling armatures,
As bright as frogs' eyes, giggling in the girth
Of steely gizzards—axle-bound, confined
In coiled precision, bunched in mutual glee   75
The bearings glint,—O murmurless and shined
In oilrinsed circles of blind ecstasy!

Stars scribble on our eyes the frosty sagas,
The gleaming cantos of unvanquished space. . .
O sinewy silver biplane, nudging the wind's withers!   80
There, from Kill Devils Hill at Kitty Hawk
Two brothers in their twinship left the dune;
Warping the gale, the Wright windwrestlers veered
Capeward, then blading the wind's flank, banked and spun
What ciphers risen from prophetic script,   85
What marathons new-set between the stars!
The soul, by naphtha fledged into new reaches,
Already knows the closer clasp of Mars,—
New latitudes, unknotting, soon give place
To what fierce schedules, rife of doom apace!   90

Behold the dragon's covey—amphibian, ubiquitous
To hedge the seaboard, wrap the headland, ride
The blue's cloud-templed districts unto ether. . .
While Iliads glimmer through eyes raised in pride
Hell's belt springs wider into heaven's plumed side.   95
O bright circumferences, heights employed to fly
War's fiery kennel masked in downy offings,—
This tournament of space, the threshed and chiselled height,
Is baited by marauding circles, bludgeon flail
Of rancorous grenades whose screaming petals carve us   100
Wounds that we wrap with theorems sharp as hail!

Wheeled swiftly, wings emerge from larval-silver hangars.
Taut motors surge, space-gnawing, into flight;
Through sparkling visibility, outspread, unsleeping,

Wings clip the last peripheries of light. . .   105
Tellurian wind-sleuths on dawn patrol,
Each plane a hurtling javelin of winged ordnance,
Bristle the heights above a screeching gale to hover;
Surely no eye that Sunward Escadrille can cover!
There, meaningful, fledged as the Pleiades   110
With razor sheen they zoom each rapid helix!
Up-chartered choristers of their own speeding
They, cavalcade on escapade, shear Cumulus—
Lay siege and hurdle Cirrus down the skies!
While Cetus-like, O thou Dirigible, enormous Lounger   115
Of pendulous auroral beaches,—satellited wide
By convoy planes, moonferrets that rejoin thee
On fleeing balconies as thou dost glide,
—Hast splintered space!

                    Low, shadowed of the Cape,
Regard the moving turrets! From grey decks   120
See scouting griffons rise through gaseous crepe
Hung low . . . until a conch of thunder answers
Cloud-belfries, banging, while searchlights, like fencers,
Slit the sky's pancreas of foaming anthracite
Toward thee, O Corsair of the typhoon,—pilot, hear!   125
Thine eyes bicarbonated white by speed, O Skygak, see
How from thy path above the levin's lance
Thou sowest doom thou hast nor time nor chance
To reckon—as thy stilly eyes partake
What alcohol of space. . . ! Remember, Falcon-Ace,   130
Thou hast there in thy wrist a Sanskrit charge
To conjugate infinity's dim marge—
Anew. . . !

            But first, here at this height receive
The benediction of the shell's deep, sure reprieve!
Lead-perforated fuselage, escutcheoned wings   135
Lift agonized quittance, tilting from the invisible brink
Now eagle-bright, now
                  quarry-hid, twist-
                        -ing, sink with

Enormous repercussive list-
                    -ings down
Giddily spiralled
                    gauntlets, upturned, unlooping
In guerrilla sleights, trapped in combustion gyr-   140
Ing, dance the curdled depth
                    down whizzing
Zodiacs, dashed
                    (now nearing fast the Cape!)
                        down gravitation's
                            vortex into crashed
. . . dispersion . . . into mashed and shapeless débris. . . .
By Hatteras bunched the beached heap of high bravery!

★

The stars have grooved our eyes with old persuasions   145
Of love and hatred, birth,—surcease of nations. . .
But who has held the heights more sure than thou,
O Walt!—Ascensions of thee hover in me now
As thou at junctions elegiac, there, of speed
With vast eternity, dost wield the rebound seed!   150
The competent loam, the probable grass,—travail
Of tides awash the pedestal of Everest, fail
Not less than thou in pure impulse inbred
To answer deepest soundings! O, upward from the dead
Thou bringest tally, and a pact, new bound,   155
Of living brotherhood!

                    Thou, there beyond—
Glacial sierras and the flight of ravens,
Hermetically past condor zones, through zenith havens
Past where the albatross has offered up
His last wing-pulse, and downcast as a cup   160
That's drained, is shivered back to earth—thy wand
Has beat a song, O Walt,—there and beyond!
And this, thine other hand, upon my heart
Is plummet ushered of those tears that start
What memories of vigils, bloody, by that Cape,—   165
Ghoul-mound of man's perversity at balk

And fraternal massacre! Thou, pallid there as chalk,
Hast kept of wounds, O Mourner, all that sum
That then from Appomattox stretched to Somme!

Cowslip and shad-blow, flaked like tethered foam   170
Around bared teeth of stallions, bloomed that spring
When first I read thy lines, rife as the loam
Of prairies, yet like breakers cliffward leaping!
O, early following thee, I searched the hill
Blue-writ and odor-firm with violets, 'til   175
With June the mountain laurel broke through green
And filled the forest with what clustrous sheen!
Potomac lilies,—then the Pontiac rose,
And Klondike edelweiss of occult snows!
White banks of moonlight came descending valleys—   180
How speechful on oak-vizored palisades,
As vibrantly I following down Sequoia alleys
Heard thunder's eloquence through green arcades
Set trumpets breathing in each clump and grass tuft—'til
Gold autumn, captured, crowned the trembling hill!   185

Panis Angelicus! Eyes tranquil with the blaze
Of love's own diametric gaze, of love's amaze!
Not greatest, thou,—not first, nor last,—but near
And onward yielding past my utmost year.
Familiar, thou, as mendicants in public places;   190
Evasive—too—as dayspring's spreading arc to trace
        is:—
Our Meistersinger, thou set breath in steel;
And it was thou who on the boldest heel
Stood up and flung the span on even wing
Of that great Bridge, our Myth, whereof I sing!   195

Years of the Modern! Propulsions toward what capes?
But thou, *Panis Angelicus,* hast thou not seen
And passed that Barrier that none escapes—
But knows it leastwise as death-strife?—O, something
        green,
Beyond all sesames of science was thy choice   200

Wherewith to bind us throbbing with one voice,
New integers of Roman, Viking, Celt—
Thou, Vedic Caesar, to the greensward knelt!

And now, as launched in abysmal cupolas of space,
Toward endless terminals, Easters of speeding light—   205
Vast engines outward veering with seraphic grace
On clarion cylinders pass out of sight
To course that span of consciousness thou'st named
The Open Road—thy vision is reclaimed!
What heritage thou'st signalled to our hands!   210

And see! the rainbow's arch—how shimmeringly stands
Above the Cape's ghoul-mound, O joyous seer!
Recorders ages hence, yes, they shall hear
In their own veins uncancelled thy sure tread
And read thee by the aureole 'round thy head   215
Of pasture-shine, *Panis Angelicus!*
                              Yes, Walt,
Afoot again, and onward without halt,—
Not soon, nor suddenly,—No, never to let go
    My hand
              in yours,
                    Walt Whitman—
                                      so—
                                              1930

VIII

ATLANTIS

> *Music is then the knowledge of that which*
> *relates to love in harmony and system.*
>   —PLATO

Through the bound cable strands, the arching path
Upward, veering with light, the flight of strings,—
Taut miles of shuttling moonlight syncopate
The whispered rush, telepathy of wires.

Up the index of night, granite and steel—   5
Transparent meshes—fleckless the gleaming staves—
Sibylline voices flicker, waveringly stream
As though a god were issue of the strings. . . .

And through that cordage, threading with its call
One arc synoptic of all tides below—   10
Their labyrinthine mouths of history
Pouring reply as though all ships at sea
Complighted in one vibrant breath made cry,—
"Make thy love sure—to weave whose song we ply!"
—From black embankments, moveless soundings hailed,   15
So seven oceans answer from their dream.

And on, obliquely up bright carrier bars
New octaves trestle the twin monoliths
Beyond whose frosted capes the moon bequeaths
Two worlds of sleep (O arching strands of song!)—   20
Onward and up the crystal-flooded aisle
White tempest nets file upward, upward ring
With silver terraces the humming spars,
The loft of vision, palladium helm of stars.

Sheerly the eyes, like seagulls stung with rime—   25
Slit and propelled by glistening fins of light—
Pick biting way up towering looms that press
Sidelong with flight of blade on tendon blade
—Tomorrows into yesteryear—and link
What cipher-script of time no traveller reads   30
But who, through smoking pyres of love and death,
Searches the timeless laugh of mythic spears.

Like hails, farewells—up planet-sequined heights
Some trillion whispering hammers glimmer Tyre:
Serenely, sharply up the long anvil cry   35
Of inchling æons silence rivets Troy.
And you, aloft there—Jason! hesting Shout!
Still wrapping harness to the swarming air!
Silvery the rushing wake, surpassing call,
Beams yelling Æolus! splintered in the straits!   40

From gulfs unfolding, terrible of drums,
Tall Vision-of-the-Voyage, tensely spare—
Bridge, lifting night to cycloramic crest
Of deepest day—O Choir, translating time
Into what multitudinous Verb the suns   45
And synergy of waters ever fuse, recast
In myriad syllables,—Psalm of Cathay!
O Love, thy white, pervasive Paradigm . . . !

We left the haven hanging in the night—
Sheened harbor lanterns backward fled the keel.   50
Pacific here at time's end, bearing corn,—
Eyes stammer through the pangs of dust and steel.
And still the circular, indubitable frieze
Of heaven's meditation, yoking wave
To kneeling wave, one song devoutly binds—   55
The vernal strophe chimes from deathless strings!

O Thou steeled Cognizance whose leap commits
The agile precincts of the lark's return;
Within whose lariat sweep encinctured sing
In single chrysalis the many twain,—   60
Of stars Thou art the stitch and stallion glow
And like an organ, Thou, with sound of doom—
Sight, sound and flesh Thou leadest from time's realm
As love strikes clear direction for the helm.

Swift peal of secular light, intrinsic Myth   65
Whose fell unshadow is death's utter wound,—
O River-throated—iridescently upborne
Through the bright drench and fabric of our veins;
With white escarpments swinging into light,
Sustained in tears the cities are endowed   70
And justified conclamant with ripe fields
Revolving through their harvests in sweet torment.
Forever Deity's glittering Pledge, O Thou
Whose canticle fresh chemistry assigns
To rapt inception and beatitude,—   75
Always through blinding cables, to our joy,
Of thy white seizure springs the prophecy:

Always through spiring cordage, pyramids
Of silver sequel, Deity's young name
Kinetic of white choiring wings . . . ascends.   80

Migrations that must needs void memory,
Inventions that cobblestone the heart,—
Unspeakable Thou Bridge to Thee, O Love.
Thy pardon for this history, whitest Flower,
O Answerer of all,—Anemone,—   85
Now while thy petals spend the suns about us, hold—
(O Thou whose radiance doth inherit me)
Atlantis,—hold thy floating singer late!

So to thine Everpresence, beyond time,
Like spears ensanguined of one tolling star   90
That bleeds infinity—the orphic strings,
Sidereal phalanxes, leap and converge:
—One Song, one Bridge of Fire! Is it Cathay,
Now pity steeps the grass and rainbows ring
The serpent with the eagle in the leaves . . . ?   95
Whispers antiphonal in azure swing.

                                            1930